I0189501

The Quick and Easy Guide to United Methodist Polity

Anne L. Burkholder and
Thomas W. Elliott, Jr.

The Quick and Easy Guide to United Methodist Polity

Second Edition

Abingdon Press™

THE QUICK AND EASY GUIDE TO UNITED METHODIST POLITY, SECOND EDITION

Copyright © 2025 by Abingdon Press

All rights reserved.

No part of this work may be reproduced or transmitted in any form or by any means, electronic or mechanical, including photocopying and recording, or by any information storage or retrieval system, except as may be expressly permitted by the 1976 Copyright Act, the 1998 Digital Millennium Copyright Act, or in writing from the publisher. Requests for permission can be addressed to Permissions, Abingdon Press, 810 12th Ave. South, Nashville, TN 37203, or emailed to permissions@abingdonpress.com.

ISBN: 9781791037130

Scripture quotations, unless paraphrased by the author or noted otherwise, are from the Common English Bible. Copyright © 2011 by the Common English Bible. All rights reserved. Used by permission. www.CommonEnglishBible.Com.

MANUFACTURED IN THE UNITED STATES OF AMERICA

To Dr. Jan Love, Dean Emerita, Candler School of Theology
Methodist Extraordinaire and Best Boss Ever

What is the end of all ecclesiastical order? Is it not to bring souls from the power of Satan to God, and to build them up in his fear and love? Order, then, is so far valuable as it answers these ends; and if it answers them not, it is nothing worth.
June 25, 1746, letter to "John Smith," Wesley, Works, *12:80–81.*

The outreach of the church springs from the working of the Spirit. As United Methodists, we respond to that working through a connectional polity based upon mutual responsiveness and accountability. Connectional ties bind us together in faith and service in our global witness, enabling faith to become active in love and intensifying our desire for peace and justice in the world.
—The Book of Discipline of The United Methodist Church, ¶102, *"Distinctive Wesleyan Emphasis: Nurture and Mission of the Church"*

Contents

Contents

Contents

Contents

Contents

Contents

Contents

Contents

Contents

Contents

Contents

Foreword to the Second Edition

Have you ever opened *The Book of Discipline* and thought "How in the world do I navigate this?" You aren't alone. Anne Burkholder and Thomas Elliott Jr. have, once again, masterfully catered to both those with basic questions about United Methodist Church functioning and those for whom United Methodist polity strangely warms their hearts. As a self-identified Metho-nerd, I can attest that this resource makes both everyday work and denominational exploration infinitely more accessible!

Woven throughout this work are not merely explanations but thoughtful insights into how our polity is lived, connectional, and profoundly theological in nature. Anne and Thomas boldly expand our understanding of polity, theology, and ecclesiology beyond *The Book of Discipline*! (Metho-nerds, try not to gasp too loudly.) They reveal the essential truth that The United Methodist Church exists beyond its written regulations, illuminating the non-textual complexity, beauty, and potential of our beloved denomination. References to other foundational United Methodist resources—including the *United Methodist Hymnal* and *Book of Worship*—connect our polity outward toward our worship practices and spiritual formation. And for anyone overwhelmed by the alphabet soup of United Methodist acronyms and initialisms, they provide clear definitions that demystify our organizational language.

As someone who seeks humor in the most unexpected places, I particularly appreciate the occasional witty quotes introducing each entry—some capable of inducing genuine, unrestrained laughter even when discussing parliamentary procedure!

From a historian's perspective, one of this resource's most valuable aspects is the historical context provided for each entry. These historical snapshots contextualize the development of our church as it responds to social, cultural, and religious changes worldwide. While perhaps not the most immediately practical element, understanding how and why The United Methodist Church functions (or occasionally dysfunctions) provides crucial insight. One of the most common requests I receive at the General Commission on Archives and History is "When did Paragraph X come into existence in *The Book of Discipline* and why?" This guide directly addresses such questions. Consider the entry on "accessibility"—we learn that the "earliest mention" of "accessible structures" appeared in 1964, predating the Americans with Disabilities Act by twenty-six years! Such revelations demonstrate how The United Methodist Church has historically approached persons with diverse accessibility needs and continues to serve as a beacon of inclusivity.

Each general agency receives thoughtful treatment—defined, its mission outlined, and its history provided. These entries familiarize both clergy and laity with the myriad ways our connectional church exists to serve, support, and resource local congregations and annual conferences. But Anne and Thomas go further, recognizing advocacy organizations beyond official structures. They acknowledge "Affinity Groups" whose largely United Methodist membership advocates for various causes within our denomination—groups like Reconciling Ministries Network, United Methodists for Kairos Response, and Methodist Federation for Social Action. Crucially, these groups are positioned as authentically Wesleyan at their core, creating vital space for movement members to engage with those shaping our denominational policies.

This edition reflects watershed developments following the 2020/2024 General Conference, particularly the removal of restrictive language and the potential regionalization of The United Methodist Church. Updated entries on "appointment of clergy" note that bishops can now appoint LGBTQ+ identifying persons within their conferences or across conference lines when necessary. Entries regarding annual conference boundaries now reference both "regional and jurisdictional conferences" establishing those parameters. Agency name changes are incorporated throughout—The United Methodist Board of Pensions is now Wespath; United Methodist Women does business as United Women in Faith.

Especially valuable is the Appendix detailing the history of the Commission on a Way Forward and presenting the text of Paragraph 2553 in both its disaffiliation format and as printed in the 2020/2024 *Book of Discipline*—two paragraphs sharing the same number but embodying profoundly different intentions and interpretations. The authors wisely acknowledge that while the disaffiliation paragraph from the 2019 Special Called session never appeared in an official *Book of Discipline*, its historical significance and practical impact require documentation and understanding.

This resource stands as an indispensable companion alongside standard polity texts like Laceye Warner's *The Method of Our Mission: United Methodist Polity & Organization* and Thomas Frank's *Polity, Practice, and the Mission of The United Methodist Church*. Yet its distinctive accessibility extends its usefulness beyond those enrolled in formal UM polity courses. I enthusiastically recommend it for youth pastors, confirmation leaders, and even young people curious about the complex beauty of The United Methodist Church.

In this season of denominational transformation, Anne and Thomas have given us more than a reference work—they've provided a navigational compass that simultaneously honors our rich heritage while illuminating the path forward. For this gift of clarity and insight, I join countless others in expressing profound gratitude.

Ashley Boggan, PhD
General Secretary of the General Commission on Archives and History

Foreword to the First Edition

What happens when two experienced pastors, now immersed in the formation of clergy for the various ministries of the Church, start thinking about polity? With the *Book of Discipline* in hand, they remember their own experience in local churches and annual conferences. They think back to the origins of Methodism and its evolving character over time. They reflect on the individual and communal vocation of God's people proclaimed in Scripture. They consider the reasoning that supports a particular point of church discipline. And they plan where they might go for more information in order to explore a subject further.

This balanced approach, weaving together and integrating Scripture, tradition, reason, and experience, is exemplified in *The Quick and Easy Guide to United Methodist Polity*. Here Anne Burkholder and Tom Elliott model a way for pastors and lay leaders to think about their responsibilities and actions and weigh their decisions. The authors show how reflection and action belong together and strengthen the work of the Church. For pastors and laity are not alone in their particular situation, or the first to face a problem, or left to guesswork. They are part of a great living tradition that makes thoughtful decisions and productive actions possible.

Especially for pastors in their first appointment or laity in their first year of membership on a local church board or committee, nothing about United Methodist polity may seem "quick and easy." Completing the reports for charge conference can distract anybody from remembering which decisions can be made only in a charge conference session. Candidates for ministry can quickly feel overwhelmed by the application and interview process. A new chair of the Finance Committee may find the weight of fiduciary responsibility heavier than she expected.

Further, because local churches are human communities, anything can get complicated fast. A property deed long assumed to be in a safety deposit box turns up missing. A newly hired staff member is discovered to have a problematic past. A proposal to start a new program exposes long-hidden divisions and hurts in the congregation. Nobody volunteers to serve on the Pastor/Staff Parish Relations Committee. What do I do as a leader, especially when one or more of these and other complications are all happening at once?

Burkholder and Elliott set a tone here that should give any leader confidence. They demonstrate how the *Book of Discipline* provides a basic framework for powers, duties, and decisions. They show how essential ministries of the Church, such as missions or stewardship, build on the *Discipline* by continuing its spirit beyond the words on the page. They draw on the Wesleyan wisdom accumulated across generations for understanding how a leader can best approach a problem.

Polity means little, after all, except as it is practiced. In Wesleyan tradition, polity is more like a rule of life than a rule book. That is, it's a pattern for how to work together as a community called to witness and service; but that pattern must be lived out in experience. Look at how the authors explore worship here, for example. In less than fifty lines of text, they draw on foundational understandings of worship from Wesley and from the Articles of Religion originating in the Church of England; they point the reader to key passages in the *Discipline* about who conducts worship; they evoke the promise of worship as a means of grace or divine ordinance; and in the four entries following they explore aspects of worship that everyone needs to know in order to practice it: how to plan it, what to wear, and so on. But like any good coach or mentor, they can't practice it for us, the readers. Worship must be lived. Today's *Book of Discipline* can be forbidding. Many families with Methodist roots have one of the *Disciplines* from the nineteenth century as an ancestral keepsake. They were sized to fit easily in a pocket or handbag; they were relatively short; they were written in an elevated, even inspirational, style. The bishops' collective letter of introduction in the front of the book appealed for a copy to be found in every Methodist home.

The bishops' letter with its appeal remains in the front of the book, but it no longer fits a pocket or handbag. The United Methodist Publishing House must fulfill its mandate to issue the book as adopted by each General Conference even as the book has grown past eight hundred pages. Resizing the book pages and using thinner paper has made it a bit more manageable, but there's no escaping the fact that over the generations the Church has gotten more complex and legislative paragraphs longer and more detailed. One way to look at this is that the book has grown as the Church has grown. What began as a modest eighteenth-century "society" or parachurch organization for spiritual renewal in England, drawing less than 1 percent of English people into its membership, grew like Topsy in the new United States of America and continues to draw thousands of new followers around the world, particularly in sub-Saharan Africa. With US membership of over seven million in over thirty-two thousand local churches and global membership of over twelve million in one hundred twenty different countries, United Methodism has become a very large organization.

The denomination's size is not a new phenomenon. In 1850, about a third of all church members in the US were either Methodist Episcopal or Methodist Episcopal, South. Both branches developed extensive "connectional" work in publishing, education, missions, and social witness, often drawing independent voluntary associations into formal relationship as church-wide boards of the denomination. By the early twentieth century, the *Discipline* was already getting considerably longer, mainly because the work of the denomination as a whole—the "general" ministries administered by boards and agencies—needed a clear and trustworthy governance structure. Those sections alone in today's *Discipline* occupy over two hundred pages.

Over the last generation, the annual conference has grown into a more permanent regional unit with a more elaborate administrative structure as well. When The United Methodist Church was formed in 1968, the uniting denominations had over one hundred twenty U.S. annual conferences between them. These conferences were small enough to meet in local churches or church-related college auditoriums or gymnasiums. They devoted most of their time to the "conference relations" of clergy, together with worship and inspiration to support the connectional mission of the Church. Today these conferences have been consolidated into fifty-six in the US. They often meet in convention centers. Most have a central office building and staff. One hundred pages of the *Discipline* are now devoted to their powers and responsibilities.

Meantime, the central historic function of the annual conference as the home base of clergy—the covenant of ministry through which all are held accountable in mutual support and trust—has become more elaborate. The Church continually seeks to adapt its forms of ministry to particular situations, and this has resulted in well over a dozen categories of conference relation or status that must be managed through a whole process of candidacy, testing of call, mentorship, and final approval by the conference. These matters now also occupy about one hundred pages of the *Discipline*.

Given the growth indicated in these three examples (comprising half the *Book of Discipline*), and the countless nuances that General Conference has been persuaded must be addressed and governed through Church discipline, it's easy to forget that the *Discipline* evolved from "holy conferencing" and "Christian conversation" about the practices of faith and ministry. Such terms may strike the ear as nostalgic or wishful thinking, given the size and diversity of conferences and the sometimes politically charged atmosphere that pervades them. But the instinct is true to Methodist character and the essence of the Wesleyan heritage.

Conversation is original or constitutive for Methodism, and will be essential for the Church's flourishing in the future. John Wesley's "Large Minutes" to which this book refers were titled "Minutes of Several Conversations Between The Rev. Mr. Wesley and Others" and provided a consolidated record of topics discussed in conference. They were in a question-and-answer format, exploring the practices of ministry in varied situations and circumstances. This Q-and-A structure continued in *Books of Discipline* well into the twentieth century until a more legislative style of numbering and wording was adopted.

One of the strengths of Burkholder and Elliott's text is that it does not stop with what's on the page in the current *Discipline*. Rather they open a conversation with voices of the past, with historic practices, and with the current responsibilities of leaders. They evoke the dynamic through which United

Methodists arrive at decisions that, on the one hand, get written down and adopted as paragraphs in the *Discipline*, and on the other hand, must be acted on in the living realities of actual congregations and communities.

Conversation is open-ended. It has no permanently fixed outcome but is responsive to change. It is best advanced at an open table where all voices are heard. Conversation teaches, explores, and records current understandings of the practices of faith. It is a means of grace.

A *Quick and Easy Guide* invites more conversation. Book in hand, pastors and lay leaders can use it as a platform that will get them started toward engaging more deeply with the challenges and possibilities of Christian community. So turn the page. Let the conversation begin.

Thomas Edward Frank

Pentecost 2017

Preface to the Second Edition

This second edition of *The Quick and Easy Guide to United Methodist Polity* (hereafter referred to as "this guide") is a response to the 2020/2024 General Conference of The United Methodist Church. It reflects the "new" United Methodism that fully includes LGBTQ+ persons and seeks to honor the indigenization of the Church in many cultures and places. Following the 2019 special called General Conference and the disaffiliation of numerous congregations and several central conferences, new and important questions have arisen: How do United Methodists throughout the world now define what we hold in common? How is our connection affected when all can modify some parts of the *Discipline*? What are the roles and functions of our spiritual practices? What are the ministry and mission of our Church, to which God is calling us in the neighborhood and world? What does it *REALLY* mean to live in covenant with one another under the authority of the *Discipline* as a truly international church of God's people called United Methodist?

And yet, our original questions remain. Can United Methodist pastors vote in local church decisions? Must the pastor always be present at the Pastor/Staff Parish Relations Committee? What forms do pastors need for charge conference? Who has what authority for hiring and firing staff? Where should a person go to learn about the candidacy process? What is the process for buying additional church property? Are the new "Social Principles," a part of the new *General Book of Discipline*, legally binding for members of The United Methodist Church? Where does one go to understand the candidacy process for receiving a license for pastoral ministry, for getting commissioned, and being ordained if we have regional conferences that do these things differently?

Who is now allowed to be married in our church? Why does my church have an "Administrative Board and Council on Ministries," when the *Book of Discipline* (*Discipline*) recommends a "Church Council"?

This second edition of this guide addresses these and many other questions related to the practices of United Methodist ministry. Written with lay and clergy practitioners in mind, this guide rises out of several convictions that give shape and form to what we mean by United Methodist polity.

First, as reflected in the *Discipline*, there is the conviction that United Methodist polity is necessarily theological and thus it is important to think theologically about the order of our church.

John Wesley set the pace when he resourced the establishment of the nascent Methodist Episcopal Church in America at the Christmas Conference (1784) with a doctrine (his revision of *The Articles of Religion*) and a liturgy known as *The Sunday Service of the Methodists in North America* (his abridgement of *The Book of Common Prayer*). He provided a hymnbook that was accepted, the conference adopted a modified version of the General Rules, and the "Large Minutes" were adapted to American Methodism. These later became known as the *Doctrines and Discipline of the Methodist Episcopal Church* or our *Book of Discipline*.

In establishing the first constitution of the church, the 1808 General Conference protected *The Articles of Religion* and the General Rules with restrictive rules. Though not included initially in doctrinal norms, Mr. Wesley's *Explanatory Notes Upon the New Testament* and four volumes of *Sermons* continued as traditional sources giving preaching its distinctive Methodist character.

In The United Methodist Plan of Union (1968) both the Methodist *Articles of Religion* and the Evangelical United Brethren *Confession of Faith* were deemed congruent and accepted as doctrinal standards, along with the General Rules that were protected by restrictive rules in the Constitution. Because the first restrictive rule was never formally defined, Wesley's *Sermons* and *Explanatory Notes on the New Testament* were understood specifically to be "present existing and established standards of doctrine" (¶ 104).

In 1988, the General Conference updated our theological statement by adding a significant development, "Our Theological Task." Whereas "Our doctrinal affirmations assist us in the discernment of Christian truth in ever-changing contexts. Our theological task includes the testing, renewal, elaboration, and application of our doctrinal perspective in carrying out our calling 'to spread scriptural holiness over these lands'" (¶ 105). In the very nature of our Christian lives United Methodists are compelled to think theologically!

Through subsequent years, General Conference has continued to bring clarity to our theological convictions by adopting significant statements on denominational understanding of Baptism ("By Water and the Spirit," 1996) and Holy Communion ("This Holy Mystery," 2004), and has been working on a statement on the nature and mission of the church. We have a long tradition of thinking theologically about our polity and a church with a theological task to continue to engage.

Second, United Methodist polity is, as described by Dr. Thomas E. Frank in his seminal text, *Polity, Practice, and the Mission of The United Methodist Church*, characterized by discipline and community. In reference to the use of the term "discipline," Frank describes how in our history, "discipline" and "methods" were "peculiarly related." "Disciplines of growth in the Christian life" were directly related to "practices of love in Christian community." Discipline was exercised in the early Methodist societies, classes, and bands through self-examination and mutual accountability. In 1743, John Wesley published the pamphlet on the "Nature, Design, and General Rules of the United Societies" with an emphasis upon the means of grace and holy living (Frank, 46). So, even these early Methodist forms were created to undergird the theological and spiritual life of the church. Early Methodist conferencing yielded the "Large Minutes," a record of conversations between Wesley and his preachers, which gave order to the expanding Methodist movement in England and North America. General and annual conferences have proceeded over the past two hundred years, with an ever-increasing democratic spirit, to engage in the legislative work of the Church and vote on critical issues regarding the Church's life and ministry (ibid). The uniqueness of this character is preserved throughout the pages of this guide.

Third, the breadth of United Methodist polity includes more than what is recorded in the *Discipline*. Consider the following:

Robert and Elizabeth Strawbridge, Philip Embury, and Captain Thomas Webb, laity in the early movement, established Methodist societies, respectively, in Maryland, New York City, and Philadelphia. Sunday school gradually replaced the class meetings in most Methodist churches.

Caucuses, like Black Methodists for Church Renewal (BMCR) and Methodist Associated Representing the Cause of Hispanic Americans (MARCHA), though not established by the General Conference, serve a critical advocacy role in the Church and world.

The Council of Bishops offers guidance to the Church through timely, pastoral letters and statements like "In Defense of Creation" and "The Bishop's Initiative on Children and Poverty," and even most recently "The Bishops' Pastoral Letter on Violence in Israel and Palestine."

Local churches, conferences, and general agencies adopt local operating policies and procedures.

By including material beyond, yet connected to, the *Discipline*, this guide provides the user with a much fuller representation of the breadth and depth of the Church's polity from class to church to conference, and of United Methodism as a whole.

Fourth, United Methodist polity invites us to think about what it means to commit to a "rule of life," as both individuals and the Church. For centuries, religious societies and churches have developed and utilized rules to guide the life of a community of faith, and Methodism is no exception. Incredibly early in the Methodist movement, John Wesley published the "General Rules for the United Societies" where we find three rules for translating faith into action, in the words of John Wesley: (1) do no harm; (2) do good; and (3) attend upon the ordinances of God. This grace-based practical theology gave rise to the need for the structure, practices, and rules that evolved over two hundred years into The United Methodist Church. This text, then, points to the theological and historical frameworks that undergird our polity.

With today's continuing international expansion of United Methodism and the indigenization of the Church in many cultures and places, including the landscape of North America, new questions have arisen: What do or should United Methodists throughout the world hold in common? What is the nature of our connection? What are the role and function of our spiritual practices? What are the ministry and mission of our Church, to which God is calling us in the neighborhood and world? What does it *really* mean to live in covenant with one another under the authority of the *Discipline* as an international church of God's people called United Methodist?

The *Discipline* is the place where we anchor our understanding of how God is calling us as United Methodists to be in covenant with one another. This guide, in all its multifaceted entries, invites us to think about the life we hold in common, together, as United Methodists.

Finally, United Methodist polity is about ordering the life of the Church for the mission of God in the world. John Wesley preached in the field and discovered a need to organize people into societies for spiritual growth. As societies grew, once again he found a need to resource them with preachers. To give guidance and direction to these spiritual leaders, Wesley organized conferences.

From this illustration of Wesley, we learn how form follows function, how structure is shaped by mission, how ecclesiology grows from missiology. Not only does this realization help us think about the posture of our local churches and the work we do as pastors and laity but it also challenges us to ask, "What is the trajectory of our Church?" Indeed, how are we "mak[ing] disciples of Jesus Christ for the transformation of the world"? By making the polity of The United Methodist Church more accessible, this guide will show how the mission of the Church is served by its polity.

Acknowledgments

What a privilege it is for us to have this opportunity to create a second edition of this book, especially in response to the 2020/2024 General Conference! The first edition grew out of our love for The United Methodist Church, and a vision for how our experience and teaching could help the church. This second edition is motivated by a desire to bring it in alignment with the new UMC's inclusive vision for itself and to bring a stronger emphasis to the theological and doctrinal underpinnings of its polity.

It is worth repeating from the first edition how strongly The UMC we truly are, and grateful to be so. The denomination had a very strong formational impact on both of us as cradle Methodists, shaped early on by osmosis in the tradition, and confirmed in and through Methodist life. Methodism is in our bones!

For Anne, her earliest memory of faith was the baptism of her baby sister in the school auditorium of a new church start just outside of Cincinnati. They followed a ritual that was the same in every Methodist church her family attended as they moved fifteen times with the Air Force before she left for college. Her first experiences of integration took place at summer youth camp in Fruitland, Florida, and the 1968 merger of The EUB and The Methodist Church that united two neighboring Methodist churches in Oxon Hill, Maryland. On to Florida State University's Wesley Foundation where she sang in a choir with and from Florida A&M, and then on to seminary at Candler School of Theology, she was formed by the ever-changing landscape of the denomination and shifting culture of the South. She became a member of the Florida Conference and served as an urban ministries director, church pastor, chairperson of the board of ordained ministry, district superintendent, and director of connectional ministry. She went on to serve as the associate dean of Methodist Studies at Candler School of Theology and as Professor in the Practice of Ecclesiology and Church Leadership for fourteen years, and is now retired.

Tom was raised at Decatur First United Methodist Church in Decatur, Georgia, and grew up in the sawdust of the annual Salem Campmeeting in Newton County, Georgia. When Tom began volunteering as a song leader for the junior high youth at his church, little did he know that this experience would eventually lead him into full-time ministry. Following seminary at Candler School of Theology, Tom served for twenty-six years as a pastor of local churches in the North Georgia Conference of The UMC. He also taught as an adjunct instructor at Reinhardt College and in the Methodist Studies Department at Candler before joining the faculty full-time as director of Contextual Education II, Teaching Parish, and Internships as well as Professor in the Practice of Practical Theology and Methodist Studies.

Our earlier practical experiences and teaching helped us understand just how complex and confusing our polity can be. We have sought to create a tool that assists not only church clergy, lay leaders, and seminarians, but all United Methodists by simplifying access to our polity: the *Book of Discipline*, legal and financial sources, and historical rationales for why we do things the way we do.

Despite the challenges and opportunities faced by the Church in the world today, we love The United Methodist Church and the richness of our theological tradition, spiritual practices, and worldwide connections. We give thanks for the churches and the ministries that have shaped and formed us, for the privilege to serve, for the amazing place that is the Candler School of Theology at Emory University, where we are honored to teach and administer, and for all our students who have taught us polity.

We are grateful for...

Cameron Merrill, editor, and Abingdon Press for this opportunity to improve on the original! Cameron has always been available with ready answers to our questions or knew who to ask when he did not have the answers.

Ashley Boggan, general secretary of the General Commission on Archives and History (GCAH), author, and professor for her gracious foreword for this second edition. Her knowledge of UM History and appreciation for

The UMC is simply the best. We witnessed her vision for getting folks excited about church history and polity when she led trivia games with seminary students at the 2020/2024 General Conference in Charlotte.

Tom Frank, mentor and friend who helped both of us get started teaching polity, sharing his syllabus and making suggestions about how to go about it, wrote our first foreword (included) and gave us big hugs at the 2020/2024 General Conference, delighted to hear that we were writing a second edition. Tom, we continue to be humbled by your delight in and contribution to this project.

Carlene Johnson, our former student and teaching assistant, and now project editor. Carlene is a brilliant thinker and a fabulous wordsmith, another cradle Methodist and a double "PK"; she holds degrees in both law and theology. She has been a delegate to four General Conferences, served at a General Agency and on the Florida Conference Committee on Investigation, chaired the Florida Conference's Standing Rules Committee, and now rises to the role of parliamentarian for the Florida Conference.

Jan Love, dean emerita, to whom this edition is dedicated; and Jonathan Strom, dean, for support of our academic and Methodist endeavors; Russ Richey, dean emeritus, William R. Cannon Distinguished Professor Emeritus of Church History, for reinforcing our Methodist ethos at Candler and for his legacy of leadership and ongoing scholarship; and Rex Matthews, professor emeritus in the practice of historical theology and Wesleyan studies, colleague, and friend.

United Methodist and contextual education colleagues at Candler for their constant inspiration and support: Brett Opalinski, current assistant dean of Methodist studies and assistant professor in the practice of spiritual formation and church leadership. Amy Walker, associate director of Methodist studies; Jess Cusik, academic program associate; Carmen Toussaint, assistant director of programs, Office of Contextual Education; and Letitia Campbell, director of contextual education I and CPE assistant professor in the practice of ethics and society. Larry Goodpastor, bishop, colleague, reader, and friend. The entire Candler faculty for the dialogue we have always shared about formation of ministers and the contributions that each of our disciplines and traditions makes to the whole.

This new edition was due to be written shortly after the special called 2019 and originally scheduled 2020 General Conference. Given the circumstances of the pandemic in 2020, the establishment of a disaffiliation process due to paragraph 2553, the postponements of the 2020 conference, and the changes that have continued to take place in our culture, this is, joyfully and thankfully, a different book than it would have been.

So, we still offer this book because we love the Church, and we believe in the ministry and mission of Jesus Christ in the world. We know as well that United Methodist ministry can and will be filled with both challenges and opportunities—and this is a much-needed resource.

The focus of this resource is on polity lived out by clergy and lay practitioners primarily in the North American United Methodist Church context, especially in the local church and extension ministry. This is especially the case because of the dramatic transformation through which the denomination is moving and the pending constitutional amendments.

As teachers and practitioners, we recognize that UM polity is complex, and we apologize in advance for the limitations of this text and for any mistakes herein (any errors are our own!). A text that covers a subject as vast as the polity of The UMC will not address every question, speak to every situation, or serve every person's need or interest. However, we want to continue improving this resource, so we welcome your insights and input, and would like to hear from you.

How to Use This Book

We recognize that United Methodists (UMs) have their own unique language in both written and oral forms of polity. *The Quick and Easy Guide to United Methodist Polity* functions as a comprehensive annotated index to the *Book of Discipline* and the non-disciplinary practices that make up our polity. It is designed to aid students in Licensing School for Pastoral Ministry, Course of Study, and seminary polity courses appreciate and understand the importance of our polity. It will help direct clergy and lay leaders to the relevant sections of the *Discipline* for the particular subject they are researching. It is for anyone who needs a starting point for understanding a particular issue in the practice of UM ministry. It is in no way designed to replace the *Discipline* but designed to assist UMs with appreciating and using it! The guide also points to additional UM resources provided by the general agencies and important texts that speak to particular polity-related matters.

In summary, this guide will provide context for understanding and applying the *Discipline*, point toward relevant material and disciplinary paragraphs for issues faced in ministry settings, reduce the time for research and potential for error (confusion) by those who interpret polity and the *Discipline*, and facilitate the leadership of clergy and laity by making polity and the *Discipline* more accessible.

Readers need to be aware of several features of the text:

1. Each entry appears in alphabetical order.

2. Each entry follows the same pattern.

   a. It begins with a relevant and sometimes humorous quotation from an early Discipline, historical Methodist figure, or other interesting historical resource.

b. A definition or explanation of the entry then follows.

c. Paragraph numbers from the 2020/2024 Discipline are included in parentheses.

d. In some entries, references to other important UM texts, such as The United Methodist Hymnal or The Book of Worship, are also included in parentheses within these paragraphs.

e. Note that some entries have no references to the Discipline, because they are not mentioned there. The authority behind such a practice or rule will come from a different source that will be referred to in the text.

f. A brief description of the history of the entry then follows. The historical paragraph provides context and depth, helping to explain the origin of a particular doctrinal statement, practice, or rule and why United Methodists act and believe what United Methodists do.

g. Each entry concludes with "See also:" a notation that directs the reader to an additional source of information.

3. Within each entry the reader will find what appear to be randomly italicized words or phrases. They are not random by any means! The words in italics are terms that are also included as entries in this guide. The italicized terms provide a means for cross-referencing one's research within the text. (Note: cross-reference terms are italicized within quotations without note.) Because the entries are in alphabetical order, the reader should be able to skip around the text with relative ease.

4. Some commonly used acronyms and abbreviations are used consistently for particular resources and for the general agencies of the Church. The list is certainly not comprehensive of the Church's unique vocabulary but does reflect those used in the text. Please review the acronyms listed below and refer to them as necessary.

5. A list of sources is found below as well. Traditional footnotes and endnotes have been avoided; sources are referenced within the text and paraphrased.

Acronyms and Abbreviations

The United Methodist Church and Its Predecessor Denominations

EA—Evangelical Association

EC—Evangelical Church

EUBC—Evangelical United Brethren Church

MC—Methodist Church

MEC—Methodist Episcopal Church

MECS—Methodist Episcopal Church, South

MPC—Methodist Protestant Church

UBC—United Brethren Church

UM—United Methodist

UMC—The United Methodist Church

Official Texts of The United Methodist Church

Discipline—*The Book of Discipline of The United Methodist Church* and its various antecedents.

BOR—*The Book of Resolutions of The United Methodist Church*, 2020/2024

BOW—*The United Methodist Book of Worship*

BWTS—By Water and the Spirit

THM—This Holy Mystery

UMH—*The United Methodist Hymnal*

General Agencies, Committees, and Offices

ACEIR – Advisory Committee on Ecumenical and Interfaith Relationships (New Name for the Office of Christian Unity and Interfaith Relationships (OCUIR)

CFO—Committee on Faith and Order

CT—Connectional Table

GBCS—General Board of Church and Society

GBGM—General Board of Global Ministries

GBHEM—General Board of Higher Education and Ministry

GBOD—General Board of Discipleship (Discipleship Ministries)

GCAH—General Commission on Archives and History

GCFA—General Council on Finance and Administration

GCORR—General Commission on Religion and Race

GCOSROW—General Commission on the Status and Role of Women

GCUMM—General Commission on United Methodist Men

UMCom—General Commission on Communication

UMW—United Methodist Women

Wespath—Wespath

SOURCE ABBREVIATIONS FOR MULTIPLE REFERENCES IN QUOTATIONS

Bangs, vol. 1, p.#	Bangs, Nathan. *A History of the Methodist Episcopal Church*. Volume I, 12th ed. (New York: Carlton & Porter, 1860).
Bangs, vol. 2, p.#	Bangs, Nathan. *A History of the Methodist Episcopal Church*. Volume II, 3rd ed. (New York: Carlton & Porter, 1853).
Bangs, vol. 3, p.#	Bangs, Nathan. *A History of the Methodist Episcopal Church*. Volume III (New York: G. Lane & C. B. Tippett, 1845).
Bangs, vol. 4, p.#	Bangs, Nathan. *A History of the Methodist Episcopal Church*. Volume IV (New York: Carlton & Porter, 1853).
BOW, p.#	The United Methodist Publishing House. *The United Methodist Book of Worship* (Nashville: The United Methodist Publishing House, 1992).
Discipline, 1785	*A Form of Discipline for the Ministers, Preachers, and Members of the Methodist Episcopal Church in America.* Considered and approved at a Conference Held at Baltimore, Maryland, on Monday the 27th of December, 1784 (New York: W. Ross, in Broad Street, 1787).
Discipline, 1787	*A Form of Discipline for the Ministers, Preachers, and Members of the Methodist Episcopal Church in America.* Considered and approved at a Conference Held at Baltimore, Maryland, on Monday the 27th of December, 1784... Arranged under proper Heads... (Elizabeth-Town: Shepard Kolloc, 178_ [date indecipherable]).

5

Discipline, 1789	*A Form of Discipline for the Ministers, Preachers, and Members of the Methodist Episcopal Church in America.* Considered and approved at a Conference Held at Baltimore, Maryland, on Monday the 27th of December, 1784… Arranged under proper Heads… the 5th edition (New York: William Ross, in Broad-Street, 1789).
Discipline, MC, year	*Doctrines and Disciplines of the Methodist Church.*
Discipline, MEC, year	*Doctrines and Disciplines of the Methodist Episcopal Church.*
Discipline, MPC, year	Forlines, C. E., ed. *Constitution and Discipline of the Methodist Protestant Church* (Baltimore, Pittsburgh: The Board of Publication of the Methodist Protestant Church, 1936).
Discipline, UMC, year	The United Methodist Publishing House, *The Book of Discipline of The United Methodist Church* 1968, 2002, 2006, 2016 (Nashville: The United Methodist Publishing House, 2002, 2006, 2016).
Frank, p.#	Frank, Thomas E. *Polity, Practice, and the Mission of The United Methodist Church* (Nashville: Abingdon Press, 2006).
General Minutes, 1784	*The General Minutes of the Conferences of the Methodist Episcopal Church in America* (London: 1786) or *Minutes of Several Conversations Between The Rev. Thomas Coke, LL.D., The Rev. Francis Asbury and Others at a Conference… Begun in Baltimore… Monday, the 27th of December in the Year 1784.*
Harmon, EE, p.#	Harmon, Nolan B. *Ministerial Ethics and Etiquette* (Nashville: Cokesbury Press, 1928).

Harmon, *Under-standing*, p.#	Harmon, Nolan B. *Understanding the United Methodist Church* (Nashville, Abingdon Press, 1974).
Hickman, p.#	Hickman, Hoyt. *United Methodist Altars: A Guide for the Local Church* (Nashville: Abingdon Press, 1996).
MEA I, p.#	Richey, Russell E., Kenneth E. Rowe, and Jean Miller Schmidt. *The Methodist Experience in America*. Volume I (Nashville: Abingdon Press, 2010).
MEA II, p.#	Richey, Russell E., Kenneth E. Rowe, and Jean Miller Schmidt. *The Methodist Experience in America*. Volume II (Nashville: Abingdon Press, 2009).
Vickers, p.#	Vickers, John A., ed. "First Journal to North America." *The Journals of Dr. Thomas Coke* (Nashville: Kingswood Books, Abingdon, 2008).
John Wesley, *Works*, vol. #, p.#	*The Works of John Wesley*, Bicentennial Edition, various volumes (Nashville: Abingdon Press, 1984– Present).

Entries

Accessibility

¶1248. Art. 15. Architecture—The National Division shall make provision for the fulfillment of the following purposes in its architectural work: 1. To prepare up-to-date church plans of a general nature. . . .

8. To consult with local churches and architects to ensure in church building plans proper facilities for physically handicapped persons. —*Discipline*, MC, 1964.

The UMC is called to be inclusive of all people, and "a further mark of inclusiveness is the setting of *church* activities in facilities accessible to persons with disabilities" (140). This is promoted through a Disability Awareness Sunday (262), an annual conference committee on disability concerns (653), an annual accessibility audit in the *local church* conducted by the *Board of Trustees* (2533.6), and included in the trustee report to the *charge conference* (2550.10) and accessibility plans for the planning and financing of buildings (2544). *Clergy* with disabilities are not excluded from licensing, commissioning, or ordination when able to perform ministerial duties (315, 324.8). Nor is anyone excluded from participating in the sacraments of *Baptism* and *Holy Communion* because of physical, neurological, mental, psychological, or developmental conditions or abilities. When becoming a member of the Church, persons with disabilities who are unable to answer for themselves may have a guardian respond to the vows on their behalf (214). Persons with disabilities are also mentioned in the Social Principles with regard to fair treatment by Media (161.G), and law enforcement (163), and in the Social Creed (164). Lastly, persons with disabilities are to have full access to participation in *church conferences* (248) and to be elected as church leaders (249).

The expectation for accessible structures is first found in the *Discipline* (the earliest mention is found in 1964) of The MC, preceding the Americans with Disabilities Act of 1990 that required accessibility accommodations to be in place within thirty years. Oversight for these architectural accessibility concerns was lodged within The MC Board of Missions.

See also: www.gcfa.org/resource/local-church-forms; information@umcdmc.org.

Adult Ministry

> When the secretary had called all the names and marked them in his book the minister rose from his seat and passed into the Bible-class room. The men and women who were seated on the seats at the sides of the platform followed him. This was the Bible class and the minister was the teacher. . . .
> —"An Hour and a Half in a Country Sunday School. . . ." (New York: Published by Carlton and Porter for the Sunday-school Union of the Methodist Episcopal Church, 1858), RRS, Vol 2, 311.

Age-level ministries are encouraged by the *Discipline*, including those that focus on adults, senior adults, and young adults (253). In the US, young adults range up to the age of thirty. Outside of the US, young adults include those who are up to thirty-five. Adult ministry focuses on "the hopes, concerns, and needs of adults in the community to determine how the congregation might serve them and how they might serve one another as Christian disciples and good neighbors." Ranging from bringing new adult Christians through baptism, discovering their spiritual gifts, and figuring out how God calls them to service in the church and the world, adult ministry focuses on all age groups through small group ministries, classes, and projects. A coordinator for adult ministries is often elected as a member of the leadership team of the *church*.

See also: https://www.umcdiscipleship.org/resources/adult-ministries -coordinator; www.umcdiscipleship.org/articles/adult-discipleship-in-a -continually-changing-world.

Advisory Committee on Ecumenical and Interfaith Relationships – *See* Bishop

Affiliate/Associate Members (Local Church)—*See* Professing Member

Affinity Groups

> The Spirit which gave Methodism birth was a spirit of service. Wesley's philanthropy at Oxford began with his sympathy for prisoners . . . releasing prisoners held for debt, helping the poor with money and medicine, maintaining children at school . . . (But) is the church to be content merely to carry forward on a larger scale than ever before the services which it has already established? Or will it seek also the creation of a society in which many of those services will be forever unnecessary? . . . will it give itself also to the utmost to build that kind of a social order in which there shall be no opposing camps . . . ? —Harry F. Ward, executive of the MFSS, "Social Service and the Church."

In addition to official caucuses, The UMC has unofficial affinity groups. These are non-disciplinary, but usually incorporated means of connecting like-minded and action-oriented people. Such groups include but are surely not limited to the Reconciling Ministries Network (RMN) Creation Justice, United Methodists for Kairos Response (UMKR), and the historic Methodist Federation for Social Action (MFSA).

These groups make their voices heard in a number of compelling ways depending on the timeliness of particular issues. Members will often submit legislation, demonstrate at General Conference, and mobilize local churches and members through different strategies and programs. They raise their own funds and usually have some paid staff. Their activism has led the Church in new directions by creating awareness and moving members toward personal and collective strategies.

11

The MFSS, the forerunner to MFSA, began in 1906 focusing its attention on the unconscionable conditions of industrial workers and child labor. They advocated for better working conditions, an eight-hour workday, the elimination of child labor, and the improvement of education for children. They supported the unionization of workers and often called the church to support strikes. In 1908, they succeeded in getting the original Social Creed passed through the *General Conference.*

Alternate Church Council Structure—*See* Local Church Structure—How to Change It

Annual Conference

In June 1744, I desired my brother and a few other Clergymen to meet me in London, to consider how we should proceed to save our own souls and those that heard us. After some time, I invited the Lay Preachers that we had in the house to meet with us. We conferred together for several days and were much comforted and strengthened thereby. —John Wesley, "THOUGHTS upon Some Late OCCURRENCES," *Arminian Magazine* Consisting of Extracts and Original Treatises on Universal Redemption, Jan. 1778–Dec. 1797 no. 8 (1785): 267–69.

As a part of the constituted *Church* structure (Article IV) the "Annual Conference is the basic body of The UMC" (370) with the right of voting on *Constitution of The United Methodist Church* amendments, electing lay and *clergy* delegates to the legislative bodies of the *Church*—the *General Conference, jurisdictional conferences*, and *central conferences*—and attending to matters of *ordination*, character, and the conference relations of clergy (34. Article II). An annual conference fulfills the *mission statement of the denomination* by "equipping its *local churches* for ministry and by providing a *connection* for ministry beyond the *local church*" (601).

The boundaries of annual conferences are set by the *regional and jurisdictional conferences* (28. Article V.4). The *bishop* sets the time for annual conference

(603.2) and may call a special session for a specific purpose (603.5). The location is chosen by the annual conference or a special committee always paying attention to concerns for accessibility and sustainability (603.4).

The *clergy* membership is composed of "*deacons* and *elders* in *full connection, provisional members, associate members,* and *local pastors*" (33. Article I; 370; 602). The *lay member of the annual conference* is elected from the *professing members* of each *charge* and includes diaconal ministers, deaconesses, home missioners, and lay leadership positions throughout the annual conference (33. Article I). Special provisions are made so that the *lay membership* is always equal to the number of *clergy* members (33. Article I). With the exception of lay participation in the *Board of Ordained Ministry*, the Committee on Investigation, and the *District Committee on Ordained Ministry*, laity are restricted from voting on *clergy* matters in the annual conference (34. Article II).

To accomplish the mission of The UMC, annual conferences have flexibility in designing structure for administrative and ministry needs (610) provided that the following mandated structures are included: Council on Finance and Administration (611), *Committee on Equitable Compensation* (624), *Board of Ordained Ministry* (634), Administrative Review Committee (635), Committee on Episcopacy (636), Board of Pensions (638), Board of Trustees (640), United Methodist Women (647), and United Methodist Men (648). In addition, conferences shall have in some form a: Board of Laity (630), Committee on Ethnic Local Church Concerns (631), Board of Global Ministries (632), Board of Higher Education and Campus Ministry (633), Episcopal Residence Committee (637), Commission on Archives and History (641), structures related to Christian unity and interreligious relationships (642), Commission on Religion and Race (643), Commission on the Status and Role of Women (644), Commission on the Small Membership *Church* (645), Commission on Communication (646), Council on Youth Ministry (649), Council on Young Adult Ministry (650), Council on Older Adult Ministries (651), Committee on Disability Concerns (653), and Committee on Native American Ministry (654). Annual conferences are encouraged to have a Committee on Hispanic/Latino Ministries (655) and a Committee on

Criminal Justice (657). When annual conferences are considering merging or division, they are required to create a Joint Distributing Committee (639).

Since John Wesley's first meetings with preachers in 1742 and 1744, Methodists have been conferencing. In 1773, Thomas Rankin held the first conference with the North American preachers, and the annual conference began meeting in multiple sessions. The first *General Conference* was called in 1792, after this system became challenging, and in 1796, the concept of "conference" was expanded beyond membership to include six geographically defined annual conferences. Initially, conferences comprised traveling preachers, but eventually included *Lay Members of the Annual Conference* by the early twentieth century.

See also: Russell E. Richey, *The Methodist Conference in America: A History* (Nashville: Kingswood Books, 1996); www.umc.org/who-we-are/annual-conferences.

Appointment of Clergy

Our plan of itineracy is based upon the world-parish conception of Methodism. A preacher in one place must be ready to be a preacher in all places. "Go ye into all the world, and preach the gospel to every creature" has been a command that United Methodism has taken seriously. "Go ye"—not "wait until the people come to you." . . . in the itinerant system, the appointive power tells each preacher what is to be his [or her] church and tells each church who is to be its preacher. —Harmon, *Understanding*, 121.

Bishops "make and fix all appointments" of *clergy* in their *episcopal* areas, taking into consideration "the gifts and evidence of God's grace" of the persons appointed and "the needs, characteristics, and opportunities of congregations and institutions" (425). Bishops may appoint LGBTQ elders across conference lines when a suitable appointment is not available and/or if the elder needs to move for safety reasons (425.2). Appointments may include a circuit, station, cooperative parish, ecumenical shared ministry, *extension ministry*, a *church* of another denomination, or a staff position in one of these ministries (338). Appointments are made in commitment to open *itineracy* (425) through a mandatory consultation process involving the *bishop*, *district superintendent*, *pastor*, and *Pastor/Staff Parish Relations Committee* of the *local church* (426). A profile of the congregation, the annual review of the *pastor*, and the demographics of the community are utilized in this process (427). A *pastor*, a *Pastor/Staff Parish Relations Committee*, a *district superintendent*, or a *bishop* may initiate a pastoral change (428). The length of an *appointment* is determined by the "long-term pastoral needs" of the *pastors*, *charges*, and communities (429). Though appointments are reported by the *bishop* at the regular session of the *annual conference* (429), they may be made at any time by the *bishop* and *Cabinet* (430). On some occasions, appointments may be made on a less than full-time basis by request of a clergyperson or the *bishop* (338.2). Interim appointments may be utilized in some situations (338), and appointments may be made to an *extension ministry* (343).

The appointment system dates to John Wesley's era when he appointed preachers, rotating them among the circuits while attempting to match up their gifts and graces. Contrary to the stereotype of Francis Asbury as an arbitrary authoritarian when it came to appointments, Asbury's *Journal*, as interpreted by John Wigger in his book *American Saint*, reveals the extraordinary efforts it took to match up and deploy traveling preachers to the constantly expanding circuits, doing what he could to "balance the concerns of the preachers with the needs of the societies" (280–281). Methodism has followed a very similar pattern, with the *bishop* consulting with the *district superintendents* about pastoral appointment making. Following the establishment of The UMC in 1968, this process grew to include a consultation on behalf of the *bishop* by the *district superintendent* with the *pastor* and *Pastor/Staff Parish Relations Committee* of the *local church*. The current consultation process in appointment making was formally defined in the 1976 *Discipline*, ¶528.

See also: John Wigger, *American Saint: Francis Asbury and the Methodists*, reprint ed. (New York: Oxford University Press, 2012).

Apportionments

If it be said that systematic giving by all the people would at once solve the problem of our Church benevolences and relieve the overtaxed, it may be instantly answered that system in asking is absolutely essential to systematic giving. We must devise a more systematic method for financing our connectional benevolences. For our own work we need, first of all, an equable basis of apportionment. This can be secured only by coordination of all the factors that indicate the relative ability of Conferences and Churches.
—Joseph B. Hingeley, ed., "Episcopal Address," Methodist Episcopal Church, Journal of the General Conference (New York, Cincinnati: Methodist Book Concern, 1912), 200.

Apportionments represent the philosophy that together we can accomplish more than we can as individuals, *local churches*, *districts*, or *annual conferences*. As a part of the *general funds* of the *Church*, apportionments are the approved method of churchwide giving that supports the connectional ministry and mission of The UMC (808–818). Apportionment amounts are based on the formula recommended by the *GCFA* and approved by the *General Conference* (806.1 c). These amounts are then communicated to each *annual conference* through the Conference Council on Finance and Administration (613.3), and, from there, apportioned amounts are sent to *districts* and *local churches* (247.14). As a part of fulfilling the mission of The UMC, *pastors* are to lead the *local church* in "full and faithful payment of all apportioned ministerial support, administrative, and benevolent funds" (340.2 *c*) (2) (*e*)).

Nine major funds make up the general UMC apportionments. World Service Fund underwrites the mission of The UMC in the world (812). General Administration Fund pays for *General Conference*, *Judicial Councils*, and other administrative agencies (813). Interdenominational Cooperation Fund supports the ecumenical activities of the Council of Bishops (814). Black College Fund supports capital and operating budgets for Black colleges (815). Ministerial Education Fund provides financial support for the *education* of *ordained* ministers (816). Central Conference Theological Education Fund provides resources to UM-owned seminaries outside the United States (817). Central Conference Higher Education Fund provides support to UM-owned colleges and universities (818). Episcopal Fund underwrites salaries and work expenses for bishops (819). Africa University Fund supports the UM university in Africa (810.1). *Annual conferences* may also establish apportionments for special missional emphases (613-615).

An early example of apportioned-type giving is found in the class meetings, where participants were expected to give a penny a week and a shilling a quarter toward the relief of the poor, support of traveling preachers, and payment on the Methodist preaching houses. Based in this type of practice, The UMC eventually developed a system of *general funds* to support special initiatives and missions.

See also: https://www.gcfa.org/reports.

Archives of the Local Church—*See* Local Church Historian

Articles of Religion

> Resolved . . . That the General Conference do earnestly recommend the superintendents to make the most careful inquiry in all the annual conferences, in order to ascertain whether any doctrines are embraced or preached contrary to our established Articles of Faith; and to use their influence to prevent the existence and circulation of all such doctrines. —Resolution adopted at the 1816 General Conference, Bangs, vol. 3, 48.

The Articles of Religion (3., Art. III) are part of the doctrines of The UMC. Though these articles do not contain any uniquely Wesleyan emphases—like statements on prevenient grace, assurance, or Christian perfection—together with the Confession of Faith, The Standard Sermons of Wesley, The Explanatory Notes Upon the New Testament, and The General Rules, they serve as the basis for UM Doctrinal Standards.

The Articles of Religion in their present form are John Wesley's revision and distillation of the Thirty-Nine Articles of the Church of England, which he sent to America in 1784 to serve as a doctrinal statement for The MEC.

Added to the original articles was Article XXIII, "Of the Rulers of These United States of America" to acknowledge that the MEC recognized the independence of the United States of America. With the establishment of the first Methodist Constitution in 1808, the Articles of Religion were established as doctrinal standards for The MEC and, through the first Restrictive Rule (18., Art. I), were protected from revocation, alteration, or change. Through legislative enactment, the following two articles were added later in 1939: "Of Sanctification" and "Of the Duty of Christians to the Civil Authority" (104).

See also: Scott J. Jones, *United Methodist Doctrine: The Extreme Center* (Nashville: Abingdon Press, 2002), 48–52.

Asbury, Francis

> Whither am I going? To the New World. What to do? To gain honor? No, if I know my own heart. To get money? No: I am going to live to God, and to bring others so to do. —Francis Asbury (Elmer T. Clark, J. Manning Potts, and Jacob S. Payton, eds., *The Journal and Letters of Francis Asbury*, vol. 1 [London: Epworth Press, 1958], 4).

Francis Asbury was the person most responsible for shaping Methodism in America. He was appointed by John Wesley to the colonies at the age of twenty-six to organize and oversee the Methodist mission. He never returned to England. At the Lovely Lane Chapel Christmas Conference in December 1784, Asbury was ordained a deacon, an elder, and a general superintendent (soon to be called a bishop), all in the same service. A disciplined, ascetic, and autocratic man, Asbury traveled, led, and consistently reorganized the Methodists for forty-five years (1771–1816), in response to the growth, controversies, and cultural changes taking place in the young United States.

Key elements of today's Methodism are grounded in practices begun by Asbury. Itinerancy and conferencing, commitment to an educated clergy, the episcopacy, and the ability to adapt to cultural changes are the most prominent.

See also: Wigger, John. *American Saint: Francis Asbury and The Methodists.* Oxford, University of Oxford Press, 2009. Especially the Introduction.

Assessment of Local Church Potential

Quest. 1. Is it advisable for us to preach in as many Places as we can, without forming any Societies?

Answer: By no Means: We have made the Trial in various Places; and that for a considerable Time. But all the Seed has fallen by the wayside. There is scarce any Fruit remaining.

Quest. 2. Where should we endeavor to preach most?

Answer: 1. Where there are the greatest Number quiet and willing Hearers. 2. Where there is the most Fruit. —*Discipline*, 1785, §XIV. "Rules by which we should continue, or desist from, Preaching at any Place."

With transitioning communities and neighborhoods surrounding *local churches*, it is important for a congregation to think about how it is being called to respond in ministry and *mission* to its neighborhood. The *Discipline* has a helpful process for the Assessment of Local Church Potential (212-213). The process is designed to assist *local churches*, *pastors*, and *district superintendents* with evaluating the vitality of a *local church*, the best directions for building relationships with neighbors, or determining whether a *local church* should be merged or discontinued. This process became a part of the *Discipline* in 1996.

See also: www.umcdiscipleship.org/resources/denomination-launches -resources-to-increase-church-vitality.

Associate Member (Annual Conference)

Clergy delegates include Full Elders, Full Deacons, Associate Members, Provisional Elders, Provisional Deacons, Full-time Local Pastors, part-time Local Pastors, Retired Elders, Retired Deacons, Retired Associate Members, and Retired Provisional Members who retired before 2013. —Letter to the lay and clergy members of the South Georgia Annual Conference of 2016, sgaumc-email.brtapp.com/viewemail/428578.

Associate members of the annual conference are licensed local pastors (315.2 b) who itinerate and have the same security of appointment as provisional members of the annual conference and full connection members of the annual conference (321).

Eligibility for associate membership includes a person having: reached the age of forty, earned sixty hours of credit toward a BA from a school listed by the University Senate, completed Course of Study school and four years of service as a full-time local pastor, and received a three-fourths majority recommendation by the Board of Ordained Ministry to the clergy executive session (322).

Associate members are amenable to the annual conference, may serve on conference committees, and vote on all items except amendments to the Constitution of The United Methodist Church and on matters of ordination, character, and the conference relations of clergy.

Though associate members serve on conference committees, they are not eligible to be delegates for election to General Conference, jurisdictional conferences, or central conferences. Associate members are subject to the provisions of leave, retirement, minimum salary, and pension (321). All associate members shall be members and participants in the Fellowship of Local Pastors and Associate Members (323).

Upon meeting the necessary conditions (324.6), associate members may be received as provisional members (322.4). Associate members retain their clergy status at retirement (358).

The category of associate member was added in 1980. Prior to this development the 1964 MC *Discipline* allowed for admission of local pastors to the "traveling ministry." It provided a means by which local pastors could enter "on trial"—that is, they were ordained deacons (the pre-1996 system term) and could eventually enter into full connection and be ordained as elders. To enter into full connection in this manner there had to be "special conditions" and "exceptional promise" demonstrated by the candidate.

With the change in ministry orders in 1996, the General Conference eliminated this category with the provision that those who met the requirements could be elected as full members of the annual conference and ordained elders. The 2004 General Conference later restored this category so that local pastors who met the requirements could have a permanent relationship in the annual conference.

While some local pastors seek associate membership today, most local pastors who want to move beyond the local pastor status will more often attempt to fulfill the alternative path to ordination through the Advanced Course of Study, allowing them to seek provisional membership and then be ordained and receive full connection.

See also: Thomas Edward Frank, *Polity, Practice, and the Mission of The United Methodist Church: 2006 Edition* (Nashville: Abingdon Press, 2006), 209–10; Jack M. Tuell, *The Organization of The United Methodist Church, 2009–2012 Edition* (Nashville: Abingdon Press, 2009), 86–87.

Baptism

> By baptism we enter into covenant with God; into that everlasting covenant, which he hath commanded forever. By baptism we are admitted into the Church, and consequently made members of Christ, Its Head. —John A. Wesley, *A Treatise on Baptism* (New York: N. Bangs and T. Mason for the Methodist Episcopal Church, 1824).

Baptism "is the *sacrament* of initiation and incorporation into the Body of Christ." The *clergy* are obligated to instruct the congregation, help members teach others about baptism, and offer the opportunity for baptism to all. They are also obligated to offer *confirmation* classes and entry into the life of the *church* as *professing members* to all who are baptized. Members of the congregation who are baptized should also be reminded of the meaning of their baptism and its importance to the Christian faith (216, 340.2 *b*)).

In baptism, God's grace is extended to, recognized, and claimed for the one who is baptized. In sharp contrast to believer's baptism, this *sacrament* is a means of grace and a work of God. It is not an action—or work—of the new believer who agrees to baptism as a mark of conversion and acceptance of Christ as Lord and Savior. When we baptize a person who can understand what is taking place, baptism is a means of grace that celebrates the acceptance of justifying grace, while at the same time beginning the process of sanctification in the life of the new believer.

United Methodists baptize infants and persons who cannot answer for themselves. When we baptize a person who cannot respond with a clear understanding of or conviction of faith, God's grace is fully present and active (216).

Adults seeking baptism should receive guidance and *education* from the *pastor* about the meaning of baptism. Adult *confirmation* classes are also increasingly popular, especially for adults who have had no previous experience or understanding about a life of faith and *membership* in a *church* (216.3).

United Methodists do not re-baptize. Baptism is a means of God's grace, even if a person may have "felt" it "didn't work." It was real nevertheless. God does the baptizing. It draws a person closer to God (341.7). Instead of re-baptizing, we renew the vows taken by others on our behalf or that we took at our baptism. The "Renewal of Baptism" liturgy is found in *The United Methodist Hymnal*. It is often held annually in conjunction with the celebration of the baptism of Jesus or during a retreat or at some other important occasion. (*UMH*, 32–54.)

Baptism is a congregational experience. The ritual includes a vow taken by the congregation to support the person who is being baptized. A private baptism might be appropriate only when pastoral considerations override the possibility of having the baptism in the presence of the congregation. In these cases, include on behalf of the congregation the lay leader or another member in the ritual (*UMH*).

The form of baptism, whether it be sprinkling, pouring, or immersion, does not affect the sacrament. The water is the essential element, the visible and outward physical embodiment and representation of the transmission of God's grace that cleanses an infant from original sin and, in an older child or adult, acknowledges one's regeneration through justifying grace. A youth or adult can choose the form by which he or she is baptized. We do not immerse infants and young children (BWTS).

John Wesley remained an Anglican priest all of his life. The UM view of baptism is rooted in this tradition. Wesley's views about baptism are found in the *Articles of Religion* (XXIV) and his *Treatise on Baptism*, written in 1756. In 2000, the General Conference established two types of *church* membership. *Baptized members* are those who have been baptized but have not made a profession of faith. *Professing members* have experienced justifying grace and made a profession of faith.

See also: *By Water and the Spirit*, www.umcdiscipleship.org/resources/by -water-and-the-spirit-full-text; John Wesley, *Treatise on Baptism*.

Baptized Member—*See* Baptism

Bishop

> I have accordingly appointed Dr. Coke and Mr. Francis Asbury, to be joint Superintendents over our Brethren in North America: As also Richard Whatcoat and Thomas Vasey, to act as Elders among them, by baptizing and administering the Lord's Supper. If any one will point out, more rational and scriptural way, of feeding and guiding those poor sheep in the wilderness, I will gladly embrace it. At present I cannot see any better method than that I have taken. —John Wesley's "Pastoral Letter to the Brethren of North America" in John Hampton, *Memoirs of the Late Rev. John Wesley, A.M. with a Review of His Life and Writings, and a History of Methodism* (Sunderland: James Graham, 1791), 178–79.

The office of bishop is a "special ministry" of the *Church*, "not a separate order" (402). Elected from among the *elders* in the *annual conferences*, bishops are set apart for the superintending role of general oversight, supervision, servant leadership (48. Article III; 401) and equipping The UMC for disciple making (403). As an expression of the superintending ministry of the *Church*, "The role of the bishop is to uphold the *discipline* and order of the *Church* by consecrating, ordaining, *commissioning*, supervising, and appointing persons in ministry to the *Church* and the world" (403.1 *f*)). One of the special presidential responsibilities of the bishop is the ordination of *clergy*. Bishops ordain by the "laying on of hands" and may be assisted by other *elders*, laity, and leaders from *Church* partners in *full communion* (30.7, 333.3). Bishops also consecrate other bishops and commission *missionaries, deaconesses,* and *home missioners* (415.7).

Bishops are assisted in their oversight of the *annual conference* and clergy by *district superintendents* (55. Article X) who are appointed to serve on the bishop's *cabinet* and have distinct responsibilities (402). Bishops also preside over the sessions of *annual conferences, jurisdictional conferences, central conferences,* and *General Conferences* (415.1), and decide in matters of law (52. Article VII).

Bishops are elected by the delegations of the *jurisdictional conference* or *central conference* that has no jurisdictions (47. Article II). They are amenable to the *jurisdiction* or *central conference* where they are elected (523), and accountable to the *jurisdictional or central conference committee on episcopacy*. With the exception of bishops in *central conferences*, bishops have a lifetime tenure (51. Article VI). Bishops in each region or *jurisdiction* compose a College of Bishops that plans for the episcopal oversight of the *annual conferences* and *missionary conferences* in their territories (49. Article IV). All bishops, active and retired, are members of the *Council of Bishops* (48. Article III).

The 2012 *General Conference* approved a plan that folded the work of The UMC's denominational ecumenical agency, the General Commission on Christian Unity and Interreligious Concerns, into the *Council of Bishops*. This created the Office of Christian Unity and Interreligious Relationships (OCUIR) and gave the bishops oversight of ecumenical and interreligious relationships. In 2024 the OCUIR was converted to the Advisory Committee on Ecumenical and Interfaith Relationships (ACEIR) (431.3; 437).

The 2016 *General Conference* reestablished the Committee on Faith and Order (CFO) to "give leadership to The UMC in reflecting upon, discerning and living out matters of faith, doctrinal teaching, order, and discipline in the midst of mission and ministry in the *Church* and world" (444). This committee is "related and amenable to the *Council of Bishops*" (443). On occasion, the *Council of Bishops* offers statements, pastoral letters, and foundation documents as a way of speaking to the whole Church. Some examples include "In Defense of Creation" (1986), "Community with Children and the Poor: Renewing the Episcopal Initiative" (2001), "Our Shared Dream—The Beloved Community" (2003), and "A Way Forward" (2016 General Conference).

From the beginning, the episcopacy, understood as general superintendency, has been one of the marks of Methodist *polity*. Reading Lord Peter King's *Account of the Primitive Church*, John Wesley was convinced that "presbyters" and "bishops" were of the same order and had the same right to ordain. After failing to convince Anglican bishops to ordain priests for North America, Wesley, along with two Anglican priests, James Creighton and Thomas Coke, ordained Thomas Vasey and Richard Whatcoat, as *deacons*, and the next morning as *elders*. Then Wesley appointed Thomas Coke as a *superintendent* for the new *church* in North America. In a pastoral letter, Wesley revealed his *mission* plan for the *church* and his intention for Thomas Coke and Francis Asbury to supervise the movement. Refusing Wesley's *appointment*, Asbury insisted that the preachers elect both as *superintendents*. Asbury substituted the word "bishop" for "*superintendent*" in the conference minutes, inciting Wesley's displeasure.

Though the history of Methodism demonstrates the honor and respect given to the office of bishop and records a long struggle over the role, power, tenure, and questions of order, The UMC continues to elect and consecrate episcopal leaders.

See also: James E. Kirby, *The Episcopacy in American Methodism* (Nashville: Kingswood Books, 2000); Russell E. Richey and Thomas Edward Frank, *Episcopacy in the Methodist Tradition: Perspectives and Proposals* (Nashville: Abingdon Press, 2004). For the Committee on Faith and Order, see www .unitedmethodistbishops.org/committee-on-faith-and-order-quadrennium.

Bishops' Documents—*See Bishop*

Board of Ordained Ministry (BOOM)

That it be the duty of the bishop or bishops, or a committee which they may appoint in each annual conference, to point out a course of reading and study proper to be pursued by candidates for the ministry; and the presiding elders, whenever a person is presented as a candidate for the ministry, shall direct him to those studies which have been thus recommended. And before any such candidate shall be received into full connection, he shall give satisfactory evidence respecting his knowledge of those particular subjects which have been recommended to his consideration. —Resolution adopted at the 1816 General Conference, Bangs, vol. 3, 47.

After *General Conference*, the *annual conference* elects a Board of Ordained Ministry (BOOM) comprising *clergy* and laity for a term of four years. The responsibilities of the BOOM include: recruitment of ministerial leadership, working with the *GBHEM* to interpret ministry, developing a culture of call in the *annual conference*, the examination of candidates for ministry, training mentors for *Course of Study pastors*, and reviewing reports on candidates and student *local pastors*. It also oversees *clergy* relations, serves as a liaison to retired *clergy*, consulting with the *bishop*, supporting ministerial leadership, working with the *Orders* of *Deacons* and *Elders*, and the *Fellowship of Associate Members and Local Pastors*, evaluating ministerial leadership, validating special ministries where *clergy* are appointed, supporting diaconal ministers, certifying *lay ministers*, administering the *annual conferences* portion of the Ministerial Education Fund, and coordinates with the *GBHEM* (634). A Conference Relations Committee is established by the Board of Ordained Ministry to hear cases involving changes in *clergy* relationship (361.1). A designated representative of BOOM serves on each *district committee on ministry*, which functions as a subcommittee of the BOOM (634).

In The MECS, the earliest practices of evaluations of *clergy* qualifications at the *annual conference* are found in the committees established by the *annual conference* for the examination of candidates who had completed the *Course of Study.* In 1898, the "committee on admissions," separate from the committee on examinations, was established by The MECS. Parallel MEC *Disciplines* speak of a "Committee on Conference Relations" without identifying its responsibilities. Candidates had to submit answers to only two questions to this committee: (1) Are you in debt so as to embarrass you in your ministry? and (2) Will you wholly abstain from the use of tobacco? (146). With the reunification in 1939, this committee became the "Committee of Traveling *Elders* on Conference Relations and Ministerial Qualifications" in The MC, thus combining the tasks of examination and maintaining the records of *clergy* relationships with the *annual conference.* It was renamed again with the merger of 1968.

See also: www.gbhem.org/clergy/boards-ordained-ministry; www.gbhem .org/wp-content/uploads/2023/06/BOM-Handbook_complete.pdf.

Board of Trustees

> That no person shall be eligible as a Trustee to any of our churches or colleges, nor act as a Steward or Leader, that is not in constant church-communion, and a regular leader or member of a class. 2. That no person that is a Trustee, shall be ejected while he is in joint security for money, unless such relief be given him as is demanded, or the person who makes the loan will accept. —*Discipline*, 1789, §XXVII. "On Building Churches, and on the Order to be observed therein."

Trustees are elected by the charge/church conference (258.3) and have "supervision, oversight, and care of all real property" and "equipment" owned by the local church (2533). Qualifications for being a trustee include being of legal age and at least one-third must be professing members of the church (2525). Trustees are responsible for monitoring insurance (2533.2), monitoring use of properties by outside groups (2533.3), annual review of the parsonage (2533.4), administering bequests (2533.5), an accessibility audit (2533.6), determining the adequacy of storage of church records, archives, and historical objects (2533.7), and performing an audit of the church's carbon footprint (2533.8). Trustees make an annual report to the charge/ church conference (2550). Trustees are subject to the direction of the pastor and district superintendent (in absence of the pastor) for the religious use of the church property, such "that pews in The United Methodist Church shall always be free" (2533). Though the term "trustee" as it appears in the *Discipline* is synonymous with the term "director" in a corporation, the Board of Trustees is always amenable to the direction of the charge conference (2529). Both the annual conference (640), the district (2518), and United Methodist Institutions (2552) have a Board of Trustees.

As the Methodist movement grew, the management and financing of properties necessitated the consideration of the need for standards, rules, and legal implications for properties as they were rented, purchased, or built. In 1746, Wesley, in order to better further the movement, executed legal measures to have seven trustees manage the preaching houses in Bristol, Kingswood, and Newcastle. The arrangements required the trustees to permit Wesley and others to use the premises for preaching and teaching.

See also: Richard P. Heitzenrater, *Wesley and the People Called Methodists* (Nashville: Abingdon Press, 1995), 169; www.umc.org/what-we-believe /board-of-trustees.

Book of Discipline

> The *Book of Discipline* is the first written instrument uniting us in The United Methodist Church. We trust it shall be a vehicle aiding us in exploring the land of God's love more courageously. —The Council of Bishops, Lloyd C. Wicke, Reuben H. Mueller. *Discipline*, 1968, vi.

The Book of Discipline of The United Methodist Church (2020/2024) is the most current statement on how UMs agree to organize for life together, answering God's call to ministry and *mission* in the world. The product of over two hundred years of general conferencing, the book contains the *Constitution of The United Methodist Church*, theology, doctrine, *General Rules*, *Mission Statement of The UMC*, *Social Principles*, law, and organizational structure.

The *Book of Discipline* grew out of a process of practical theology conducted between John Wesley and his preachers, resulting in the British "Large Minutes." Initially a foundational document for the nascent North American Church, each new *General Conference* of the antecedent denominations composing The UMC has made contributions to the *Discipline* as it amends, adds to, and clarifies the text. Previous editions of this document were known as the *Doctrines and Discipline of the Methodist Episcopal Church*. With the merger of The MC and EUBC *churches* in 1968, the text became known as the *Book of Discipline*.

All persons applying for *annual conference* membership and *ordination* are expected to follow the *Discipline*. In the "Historic Examination for Admission into Full Connection," candidates are asked: "11. Have you studied our form of *Church* discipline and *polity*? 12. Do you approve our *Church* government and *polity*? 13. Will you support and maintain them?" (336).

The 2012 General Conference added "Part II, Global Book of Discipline" reflecting the worldwide nature of The UMC as a "denomination united by doctrine, discipline, and mission through our connectional covenant" (101). The 2016 General Conference changed "Global" to "General" in Part II to convey unity in terminology (i.e., General Conference, general superintendents).

To more faithfully accomplish the *mission* of the *Church*, *central conferences* are permitted to make "changes and adaptations" to the *Book of Discipline* (32. Article IV.5.), though certain parts cannot be changed (101). In consultation with the CFO, the *Standing Committee on Central Conference Matters* will bring legislative recommendations to the 2020 *General Conference* plenary session for the consideration of a "Part VI, General Organization and Administration not subject to change or adaptation by *central conferences*... and a Part VII, Additional Organization and Administration, adaptable by *central conferences*" (101).

See also www.umnews.org/en/news/gc2012-how-book-of-discipline-comes -to-be.

Book of Resolutions

> The *Book of Resolutions* is a product of The United Methodist Church, belongs to the church, and should be available to the church for the widest possible use. If the approaching General Conference is fully to respect its theme about making disciples for world transformation, it must reject all "penny-wise, pound-foolish" proposals and make every effort to put the *Book of Resolutions* into serious play at every level of the church's life.
> —A. W. Martin, Professor of Religion Emeritus, Oklahoma City University and a retired elder, Arkansas Annual Conference, The United Methodist Church, www.umc.org/news-and-media/blogs-commentaries/post/book-of-resolutions-guides-church-ministry; accessed May 25, 2017.

The *Book of Resolutions* contains The UMC's positions on current social policies, educational resources, various guidelines, and official documents (e.g., "This Holy Mystery"). Organized around the categories of the *Social Principles* (i.e., Community of All Creation, The Economic Community, The Social Community, and The Political Community), the resolutions are intended to be influential and instructive but are not considered to be *Church* law. A 60 percent affirmative vote of the *General Conference* is required for a resolution to be officially adopted and unless readopted, it expires after an eight-year period, no longer being printed in the book (511.2.*a*)). *The Book of Resolutions* is edited by the *United Methodist Publishing House* (511.2) and made available on The UMC website (511.2.*a*)).

Beginning with The MC, resolutions were kept as an appendix in the *Discipline*. Prior to the merger, resolutions did not show up in the *Discipline* at all, presumably lodged in the minutes and thus, in the journals of the *General Conferences*. In the 1976 *Book of Discipline* of The UMC, the *Book of Resolutions* was mentioned for the first time as an index of all the resolutions beginning with the uniting conference of 1968. It has been a parallel text to The UMC *Book of Discipline* ever since.

See also: https://www.umc.org/en/content/glossary-book-of-resolutions-the.

Book of Worship

I believe there is no Liturgy in the World, either in ancient or modern language, which breathes more of a solid, scriptural, rational Piety, than the Common Prayer of the Church of England. Little alteration is made in the following edition of it (which I recommend to our Societies in North America) except in the following instances. . . . The Service of the Lord's Day, the length of which has been often complained of, is considerably shortened.
—James F. White, ed., *John Wesley's Prayer Book: The Sunday Service of the Methodists in North America* (Akron, OH: OSL Publications, 1991), 1.

In 1992, *The United Methodist Publishing House* published the *Book of Worship* as an official UM resource for *worship* planning. This resource contains the explanation of liturgy and provides prayers, litanies, *rituals*, services, and observances for many occasions. It was provided for in the *Constitution of The United Methodist Church*, which states that it is a responsibility of the general *Church* to provide and revise the *UMH* and *ritual* of the *Church* (17.6).

This resource stands in a long tradition of *hymnals*, *rituals*, and books of worship in Methodist denominations dating back to John Wesley's provision of *The Sunday Service of the Methodists in North America* in 1784. Historically, the *rituals* were included in the *Discipline* as a part of the extensive appendix that included the *curriculum* for the *Course of Study*, decisions by *bishops* prior to the existence of the *Judicial Council*, occasional inclusions of resolutions and addresses by the *bishops*, and other items determined by the particular *General Conference* for that *Discipline*.

See also: www.umcdiscipleship.org/worship/book-of-worship.

Building Committee—*See* Property

Buildings—*See* Property

Cabinet

"I am fully convinced of the utility and necessity of the council of Presiding Elders in stationing the preachers," McKendree wrote to Asbury . . . in response to Asbury's continued objections Asbury would form a plan to station the preachers as he had always done, and then McKendree would review this plan with the "assistance" of the presiding elders. "But I still refuse to take the whole responsibility upon myself" McKendree wrote.
—John Wigger, *American Saint: Francis Asbury and the Methodists* (New York: Oxford University Press, 2009), 382.

The Cabinet is an expression of the superintending leadership of The UMC (424) and comprises the *bishop* and *district superintendents* (424). The number of *district superintendents*, appointed by the *bishop*, differs according to the size and needs of the *annual conference*. Each *annual conference* has its own cabinet, while the *bishop* may serve an *episcopal area* that includes more than one cabinet. While each *bishop* leads his or her cabinet in a different way, the cabinet is an epicenter of conference-wide missional strategy. When considering matters of the *annual conference* program, members of the extended cabinet, such as the director of *connectional ministries* and director of ministerial services, will be included (424.6). The cabinet identifies missional strategies for new *church* development, congregational transformation, and *church* closures. The *appointments of clergy* are a key part of this missional strategy. These appointments are then "fixed" by the *bishop* during the *annual conference* session.

At a very early stage in Methodist history, Francis Asbury began appointing presiding *elders* to areas that eventually formed into *annual conferences*. The position was made official in 1792. As the number of *annual conferences* grew westward, the *bishops* had greater difficulty with handling the *clergy*-relations matters between the annual meetings of each conference, because they did not reside in specific conferences over which they presided. They were truly itinerant in that they literally traveled from conference to conference "throughout the connection" during their tenure as *bishops*. When *bishops* began to reside in assigned cities in The MEC in 1872, the evolution toward a resident *bishop* with a cabinet of presiding *elders* with oversight of *districts* began. With the reunification of 1939, the establishment of cabinets with a *bishop* who resided in an *episcopal area* (that might include more than one conference) and presiding *elders*, now renamed *district superintendents*, took place. Reference to the cabinet is first made briefly in the early *Disciplines* of The MC, but in the 1956 *Discipline*, responsibilities were expanded and detailed throughout significant parts of the *Discipline*.

See also: Annual conference websites.

Candidacy

Quest. 1. How shall we try those who profess to be moved by the Holy Ghost to preach? Answ. 1. Let them be asked the following Questions, viz. Do they know God as a pardoning god? Have they the Love of God abiding in them? Do they desire and seek nothing but God? And are they holy in all Manner of Conversation? 2. Have they Gifts (as well as Grace) for the work? Have they (in some tolerable Degree) a clear, sound Understanding, a right Judgment in the Things of God, a just Conception of Salvation by Faith? And has God given them any Degree of Utterance? Do they speak justly, readily, clearly? 3. Have they Fruit? Are any truly convinced of Sin, and converted to God by their preaching? —*Discipline*, 1785, §XII. "Of the Trial of those who think they are moved by the Holy Ghost to preach."

Candidacy involves the examination of persons who sense a calling to licensed or ordained ministry (310-314). This process begins in the *local church* and continues with the *District Committee on Ordained Ministry* and certification of candidacy (310). Certified candidates who have been to *License for Pastoral Ministry School* may be appointed as *licensed local pastors* (311). Candidacy must be renewed annually by the *Charge/Church Conference* and *District Committee on Ordained Ministry* (313). Wesley established a process of testing candidates to be preachers during the earliest days of the Methodist movement. It was formalized in the first *Discipline* of The MEC in 1785. A candidate became an exhorter and a helper (and possibly a local preacher) to the *elders* and *deacons* prior to ever coming before an *annual conference* for election and *ordination*. At each stage, candidates were expected to exhibit progress in their abilities, or they would not be moved on to the next stage. Testimony is given throughout our histories of young men who resigned or were expelled from ministry because they did not exhibit fruit while "on trial" and even after they became *deacons* and *elders*.

See also: www.gbhem.org/ministry/explore-your-call-to-ministry /candidacy/.

Caucuses

> How then . . . do we respond forcefully and responsibly to racism in The United Methodist Church? We unashamedly reply—black power! —"The Black Paper," issued at the organizational meeting of BMCR, Cincinnati, OH, February 1968, www.bmcrumc.org/history; accessed May 24, 2017.

Caucuses have been increasingly active in United Methodism since the 1960s. Though not officially established through the *General Conference*, caucuses are organized for various reasons and provide a voice for groups and purposes advocating for inclusion, equality in leadership, and economic justice. A member from each of the following racial/ethnic caucuses is elected to the *Connectional Table*: Black Methodists for Church Renewal (BMCR), Methodists Associated Representing the Cause of Hispanic/Latinx Americans (MARCHA), the New Federation of Asian American United Methodists (NFAAUM), Native American International Caucus (NAIC), and the Pacific Islander Caucus of United Methodists (PINCUM) (906.1 *f*)).

Black Methodists for Church Renewal was founded in February 1968; MARCHA, the Hispanic American caucus, in 1970; the Federation of Asian American United Methodists in 1975; the Native American International Caucus in 1998. In 1971, the National Women's Caucus was established to support the creation of the *GCOSROW* through *General Conference* legislation. Following the establishment of the *GCOSROW*, the caucus has continued to advocate for the full participation of women in the episcopacy and ministry. The Pacific Islander National Caucus appears to have begun in 2008, with the approval of the 2008 *General Conference* to establish a National Plan for Pacific Islander Ministry.

See also: Thomas E. Frank, *Polity, Practice, and the Mission of The United Methodist Church* (Nashville: Abingdon Press, 2006), 264–68; www.bmcrumc.org; www.marchaumc.org; www.nfaaum.org; www.glaad .org/tags/native-americaninternational-caucus-united-methodist-church; www.pincum.org.

Cemetery, Columbarium, and Memorial Garden

> The best of all, God is with us. The last words of John Wesley. —Kenneth J. Collins, *A Real Christian: The Life of John Wesley* (Nashville: Abingdon Press, 1999), 158.

Many historic *churches* have cemeteries on land adjacent to their buildings. In recent years, some *churches* have established a columbarium or memorial garden to provide members with a means to locate cremains of loved ones. The *Discipline* says nothing about *local churches* maintaining cemeteries, columbaria, or memorial gardens; *annual conferences* may provide guidelines appropriate to the state.

While it made sense culturally and logistically to locate cemeteries adjacent to rural *churches*, most cities, towns, and counties now have ordinances prohibiting the development or expansion of church-owned cemeteries. Cemeteries must also submit to numerous regulations, and they have significant maintenance demands, making it unreasonable for most congregations to manage them.

Churches that have a cemetery should establish an independent cemetery association that holds legal title to the cemetery land, has its own Board of Trustees, registers it as a nonprofit endeavor with the IRS, maintains liability insurance, records a plot plan with the names and dates of persons buried in the cemetery (many are then posted online for genealogical research), establishes an endowment for its perpetual care, and is responsible for its ongoing care and maintenance. An association frees both the congregation and *pastor* from these ongoing concerns and ensures the long-term care of the cemetery in the event that the *church* relocates or closes. The association must abide by local and state regulations for cemeteries.

Many *churches* have also established a part of their building or land as a location for a columbarium or memorial garden that can accommodate ashes of deceased loved ones. A columbarium has small compartments that hold an urn, while most memorial gardens simply allow for the internment of urns or cremains directly into the ground. Columbaria and memorial gardens must also follow local and state laws regarding structure and location. Both columbaria and memorial gardens are illegal in some communities.

While the congregation may not establish an independent association to develop and manage a columbarium, it should still establish an oversight committee to ensure that local law allows for one to exist on *church property*; establish policies, procedures, and fees for its use; maintain liability insurance; and build an endowment to ensure its long-term care. It should also have an agreed-upon plan established in the event that it might have to be moved or if it is damaged in a disaster. Local congregations must do proper research if they are considering the possibility of a columbarium or memorial garden. Many *local church* policies are accessible online.

See also: Annual Conference policies

Central Conferences—*See also* Regional Conferences

¶296. When in any of our Foreign Mission fields there is more than one Annual Conference or Mission, or more than one form of Methodism, it shall be lawful, either by order of the General Conference or by a majority vote of all the Conferences or Missions wishing to unite, with the written call of the Bishop having Episcopal Supervision of the field, to organize a Central Conference, to be composed either of all the members of those Annual Conferences or Missions, or of representatives from the same, . . . who may also provide for the admission of Laymen to such Conference, the number of Lay Delegates not to exceed that of the Clerical Delegates. —*Discipline*, MEC, 1884.

Outside the United States, *annual conferences* were organized into central conferences (39. Article II) according to the boundaries set by *General Conference* (29. Article I). Currently, there are seven central conferences: Africa, Congo, West Africa, Central and Southern Europe, Germany, Northern Europe and Eurasia, and the Philippines. The 2016 *General Conference* also approved the Southeast Asia and Mongolia provisional central conference. Though similar to *jurisdictions* in structure and function, central conferences are unique in their manner of electing *bishops*, adapting parts of the *Discipline*, and appointing a judicial court to handle legal questions and hear appeals (32. Article IV). As a support to central conferences, the Standing Committee on Central Conference Matters (2201) serves as an independent coordinating body, facilitated by the *GBGM*, to study the supervision and structure of The UMC outside the US and its relationship with other bodies of the *Church*. The committee relates directly to the *General Conference* in matters regarding affiliation and autonomy (572), *episcopal area*s (404.1), and joining The UMC (575). The committee is elected by the *General Conference* and receives funding through *general funds* allocated by the *GCFA*. Central conferences were first established in Asia (India in 1885; China in 1897), Europe (1908), and Latin America and Africa (1920s) by The MEC. Identified first as "central mission conferences" in The MEC in 1884, the term "central" was used to identify the way in which a collection of different annual mission conferences was brought together to carry out specific purposes in a central location, but also to provide greater autonomy for decision-making by indigenous leaders. The MECS followed with the term "central conference" in 1926. The MPC developed an *annual conference* in Japan and had mission work in India and China, but did not create central conferences. Though many central conferences are still affiliated with The UMC, many conferences in Asia and Latin America became fully autonomous denominations in the 1930s and 1960s.

The reunification of The MEC, MECS, and MPC in 1939 was a turning point for central conferences. At this General Conference the rights and responsibilities that central conferences still enjoy today were afforded to them. Indigenous bishops were then elected by the central conferences themselves. Internal structures such as Courses of Study for pastors were established. Their own institutions and structures gave central conferences the ability to function and structure themselves in ways appropriate to their contexts. At the time, there were six central conferences that included China, Southern Asia, Latin America, Northern Europe, Germany, and the Philippine Islands. Three of these do not exist today. The China central conference was decimated during the China-Japanese War and the Communist takeover. Southern Asia and Latin America transformed into autonomous Methodist denominations within their own countries.

See also www.umc.org/en/content/central-conferences.

Chaplaincy

> Gentlemen, . . . Yet without this it may fairly be said that the Methodist Episcopal Church, not less devoted than the best, is, by its greater numbers, the most important of all…the Methodist Church sends more soldiers to the field, more nurses to the hospitals, and more prayers to heaven than any. God bless the Methodist Church! . . . who in this our great trial giveth us the Churches! —May 18, 1864, A Lincoln. RRS, Vol 2, p. 327.

UMC clergy may become chaplains, as distinct from the role of pastor, for a wide range of institutions including but not limited to the military, hospitals, hospice, nursing home, prisons, police departments, and schools. These positions are extension ministries that open the door for extending the mission of the church into and for the transformation of the world predominantly through pastoral leadership and care and spiritual formation. Their work is predominantly ecumenical and interfaith. Some institutions allow for trained laity as well, depending on whether ability to celebrate the sacraments is a requirement. Chaplains work in either paid or volunteer capacities. Most institutions that hire chaplains require endorsement by the denomination. The *GBHEM* is the agency that contains the United Methodist Endorsing Agency.

Chaplaincy began as early as the fourth century as priests were sent out to establish chapels, most often tents, to guard sacred relics that were made available to the people. Increasingly they were assigned to specialized locations such as palaces and universities. Prior to Methodism in the US, chaplains were first sent out to troops during the Revolutionary War as members of a

Chaplaincy Corps. During the Civil War, over 500 Methodist clergy in the South served as chaplains to troops and in hospitals and "Army missionaries" often moving with regiments from their own towns. The Missionary Society and publishing house provided them with materials for the "Army Mission." Likewise, the northern church deployed over 800 of their clergy, 38 percent of the Union chaplains, whose work in conjunction with the YMCA's "Christian Commission" saw revival break out among Union troops from 1863–1865. Methodist chaplaincy gained full professional recognition because of their participation in World War II and a desire for increasing specialization. A "Commission on Chaplains" appeared for the first time in the 1944 *Discipline* and by 1948 had its own paragraph, 1595, designating its responsibilities and membership.

See also: www.gbhem.org/ministry/chaplaincy-endorsed-ministries/become -a-chaplain/. Richey, Rowe, and Schmidt, *The Methodist Experience in America: A History*, Volume 1 (Nashville, Abingdon Press: 2010), 198–207.

The Character of a Methodist

'What then is the mark? Who is a Methodist, according to your own account?' I answer: a Methodist is one who has 'the LOVE of God shed abroad in his heart by the Holy Ghost given unto him'; one who 'LOVEs the Lord his God with all his heart, and with all his soul, and with all his mind, and with all his strength'. —"The Character of a Methodist" (1742), §1.5, *Works*, Volume 9:35.

In his treatise on "The Character of a Methodist," John Wesley sought to explain in the early part of the movement that a Methodist is no more than a genuine Christian. Thus, the distinguishing marks are not "*opinions*, but *the Word of God* as the *only and the sufficient* rule both of Christian faith and practice"; nor "*words and phrases* (i.e., *any quaint or uncommon set of expressions*)"; nor "*actions*, or *customs*, or *usages* of an *indifferent* nature (our religion does not lie in doing what God has not enjoined, or abstaining from what he hath not forbidden)"; nor "laying the *whole stress* of religion on any *single part* of it." According to Wesley, the distinguishing mark is *one who has 'the love of God shed abroad in his heart by the Holy Ghost given unto him"; one who 'loves* the Lord his God with all his heart, and with all his soul, and with all his mind, and with all his strength." "God's perfect love casts out fear" is the basis for the love of neighbor, every person, all humankind, and every child of God, purifies the heart, pleases God, and provides the basis for service, becoming a living sacrifice, holy and acceptable to God. Thus, the love of God and neighbor is the basic ethic that defines Methodist Christianity.

According to Tom Frank PPM (48–50), the organizational polity of the early Methodist movement was designed to grow people in the love of God and neighbor. This challenges us to think about what our current polity fosters.

See also: www.wesleyscholar.com/wp-content/uploads/2018/09/Character.

Charge

> Quest. What are the duties of a preacher who has the charge of a circuit, station, or mission? ¶142. To preach the gospel; to celebrate the rite of matrimony, provided it does not conflict with civil laws; . . . to control the appointment of all services to be held in the Church in his charge. —*Discipline*, MECS, 1918.

Pastors are appointed to a pastoral charge, not to a *church*. A pastoral charge is the *appointment* to which a *pastor* is sent by the *bishop* and *cabinet* which may consist of one or more *churches* organized into one *charge conference* (205). A station is a charge with a single *church*, and a circuit or cooperative parish is a pastoral charge consisting of more than one *church* (205.2).

The language of "charge" as it relates to a pastoral *appointment* emerged in The MECS *Discipline* of 1918, and spoke primarily to the role of the *pastor* as "in charge." The term quickly evolved to mean the actual collection of *churches* and *missions* in which a *pastor* would be in charge, evidenced in the *Discipline* of 1922, which spoke of concerns regarding the actual "division of a charge" and referenced concerns for equal division of *property*. The term "pastoral charge" is evident in the earliest *Disciplines* of The MC, following the reunification of 1939, as having its own Official Board (forerunner of the *Church Council*), and still maintaining quarterly conferences (forerunner of the *charge conference*). By the 1964 MC *Discipline*, the entire section on the *local church* led with five paragraphs that defined the pastoral charge.

See also: Clergy locator on annual conference websites.

Charge or Church Conference

There shall be organized in each charge a Charge Conference composed of such persons and invested with such powers as the General Conference shall provide Unless the General Conference shall order otherwise, the officers of the church or churches constituting a charge shall be elected by the Charge Conference. —*Discipline*, UMC, 1968, ¶¶48, 49.

The basic unit in the UM connectional system is the charge conference (246) as set forth in the *Constitution of The United Methodist Church* (44). It shall meet annually, but it may also meet at other specified times (246.1). Any charge conference requires the approval of the *district superintendent* to meet (246.4). The charge conference consists of the elected leadership (i.e., *Church Council* or governing structure), the *pastor(s)*, and *district superintendent*, and reviews the ministry and *mission* of the *church*, making required reports (247, 249, 2550) to the *annual conference*. The removal of an officer or the filling of a vacancy requires a charge conference as well (250). The date and time are set by the *district superintendent* (246.4), and a ten-day notice of the meeting is required (246.8).

Charge conferences may be conducted as a *church* conference, allowing all *professing members* to vote in the proceedings (248). Calling a *church* conference also requires the permission of the *district superintendent*. A *church* conference is mandated for a building program (2544.7).

The reports required for the annual charge conference are usually distributed by the *district superintendent* and/or posted on the *annual conference* website. They are also located on the *GCFA* website. The *Discipline* mandates one set of reports, but others may be added by the *annual conference*.

The charge conference came into being with the 1968 merger that created The UMC. The annual charge conference replaced the historic quarterly conferences held by the circuits for the original purpose of *sacraments* and administration. With the establishment of the Official Board of local *churches* in The MC, quarterly meetings were less necessary.

See also: Annual conference websites; www.gcfa.org/forms-and-assets.

Children's Ministry

> But what shall we do for the rising generation? Who will labour for them? Let him who is zealous for God and the souls of men begin now. 1. Where there are the children whose parents are in a society, meet them at least an hour every week. 2. Talk with them every time you see any at home. . . .
>
> 5. Preach expressly on education. "But I have no gift for this." Gift or no gift, you are to do it; else you are not called to be a Methodist-preacher.
> —General Minutes, 1784, 19.

One of the historical questions for those seeking full connection is "Will you diligently instruct the children in every place?" (336, #14). United Methodist pastors and churches are committed to this through the instruction of parents, through the baptism of their infants and children, education and training in the Christian faith (216), and admonishment of the congregation in their responsibility for the nurture of children (226).

In the 1785 *Discipline*, section XXVI provided directions to preachers on the instruction of children. In each society with at least ten children, they were to meet with them for one hour per week. Upon their experience of "being truly awakened" they were then admitted into the society. Preachers who resisted were strongly admonished—in the *Discipline* itself—to do it, whether they had the gift of working with children or not, and to continue to pray for the gift until they could do it comfortably.

See also: https://www.umcdiscipleship.org/equipping-leaders/children.

Christian Year

Since ancient times, Christians have divided the day into hours, the week into days, and the year into days and seasons of special Christian signifi-

cance. This "sanctification of time" not only gives Christian meaning to the hours, days, and seasons, but also is a way of encouraging, over a period of time, a balanced presentation of the various events in the history of salvation and the various emphases of Christian teaching. Through the centuries, while there has been much variation from time to time and from church to church, the Christian Calendar in its essentials is a unifying heritage.
—*Companion to the Book of Services: Introduction, Commentary, and Instructions for Using the New United Methodist Services, Supplemental Worship Resources* 17 (Nashville: Abingdon Press, 1988), 71ff.

Since the time of the early *Church*, Christians have developed and utilized the Christian year. The primary day in the calendar is the Lord's Day (understood to be Sunday) because of the resurrection of Jesus Christ. Following this pattern, the Christian year emphasizes key events in the life and saving work of Jesus Christ.

The Christian year is divided into two cycles: the Christmas Cycle and the Easter Cycle, with the Sundays after Pentecost composing a third unit. The Christmas Cycle begins with Advent (four Sundays before Christmas) and focuses on the past, present, and future coming of Christ. Christmas celebrates the birth of Jesus and is understood as not only a day but also a season. Epiphany highlights the manifestation of God in Jesus Christ and is followed by the Season after Epiphany, which includes Baptism of the Lord Sunday and Transfiguration Sunday.

The Easter Cycle begins on Ash Wednesday, the first day of the Lenten season, and is traditionally a time of devotion and renewal for believers, and preparation for converts seeking *baptism* and *church membership*. The Season of Lent culminates with Holy Week, which includes Palm/Passion Sunday, commemorating Jesus's triumphal entry into the city of Jerusalem; Holy Thursday (sometimes referred to as "Maundy," a Latin word meaning "command"), with attention to Jesus's new commandment to "love one another; even as I have loved you" (John 13:34 RSV); and Good Friday, observing the crucifixion of Jesus. Easter celebrates the resurrection of Jesus Christ and begins the Easter Season, which culminates at Pentecost, witnessing the coming of the Holy Spirit upon the *Church*. The Sunday after Pentecost is Trinity

Sunday and begins the Season after Pentecost and culminates with Christ the King Sunday. All Saints Sunday is typically celebrated in early November.

Churches emphasize these days and the seasons of the Christian year with different colors, rituals, and lections. In some *churches*, the recognition of saints has been tied to certain days within the Christian year.

To connect the liturgical seasons more directly with Christ, Wesley made several changes to the Christian year in *The Sunday Service of the Methodists in North America*, which he prepared for The MEC in 1784. Namely, he removed the number of Sundays devoted to saints, and though retaining the lessons of the days themselves, Wesley removed any mention of Epiphany and Lent. Current versions of the Christian year are a product of the cooperative work of several Christian denominations.

See also: www.umcdiscipleship.org/worship.

Church

On April 23, 1968, The United Methodist Church was created when Bishop Reuben H. Mueller, representing The Evangelical United Brethren Church, and Bishop Lloyd C. Wicke of The Methodist Church joined hands at the constituting General Conference in Dallas, Texas. With the words, "Lord of the Church, we are united in Thee, in Thy Church and now in The United Methodist Church," the new denomination was given birth by two churches that had distinguished histories and influential ministries in various parts of the world. —www.umc.org/who-we-are/formation-of-the-united-methodist-church, accessed July 15, 2017.

From a polity perspective, the English word "church" is used in four primary ways.

First, based on the biblical term *ekklesia* meaning "called out," it defines a gathering of people who are called to be together as a congregation of persons committed to one another through their vows to God through Jesus Christ, to the denomination, and to one another.

Second, the word is often used to mean the building(s) in which the people gather to be formed as disciples through worship, spiritual formation, education, fellowship, and service, and then be sent out to participate in and contribute to the positive transformation of the world. These first two constitute what Methodists most often call a local church.

Third, "Church" (with a capital C) is used to identify a body made up of many *local churches*, along with shared structures of oversight, resources, and commitments to a particular set of doctrines, rules, and practices. These Churches are often called denominations. The UMC is a good example of a denomination that has grown too large and complex to be a denomination. Currently, references are often made to The UMC as a "general Church" rather than as a denomination.

Fourth, the word "Church" (again, with a capital C) is used to mean the one, holy, apostolic, and universal gathering of all Christians, visible and invisible, both living and dead, that is moving toward eventual consummation in the fully realized reign of God on earth and in heaven.

The earliest references to "church" in Methodism referred to The Church of England and to buildings in which the class meetings and societies met. In England, however, Wesley originally insisted on calling these buildings "meeting houses" and "chapels," so as not to be misunderstood for trying to start a new Church. In US Methodism, Asbury and others spoke of building churches as in constructing buildings for the societies and also named the new denomination The Methodist Episcopal Church. As Methodists settled into being a denomination, societies grew and stabilized and were eventually called "churches."

When several churches gather together, there is often reference to the way in which all of the Christians are taking part in the Church universal that includes all Christians.

See also: www.umc.org/en/content/formation-of-the-united-methodist -church.

Church Council

¶103. Whenever the Quarterly Conference of any charge shall desire it, it may organize, and continue during its pleasure, an Official Board to be composed of all the Members of the Quarterly Conference, including all the Trustees, except . . . as are not members of the Methodist Episcopal Church . . . shall be presided over by the Preacher in Charge, . . . may discharge the duties belonging to the Leaders and Stewards' meeting . . . devise and carry into effect suitable plans for providing for the Finances of the church. —*Discipline*, MEC, 1888.

The Church Council is the "executive agency of the *charge conference*" (244.1). It coordinates *local church administrative responsibilities* and *local church ministry responsibilities* by providing for the organizational and temporal life of the *local church*, by envisioning, planning, implementing, and evaluating the ministry and *mission* of the *local church* (252.1). Membership includes the following positions (and may include others): the chairperson of the Church Council; the *lay leader*; the chairperson and/or a representative of the *Pastor/Staff Parish Relations Committee*; the chairperson and/or a representative of the *Board of Trustees*; the *treasurer*; a *lay member to annual conference*; the president and/or a representative of the *United Methodist Men*; the president and/or a representative of the *United Methodist Women*; a young adult representative; a representative of the United Methodist Youth; and the *pastor(s)* (252.5). An alternative structure for the Church Council may be developed (244.2).

Since the merger in 1968, the *Discipline* has prescribed several different organizational models for *church* leadership including: the Administrative Council and Council on Ministries (1968); the Administrative Council (1980); and the Church Council (1996). Many *local churches* are finding alternative structures (244.2) to be useful for decision-making and for acting on plans for ministry and *mission*. Prior to the merger, The MC defined a similar body as the Official Board, which was originally described by predecessor denominations as either the Official Board or the Board of Stewards.

See also: www.umc.org/en/content/book-of-discipline-252-the-church -council.

Clergy

First, if we are "overseers over the Church of God, which he hath bought with his own blood," what manner of men ought we to be, in gifts as well as in grace . . . gifts from nature . . . understanding . . . capacity of reasoning . . . some liveliness and readiness of thought . . . a good memory . . . knowledge of the Scriptures . . . a knowledge of the original tongues (Greek and Hebrew) . . . a knowledge of profane history . . . knowledge of the sciences . . . the general grounds of natural philosophy . . . geometry . . . knowledge of the world . . . prudence . . . good breeding . . . a strong, clear musical voice, and a good delivery. —John Wesley, "An Address To The Clergy," Wesley's *Works* (Jackson, 1872), vol. 10, 481–84.

Clergy are defined as "individuals who serve as commissioned ministers, *deacons, elders,* and *licensed local pastors* (full- and part-time), who hold membership in an *annual conference,* and who are commissioned, ordained, or licensed" (142). The relationship of affiliate member of the conference has been removed from the *Book of Discipline* and thus no longer exists.

A clergyperson may not necessarily be appointed as a *pastor* of a *local church* (i.e., not all clergy serve as *pastors*), but may be appointed to an *extension ministry* (338, 343-344). In the practice of ministerial duties, clergy are amenable to the *annual conference* (370.1) and charged to maintain *confidentiality,* including confessional confidences, except in the cases of suspected child abuse or neglect or in cases where mandatory reporting is required by civil law (341.6).

Clergy complete an annual evaluation (350), and attend to their spiritual growth and *continuing education* (350). Based upon the UM understanding of historical covenants, clergy, for vocational purposes, are not considered employees of the *local church, district,* or *annual conference,* but servants of God (143). Mandatory retirement age for *clergy* is 72 years of age (358.1). Beginning with *candidacy,* clergy "for the sake of the *mission* of Jesus Christ in the world and the most effective witness of the gospel, and in consideration of their influence as clergy, to make a complete dedication of themselves to the highest ideals of the Christian life as set forth in ¶¶ 103-105; 160-164" (310.2 *d*)).

There are provisions for change in clergy conference relationship (353) including Voluntary Leave of Absence or Transitional Leave (354), Involuntary Leave of Absence (355), Maternity or Paternity Leave (356), Medical Leave Due to Medical and Disabling Conditions That Prevent Performance of Ministerial Duties (357), Retirement (358), Honorable Location (359), Administrative Location (360), Withdrawal (361), and readmission (365-369). Voluntary leave of absence includes personal, family, or transitional leave (354.2).

Some early Methodist preachers were clergy, having been ordained by the Church of England. Until John Wesley made the controversial decision to lay hands upon Thomas Coke as a general superintendent and Thomas Vasey as an *elder*, there was no such being as a Methodist clergyperson. With the ordination of Francis Asbury as a *deacon, elder*, and superintendent, and the election and *ordination* of twelve *elders* and three *deacons* at the Christmas Conference of 1784, the newly formed Methodist Episcopal Church had clergy. Major portions of the licensing, *commissioning*, and ordination evaluation processes and language in the service still echo the original services shaped by Wesley for this iconic occasion.

See also: www.gbhem.org/ministry/clergy-leaders/.

Clergy Delegate to General, Regional, and Jurisdictional Conferences

When we take a serious and impartial view of this important subject, and consider the extent of our connection, the number of our preachers, the great inconvenience, expense, and loss of time, that must necessarily result from our present regulations relative to our General Conferences, we are deeply impressed with a thorough conviction that a representative or delegated General Conference, composed of a specific number, on principles of equal representation, . . . would be much more conducive to the prosperity and general unity of the whole body, than the present indefinite and numerous body of ministers, collected together unequally from the various conferences. —Memorial from the New York Conference, sent to the General Conference of 1808, Bangs, vol. 2, 227.

The *annual conference* elects both clergy and lay delegates to the *General Conference and regional conferences*. Each *annual conference* is allotted a certain number of delegates according to the ratio for representation and elects equal numbers of clergy and lay delegates up to that number. Additional delegates are elected to complete the number allowed by the ratio for the regional *conference*. Regional conference delegates, in the order they are elected, shall be reserve delegates to the *General Conference*. In regional conferences with jurisdictions, both general and regional conference delegates serve in the jurisdictional conference. In addition, the *annual conference* shall also elect reserve delegates to the *jurisdictional conference*. These may also serve as reserve delegates to the *General Conference* (35. Article III).

Clergy delegates are elected from the *clergy* members, *elders* and *deacons* in *full connection*, and "shall be elected by the *clergy* members of the *annual conference* or provisional *annual* conference who are *deacons* and *elders* in *full connection, associate members,* and those *provisional members* who have completed all of their educational requirements and *local pastors* who have completed *course of study* or an M. Div. degree and have served a minimum of two consecutive years under *appointment* immediately preceding the election" (36. Article IV).

The original *general conferences*, held through 1808, met with the expectation that all traveling elders would attend, following the original pattern of John Wesley, who gathered all of his preachers each year. By 1808, the problems that emerged with this approach were evident. Not all of the elders would even make it to the conference due to the costs, difficulties of travel, and amount of time required to get to and participate in the conference, resulting in an uneven representation of the *annual conferences* at the *general conferences*. The 1808 *General Conference* concurred and established the delegated system in conjunction with the new *constitution* and the elements that have formed the basis of Methodist processes throughout its history.

See also: James M. Buckley, *Constitutional and Parliamentary History of the MEC* (New York: The Methodist Book Concern, 1912).

Clergy Executive Session

> Quest. 1. How is an Elder constituted? Answ. By the election of a Majority of the Conference, and by the laying on of Hands of a Bishop, and the Elders present. —*Discipline*, 1785, §V. "On the constituting of Elders, and their Duty."

The Clergy Executive Session is required to meet annually at the regular session of the *annual conference*, or at a special session called by the *bishop*, and comprises *elders* and *deacons* in *full connection* (370.5). *Elders* and *deacons* have "sole responsibility" for "all matters of *ordination*, character, and conference relations" (602.1 *a*)). Though the lay members of the *Board of Ordained Ministry* may attend the clergy executive session and have voice, only ordained *clergy* in *full connection* and *Board of Ordained Ministry* members, including *associate members* and *local pastors*, when on the *Board of Ordained Ministry*, may vote (602.1).

The clergy executive session at *annual conference* was established when laity gained the right to participate in the *annual conference*. The one area where laity were not allowed to participate was in the decision-making processes about and voting on *clergy* relations and credentialing. This is a distinctive holdover from the original American Methodist Episcopal tradition. Laity were always (as they are today) involved in approving candidates as they proceeded toward election by their peers into membership in the *annual conference*.

See also: Annual conference webpages that refer to previous or future sessions of the annual conference.

Clergy Work Expenses and Reimbursements

¶364. It shall be the duty of the Quarterly Conference of each Circuit and Station, at the session immediately preceding the Annual Conference, to appoint an Estimating Committee, . . . who shall, after conferring with the Preachers, make an estimate of the amount necessary to furnish a comfortable support to the Preacher or Preachers stationed among them. . . . The Traveling and Moving Expenses of the Preachers shall not be reckoned as a part of the estimate, but shall be paid by the Stewards as a separate item. —*Discipline*, MEC, 1884.

Tax deductions for work expenses and a reimbursable account through one's local *church* are not a part of *pastoral compensation and benefits*. They are, instead, ways of helping to lower the costs of fulfilling one's work and are tied to the self-employed tax status of *clergy*. First, for non-reimbursed expenses, one may get a tax deduction on annual federal income tax forms. Second, the *church* should create an accountable reimbursement policy and provide an account for the reimbursement of *clergy* work expenses. A reimbursement account for *clergy* work expenses incurred while performing the work of ministry should also be set up in the *church* budget. Any non-reimbursed, work-related expenses are tax-deductible for clergy. *Local churches* are responsible for developing a policy regarding accountable reimbursements and for reporting to the *annual conference* on the appropriate form the expenditures of *pastors* for the following purposes: 1) professional expenses and reimbursement; 2) allowances, in addition to base compensation, for housing and other items (some of these are considered benefits). Guidelines are available through the tax-packet found on the *GCFA* website (626). The history of US tax law is well beyond the scope of this project!

See also: www.gcfa.org/resource/tax-packet-addressing-tax-issues.

Closure/Discontinuance of a Local Church

What directions are given concerning District conferences? . . . ¶72 Ans. 5. It shall be the duty of the Conference to inquire particularly into the condition of the several charges in the District: (1) As to their spiritual state, and the attendance upon the ordinances and social meetings of the Church. (2) As to missions within the District, where new ones should be established, and what missions should be raised to circuits or stations. —*Discipline*, MECS, 1906.

According to the *Discipline*, churches "exist in and for the world" (202) and are closed when "the local church no longer serves the purpose for which it was organized or incorporated (¶¶201-204); or the local church property is no longer used, kept, or maintained by its membership as a place of divine worship of The UMC" (2549.1 *a), b)*). An assessment of local church potential that can help with determining whether a local church is serving its purpose is available in the *Discipline* (213). After a process involving the district superintendent, the congregation, legal counsel, and the District Board of Church Location and Building, and transfer of membership plan, title to the property goes to the Conference Board of Trustees, who will hold it in trust and then determine the property's disposition or future use (2549.2).

During the early years of The MC, the *Discipline* began providing guidelines about how to deal with "abandoned" property. By 1956, there was a clear process for how to handle both abandoned and discontinued properties and churches, which reflects very closely the procedures used by annual conferences today.

See also: District Superintendent's office; Beth M. Crissman and Nancy B. Rankin, *Choosing the Faithful Path: A Bible Study for Discerning a Faithful Future* (Nashville: Plowpoint Inc., 2017).

Cokesbury

I remember the time when the people who dwelt in their log cabins had no other books to read but such as they obtained from Methodist itinerants, who carried them around their circuits in their saddlebags, and after preaching sold them to the people. In this humble way the poor people in the wilderness were supplied both with the living word from the lips of God's messengers, and with the reading matter for their meditation by the fireside when the living teacher had taken his departure. —Bangs, vol. 4, 452.

Cokesbury bookstore is the virtual storefront and main distributor for *The United Methodist Publishing House*. Cokesbury sells Bibles, Christian books, Sunday school studies, spiritual formation materials, curriculum for all ages, clergy and choir robes, and *church* supplies. In addition to the online bookstore, Cokesbury offers Community Resource Consultants who help resource ministries.

On November 5, 2012, the Board of Directors of The UMPH announced the closing of thirty-eight Cokesbury full-line retail stores and nineteen seminary stores. The plan was to refocus and expand resources toward Cokesbury.com by enhancing the online store and call order centers, increasing presence at conferences, and making consultants available to *church*es and leaders.

When the original Book Concern was established by The Methodist Episcopal Church, traveling preachers and deacons acted as distributors and salespersons for the books and materials published by the printing agency of the *Church*. Throughout the history of each of the predecessor denominations, a publishing and distribution arm of the *Church* was established. "Colporteurs" or book agents were appointed by the *bishop*, some full-time, to circulate among *churches* and conferences to distribute and sell books from the Book Concern. This practice continued until the establishment of The MC in 1939.

See also: www.cokesbury.com.

College of Bishops—*See* Bishop

Colleges and Universities

Resolved, by the delegates of the annual conferences in General Conference assembled, that it be, and it is hereby, recommended to all the annual conferences to establish, as soon as practicable, literary institutions, under their own control, in such way and manner as they think proper . . . That it be the special duty of the episcopacy to use their influence to carry the above resolution into effect, by recommending the subject to each annual conference. —Resolution passed at the 1820 General Conference, Bangs, vol. 3, 106–7.

According to the *GBHEM*, The UMC is directly connected to 106 schools, colleges, and universities in the U.S., of which about 90 are colleges and universities, and relates to 700 in other parts of the world. Today, forty states and Puerto Rico have at least one UM-related school, college, university, or school of theology.

John Wesley believed that all children, both boys and girls, should have access to education. Coinciding with the formation of The MEC in 1784, one of the earliest efforts of Bishops Coke and Asbury was to establish Cokesbury College for the sons of Methodist preachers. It would be the equivalent of a college preparatory school today. After a move following a fire, constant financial problems, and a second fire that destroyed its buildings again, the Cokesbury College project was abandoned in 1796. Deeply concerned, however, that most of the "seminaries of learning" were grounded in the Reformed/Presbyterian traditions or no religious tradition at all, the 1820 *General Conference* passed a resolution that each *annual conference* establish "literary institutions" for both men and women, that would foster both "knowledge and vital piety." By the 1830s, colleges for both men and women were being established throughout the US connection. By the time of the Civil War, Methodist denominations had established over two hundred schools and colleges. Following the Civil War, between 1866 and 1904, The MEC founded eleven *historic black colleges and universities* and Gammon Theological Seminary.

Commission on the General Conference

> I arrived in New York on the Friday previous to the Conference, and wishing to know just what was the best course for me. . . . I went over to the Opera House where the Conference was to hold its session and inquire for General Fisk, finding him already conferring with grave dignitaries of the church and busy with his duties as chairman of the Committee of Arrangements. . . . He told me there was going to be a vigorous fight, but he thought the women would get in. —Francis E Willard, RRS, p. 429.

The General Conference elects a twenty-five-member commission from throughout the connection that sets the date, location, and number of members of the GC. Leadership is elected from within the membership by the members themselves. It determines proposed amendments to the Plan of Organization and Rules of Order that are voted on at the beginning of each General Conference. The Commission also makes all the necessary arrangements for delegates' travel and housing, the publication of the Advance Edition of the Daily Christian Advocate, and reports in the four official languages of the GC 512.

Prior to the establishment of the commission, general conferences were organized by a large group consisting of the Council of Bishops, the Standing Committee on Central Conference Matters, and an additional committee appointed by the Council of Bishops.

See also: www.resourceumc.org/en/content/commission-on-the-general -conference-forges-towards-2028.

Commission on a Way Forward

See appendix.

Commissioning

> We may then, if he gives satisfaction, receive him as a probationer, by giving him the form of discipline. Observe! Take on trial is entirely different from admitting a Preacher. One on trial, may be either admitted or rejected, without doing him any wrong; otherwise it would be no trial at all. Let every Deacon and Elder explain this to those who are on trial, as well as to those who are in future to be proposed for trial. —*Discipline*, 1789, §VII. "On the Method of receiving Preachers, and their Duty."

In commissioning, the *Church* acknowledges God's call in a candidate for ministry, and invokes the Holy Spirit for faithful leadership, service, proclamation, and equipping of others for ministry. Commissioned ministers are *provisional members* in the *annual conference* and participate in a residency program where their effectiveness for ministry and *ordination* is discerned. The period of commissioned ministry concludes when the *provisional member* is received as an *elder* or *deacon*, or the decision is made not to proceed toward *ordination* (325).

In 1996, the *General Conference* approved an extreme revision of the way in which Methodists had historically provided for membership in the *annual conference* and *ordination*. Methodists first brought in persons "on trial" or "on probation" prior to ordaining them as *deacons* who would then move on to become *elders*. Then changes were made that conflated "on trial" with

55

being an ordained deacon, only to be moved forward as *elders* with full connection in the *annual conference*. The status of "on trial" or "on probation" indicated that candidates for *ordination* did not yet have full connection with the *annual conference*. In 1996, two orders—*deacon* and *elder*—were established, and candidates received provisional membership as they were commissioned by the *annual conference* in anticipation of being ordained only once as *deacons* or *elders* in full connection with the conference.

See also: www. gbhem.org/ministry/explore-your-call-to-ministry /provisional-membership/.

Committee on Episcopacy (Jurisdictional and Annual Conference)—*See* Bishop

Committee on Faith and Order—*See* Bishop

Complaints (Administrative and Chargeable Offenses)

> Quest. 2. What shall be done in cases of improper tempers, words or actions, or a breach of the articles and discipline of the church? Answ. The person so offending shall be reprehended by his Bishop, Elder, Deacon or Preacher that has charge of the circuit. Should a second transgression take place, one, two or three Preachers may be called in; if not cured then, he shall be tried at the quarterly meeting. —*Discipline*, 1789, §XXXIII. "On the Manner by which immoral Ministers and Preachers shall be brought to Trial."

The *Discipline* defines a complaint as "a written and signed statement claiming misconduct or unsatisfactory performance of ministerial duties" (413, 363.2 *a)*). This is the first step in establishing a judicial process that evaluates whether an immoral action has taken place that requires disciplinary action against a person. The process applies to a *bishop* (413), a clergyperson (363), or a layperson (2704.4, 2703.3). When the effectiveness of a clergyperson is in question, the *bishop* identifies the concern, holds supervisory conversations, and determines an action plan (334.3), which leads to either fruitfulness or Administrative Location (360) with the assistance of the Conference Relations Committee of the *Board of Ordained Ministry* (362).

In the case of ministerial misconduct, the *bishop*, upon receiving a complaint, begins a "supervisory response" seeking a "just resolution" to repair harm and bring healing (363.5). If resolution is not attained, the *bishop* either dismisses the complaint or refers it to the *Church's* counsel, where it becomes a judicial process (2701-2719), if related to the chargeable offenses for *clergy* (2702.1) or laity (2702.3). A Committee on Investigation (2703) examines the allegations to see if there are reasonable grounds to bring charges resulting in a trial (2706). *Restrictive Rule* 21 ensures the right to trial for *clergy* and laity (21. Article IV), however "*church* trials are to be regarded as an expedient of last resort" (2707). The *GCFA* provides a handbook on UMC Administrative and Judicial Procedures.

From the earliest *Disciplines*, the right to some sense of due process has always been underscored and was refined through legislative processes. With the right to trial embedded in the *Constitution* through the *Restrictive Rules*, post–Civil War generations added steps to the process, which rested originally in the hands of the presiding and traveling *elders*. By the late 1880s, the presence of a committee on investigation emerged in both The MEC and MECS as a significant step in a process that could result in just resolution without having to go to a trial. A significant change in language describing the person under investigation occurred in the 1976 *Discipline* of The UMC. This *Discipline* dropped the language of "accused" and shifted to the language of "one charged" with an offense. The problem with this phrase reflected the secular notion that when one was charged with a crime, it indicated that there was already enough evidence to move to a trial if an alternative resolution could not be negotiated. This conflicted with the purpose of the committee on investigation. In 1992, the language of "complaint" entered the nomenclature, indicating that a complaint is filed against a person, and a process begins to determine if there is enough for it to transition to a chargeable offense.

Conference Staff

> ¶1296. Art. 2. Secretaries.—21. The Annual conference on nomination of the board in consultation with the Cabinet, may elect annually an executive secretary of the board, who if he is a ministerial member of the conference, shall be appointed by the bishops. The expense of his salary and of his office shall be included in the budget of the board. —*Discipline*, MC, 1964.

Conference staff help to guide the ministry and *mission* of The UMC within its boundaries (608). It is recommended that an *annual conference* have a director of connectional ministries or designated person to facilitate program and serve as a part of the extended *cabinet* (608). Each *annual conference* or *episcopal area* shall have a director of communications (609) and a conference treasurer/director of administrative services (619). These, and other designated conference staff, serve as a resource to the *annual conference* and *local church* through communications, networking, and resourcing (608). Additional conference staff may be hired by an *annual conference* in order to help fullfill its mission.

The precursors to conference staff were The MC positions of conference secretaries, who cared for a wide range of programmatic and reporting responsibilities. These included, but were not limited to, the areas of missions, education, finance, ministerial relations, and training. In addition, there were the positions of conference treasurer and secretary. Some positions were salaried as conference staff, especially if the one elected was an elder.

See also: Annual conference websites.

Confession of Faith

> Doctrinally, the Evangelical United Brethren Church belongs to the theological stream which issued from the event of God's work in Christ. It is inseparably related to sixteenth century reformation theology. This Church

proclaims no new, recent revelation. The Evangelical United Brethren Church is a thorough protestant church with a faith vitally related to the evangelical work of Luther and Calvin, modified by Arminianism, and enriched by the Christian religious experience given common people. —Paul Himmel Eller, M.A., Ph.D., *These Evangelical United Brethren* (Dayton, OH: The Otterbein Press, 1957), 121.

At the 1968 union of The Methodist Church and The Evangelical United Brethren Church, the Confession of Faith became a part of the UM Doctrinal Standards when it was deemed "congruent if not identical" in doctrinal perspective with the *Articles of Religion*, the Standard Sermons of Wesley, the Explanatory Notes Upon the New Testament, and the *General Rules* (103). The Confession of Faith is now protected by the *Restrictive Rules* (19. Article II). The Confession of Faith is shorter than the *Articles of Religion* and uses more contemporary language. It differs from the *Articles of Religion* in several main areas: on the relationship of Christians to government and participation of Christians in war, its emphasis on the expectation of full sanctification and attainment of Christian perfection, and on the relationship of Christians to *property*.

When the United Brethren in Christ and Evangelical Church united in 1946, their new *Discipline* contained the respective United Brethren Confession and Evangelical Articles. Twelve years later in 1963, the Evangelical United Brethren Church adopted a new Confession of Faith with the addition of a new article, "Entire Sanctification and Christian Perfection," representing a distinctively Wesleyan emphasis. The Confession of Faith was adopted and added to The UMC *Book of Discipline* without any changes.

See also: www.umc.org/en/content/confession-of-faith.

Confidentiality

May a minister ever take advantage of . . . a confidential statement for the purpose of helping the man who made it? Or to prevent . . . a wrong? This depends. Faith must be kept at all cost; and if a minister makes a pledge of silence, . . . and under that pledge received the . . . confidence in question, he must keep his word. At the same time, . . . [to] make a pledge binding one's future course without ascertaining beforehand something of . . . the matters in question is not wise. —Harmon, EE, 105.

Maintaining confidentiality is a key ethical principle and important practice of ministry. Confidentiality is about not just what one hears, but building trusting relationships among *clergy*, staff, and laity. As a part of the questions *provisional members* are required to answer in their *Board of Ordained Ministry* interviews, they are asked, "Will you regard all pastoral conversations of a confessional nature as a trust between the person concerned and God?" (330.5.c.(5); 335.c.(5)). In the description of the responsibilities of the *pastor*, *clergy* are directed to maintain confidentiality except in cases of child abuse and neglect, or where civil law requires reporting (340.2.*a*.(5)). In cases where there is a strong indication that a person may harm themself or another person, clergy should follow the legal guidelines of their state for requirements of reporting. Regardless, a therapeutic intervention is necessary.

The one *local church* committee that is required to hold closed meetings and maintain confidentiality is the *Pastor/Staff Parish Relations Committee* (258.2.*e*)). Confidentiality is also required during a process of investigation when a *complaint* is filed against a *clergy* member (2706.7). The *Board of Ordained Ministry* and, by extension, the *District Committee on Ministry* is required to ensure confidentiality in the review and interviewing process and the maintenance of personal information (634.2.*m*). Only during a *clergy executive session* of the *annual conference* may relevant confidential information be shared when issues related to qualifications and/or character of a clergyperson are raised (634.2.*m*). *General agencies* may hold closed meetings but are subject to restrictions on them (723). The *Judicial Council* also maintains strict rules regarding confidentiality of information and proceedings (2607).

Throughout the history of the *Church*, the confessional, which required confidentiality by the priest or *pastor*, has been an undergirding principle of ministry. In Catholicism, confession is considered a *sacrament*, and is therefore inviolable. In Methodism, confession was never considered a sacrament. In early Methodism, confession was a standard practice of the class meeting (specifically the bands) during which laypersons confessed their sins to one another. United Methodist rules on reporting what may have been heard under a condition of confidentiality are therefore guided by the rules of the state.

See also: www.resourceumc.org/en/content/team-covenants-build-trust -with-other-church-leaders.

Confirmation

Quest. What shall we do for the rising generation? Answ. 1. Where there are then children whose parents are in society 2. Procure our instructions for them, and let all who can, read and commit them to memory. 3. Explain and impress them upon their hearts. 4. Talk with them every time you see any at home. 5. Pray in earnest for them. Diligently instruct and exhort all parents . . . and if any of them be truly awakened, let them be admitted into society. —*Discipline*, 1789, §XXVI. "On the Instruction of Children."

Confirmation is both "a human act of commitment and the gracious action of the Holy Spirit strengthening and empowering discipleship" (216.1 *a*)). "Unlike baptism, which is a once-made covenant and can only be reaffirmed and not repeated, confirmation is a dynamic action of the Holy Spirit that can be repeated" (216.2 *b*)). Led by the pastor, it is the responsibility of the congregation to nurture and instruct children and youth (and adults), baptized and not, through a program of confirmation. The typical age for confirmation is at the end of the sixth grade and participation of younger children and youth desiring confirmation is at the pastor's discretion. Using the baptismal covenant service(s) (217), young people make a personal profession of faith, committing to a life of discipleship in Jesus Christ, and are confirmed. Preparation for profession of faith and confirmation should be made available for all people (216.3). There are many other occasions where the confirming presence of the Holy Spirit may be celebrated, such as a service of baptismal renewal (216.2 *b*)).

The instruction of children has always been a primary responsibility of pastors in Methodism. The children of members of the societies were of special concern as they were, for the most part, already growing up in a Christian family. They were the most accessible for the attention of the preachers through the rule that preachers were to visit from house to house. With the development of the Church School in the late 1800s, and the inclusion of children in these programs who were not necessarily members of families in the local church, a more in-depth process of education and formation became necessary.

See also: www.umc.org/en/content/beyond-baptism-what-confirmation -means-to-united-methodists; *UMH*, 32–54.

Connection

> One great object of the Centenary movement should be to promote the Connectional spirit of Methodism, and to bind anew, in cords of fraternal love and of devotion to the common cause, the East, the West, the North, and the South Unity in Christ is one of the needful marks of the true Church and to promote the unity of the American people is one of the obvious functions of the Church in this country. —Abel Stevens, *The Centenary of American Methodism* (New York: Carlton & Porter, 1865), 225, 266–68.

The outreach of the Church springs from the working of the Spirit. As UMs, we respond to that working through a connectional polity based upon mutual responsiveness and accountability. Connectional ties bind us together in faith and service in our global witness, enabling faith to become active in love, and intensifying our desire for peace and justice in the world. One of the distinctive characteristics of The UMC is connection, a structure maintained through its "chain of conferences" (*Discipline*, p. 375). The *Church* experiences connection "through episcopacy, *itineracy*, *property*, and mutual cooperation and support" (701.2). The *local church* is regarded as a "connectional society of persons who have been baptized, have professed their faith in Christ, and have assumed the vows of membership in The United Methodist Church" (203). The denomination is "bound together in a connectional covenant" (125) of common ethos, episcopacy, *itineracy, faith, doctrinal standards*, the *Constitution of The United Methodist Church, polity*, leadership, *property*, mutual cooperation and support, and *mission* (132, 701). The connectional system embraces the *mission statement of the denomination*, organizes to enable the *mission* in the *local church*, and ensures that each part of the *Church* remains faithful (701.2). This "vital web of interactive relationships" (125, 132) also includes covenant and partnership with autonomous and affiliated *churches* (125). The definition of membership in The UMC states that "All baptized or *professing members* of any local UM *church* are members of the worldwide UM connection and members of the *church* universal" (215.4).

The word "connexion" initially denoted a politician's following and could have easily been construed to mean John Wesley's own religious following. However, Wesley was careful not to set himself up as a cultic figure, and in the early Methodist movement, the term came to refer to the practice of discipline, not only in the societies, but among the preachers, leaders, helpers, and assistants.

See also: Thomas E. Frank, *Polity, Practice, and the Mission of the United Methodist Church* (Nashville: Abingdon Press, 2006); www.umc.org/en /content/organization-church-as-connection.

Connectional Ministries—*See* Conference Staff

Connectional Table

More broadly still, the CT is defined as the entity "where ministry and money are brought to the same table [,]" . . . decidedly "outside the box" of established bureaucracies with an astonishingly broad vista in its purview. The energy and optimism of new vision and fresh stewardship and coordination of the church's mission is evident here. —Frank, 280.

In order to accomplish the *mission statement of The UMC,* "The purpose of the Connectional Table (CT) is for the discernment and articulation of the vision for the *church* and the *stewardship* of the *mission,* ministries, and resources of The UMC as determined by the actions of the *General Conference* and in consultation with the Council of Bishops" (904). The Connectional Table is amenable to the *General Conference* and has authority and responsibility in collaborating with the *GCFA* on *apportionments*, approving *general agency* budgets, Churchwide appeals, and special *offerings* (905.7). Membership on the Connectional Table is representative of the whole *Church* (906).

The Connectional Table was established by the *General Conference* in 2004 and replaced the General Council on Ministries, the original management council established by The UMC in 1968. The collaborative work of the Connectional Table (especially with the *GCFA*) and its smaller size made it significantly different from the General Council on Ministries.

See also: /www.resourceumc.org/en/partners/connectional-table /home/about.

Consecration

> Dear friends, this building, which by the favor of God and human labor has been so far completed, embodies the obligation of each generation to impart its treasures of wisdom and knowledge to the generation following. For the fulfillment of this task we need not only the best that we can do but above all the blessing of almighty God. Let us, therefore, bring praise for God's aid in this undertaking, giving thanks for those who, by their gifts of their service, shall unite in fulfilling the purpose for which this building is prepared. —"Declaration of Purpose," in A Service for the Consecration of an Education Building, www.umcdiscipleship.org/resources/a-service-for -the-consecration-of-an-educational-building, accessed July 15, 2017.

Always used in the context of a worship service, the word "consecration" is used to confer sacred meaning and purpose to a person, location, or thing. The term is used in four primary ways in The UMC. First, Methodists consecrate *elders* who are elected to become *bishops*. Bishops are not ordained into their episcopal office; they remain *elders*. The consecration service takes place at the end of the *Jurisdictional Conference* or *Central Conference*, immediately following their election each *quadrennium*.

Second, Methodists consecrate bread and grape juice during *The Lord's Supper*. The prayer of consecration is repeated by the celebrant, either an *elder*, a *deacon* who has received permission from the *bishop to* act as celebrant, or a *licensed local pastor* in the setting in which one serves. In the current liturgy for Holy Communion, the prayer of consecration is embedded in "The Great Thanksgiving" and begins with the phrase, "Pour out your Holy Spirit on us gathered here, and on these gifts of bread and wine."

The third way the term is used is to consecrate or re-consecrate a building, a space such as a room or burial ground, a new program, furniture, or *worship ware* for their sacred use. Consecrated buildings are dedicated when all indebtedness on the building is retired (2545). Methodists also de-consecrate these things when they will no longer be used for sacred purposes.

The term is also used when we consecrate our *tithes* and *offerings* as we commit our pledges in a special service often called "Consecration Sunday."

See also: www.unitedmethodistbishops.org; www.umcdiscipleship.org /search/results?q=prayers+of+consecration.

Constitution of The United Methodist Church

Whereas, it is of the greatest importance that the doctrine, form of government, and general rules of the United Societies in America be preserved sacred and inviolable: and whereas every prudent measure should be taken to preserve, strengthen, and perpetuate the union of the connection: Therefore, your committee, upon mature deliberation, have thought it advisable that their third section of the form of Discipline shall be as follows, viz: The Introduction to the report that proposed the General Conference be a delegated conference and the official decision-making body of the church.
—The beginning of the Constitution, Bangs, vol. 2, 229.

The Constitution of The United Methodist Church (Constitution) was formed in 1968, as part of the merger of The MC and The EUBC, and it contains the basic elements that constitute The UMC. The Constitution is divided into the following sections:

PREAMBLE

DIVISION ONE—GENERAL: Declaration of Union (1. Article I), Name (2. Article II), *Articles of Religion* and *Confession of Faith* (3. Article III), Inclusiveness of the Church (4. Article IV), Racial Justice (5. Article V), Gender Justice (6. Article VI), Ecumenical Relations (7. Article VII), and Title to *Properties* (8. Article VIII)

DIVISION TWO—ORGANIZATION: powers, duties of the conferences, including the *General Conference* (Section I. ¶9. Article I; Section II), *Restrictive Rules* (Section III), *Jurisdictional Conferences* (Section I. ¶10. Article II; Section IV), *Central Conferences* (Section V; Section I. ¶11. Article III), *Annual Conferences* (Section VI; Section I ¶12. Article IV), Boundaries (Section VII), *District Conferences* (Section VIII), and *Charge Conferences* (Section I. ¶13. Article V; Section IX)

DIVISION THREE—EPISCOPAL SUPERVISION: the role and function of *bishops*

DIVISION FOUR—THE JUDICIARY: powers and duties of the *Judicial Council*

DIVISION FIVE—AMENDMENTS: Approved amendments and how the Constitution can be altered.

The 1808 *Discipline* was the first to establish the Constitution of The MC, which shifted powers from the *bishops* to the legislative body of the *General Conference* and instituted *Restrictive Rules* to prevent significant changes being made in the original rules, character, and ethos of Methodism. Throughout the history of its *predecessor denominations,* the Constitution of The UMC remained relatively intact, except for the time of The MPC. The MPC eliminated episcopacy, modified *itinerancy,* and instituted rights of laity following the schism of 1828–1830. The 1968 *Discipline* is the first in The MC and predecessor *churches* to name principles (i.e., *inclusiveness,* racial justice, and *ecumenical relations*) as part of the Constitution. Since 1968, sections of the Constitution have been modified, changed and altered with the needs of a growing mission. Section I, ¶5. Article V, on racial justice was added by the 2000 *General Conference*, through ratification by the *annual conferences*; it "proclaims the value of each person as a unique child of God." And last but not least, a new section has been voted on to add to the Constitution, Section I, . . . , which will be voted on for ratification by annual conferences in the next couple of years.

See also: Thomas E. Frank, *Polity, Practice, and Mission of The United Methodist Church* (Nashville: Abingdon Press, 2006), ch. 3.

Continuing Education

What general method of employing our Time would you advise us to? Answ. We advise you . . . 3. From six in the Morning till twelve . . . read in Order, with much prayer, The Christian Library, and other pious Books. . . . Read the most useful Books, and that regularly and constantly. Steadily spend all the Morning in this Employment, or at least five Hours in four and twenty. "But I have no Taste for reading." Contract a Taste for it by Use or return to your former Employment. —*Discipline*, 1785, §XVIII. "Of employing our Time profitably, when we are not travelling."

In order to lead the *church* in fulfilling the mission of disciple making, *clergy* are required to engage in spiritual formation, continuing education for ministry, and profession development throughout their careers (351). The *Pastor/Staff Parish Relations Committee* should consult with the *pastor* regarding all dimensions of work-life, health, and wellness and to arrange with the *Church Council* regarding the *pastor's* need for continual professional and spiritual development (258.2 *g*) (8)).

Clergy are entitled to a professional formation leave "at least one week each year and may include at least one month during one year of every quadrennium. . . A *clergy* member may request a formational and spiritual growth leave of up to six months while continuing to hold an *appointment* in the *local church*" (351.2-3).

Annual conferences and *general agencies* provide guidelines and multiple opportunities for continuing education. Many are now offered online.

Beginning with John Wesley, and throughout Methodist history, *clergy* were expected to continue reading and studying throughout their ministry. In 1976, annual documentation of one's ongoing continuing education was required by the Pastor/Staff Parish Relations Committee and *charge conference*. From this point forward, *clergy* were no longer just "encouraged," they were required to participate in continuing education.

Copyright Laws

> We believe that the honest minister will know when he takes what is in reality the work of another. Although the codes . . . have condemned plagiarism, it is the opinion of the writer that this sin is not as prevalent today as it once was. Ministers are better educated, they have been taught and that thoroughly to do their own thinking, and the wider reading of all people today makes plagiarism much hard to "get away with." —Harmon, EE, 145.

Music, sermons, videos, and photographs are examples of intellectual property, owned by the people who created them. "Copyrighting" is a system of registering one's material with the Library of Congress in order to legally protect one's ownership. Copyright infringement and plagiarism are unethical. These often happen when downloading material from the Internet. Sources are available for churches and individuals to purchase a license for noncommercial, educational, and spiritual uses to use materials legally while giving credit to the author/composer/producer. "Plagiarism" is similar to but not the same as copyright infringement. Plagiarism is a form of using another's material and calling it one's own. So, while it may or may not be a form of copyright infringement, depending on whether the original creator went through the process of copyrighting the material, it is definitely a form of stealing the intellectual property of another.

There are sources for royalty-free materials, especially photographs, online. Materials that are "in the public domain" are music and books for which copyrights have expired, been forfeited, or are inapplicable. "Fair Use" laws define the terms under which one can freely use the work of another. In all these situations sources should be acknowledged when you use the material of another to prevent plagiarism.

The first copyright law was established in England in 1710. The first system for copyrights in the US was established in 1790.

See also: www.umcom.org/learn/web-ministry-privacy-and-permissions; copyright.gov/about/timeline.html;fairuse.stanford.edu/overview/fair-use; www.resourceumc.org/en/content/are-you-violating-copyright-laws.

Council of Bishops—*See* Bishop

Course of Study

> Though the course of study at first was very limited in some of the conferences, and the examinations comparatively superficial, it has been gradually enlarged and improved, so much so as to require a great compass of knowledge to be able to pass an approved examination. —Bangs, vol. 3, 48.

The Course of Study is a twenty-course curriculum required to be completed to maintain *clergy* status as a *licensed local pastor* unless one already has an MDiv degree from an approved school of theology. There are five courses in four major areas: Bible, Church History and Theology, Congregational Formation, and Pastoral Identity. The Advanced Course of Study, a thirty-two-credit curriculum, taught at the master's degree level, is required if a person wants to seek *provisional membership* and *commissioning* and move toward *ordination* as an *elder*.

Full-time *local pastors* are required to attend one of the eight regional schools in the US, and complete four courses a year, with an outside deadline for completion of eight years. Part-time *local pastors* may attend a regional school, an extension school, or a satellite site. They are required to complete two courses per year, with a completion deadline of twelve years. Several regional schools offer hybrid courses. There are also six courses offered online by the *GBHEM*. The curriculum is set by the Division of Ministry of the GBHEM.

An Advanced Course of Study in conjunction with the *Discipline* (324.4) provides a path for local pastors who want to seek provisional membership.

The "original" Course of Study was created as a reading list that all candidates for full connection were expected to complete as a part of their preparation for *ordination*. Similar sets of studies were expected of persons preparing for licensing as a local preacher. In the late 1800s, the curriculum was included as a part of the *Discipline*. From the late 1880s, and into the early years of The MEC, Course of Study curriculums were published in the *Discipline* for multiple language groups as well: for Japanese and Mexican *pastors* (MECS); for German, Norwegian, Swedish, Italian, and Spanish speakers (MEC).

See also: www.gbhem.org/ministry/course-of-study/.

Cross and Flame—UM Insignia, Use and Limits

Suppose you are vacationing far from home. You drive around, looking for a church in which to worship Sunday morning. Suddenly you see a familiar sight: a Cross and Flame insignia on a sign, pointing you to the nearest United Methodist Church. You've just proved how symbols and pictures provide instant recognition, meaning and a sense of belonging. —www .umc.org/resources/a-mark-known-the-world-over, accessed June 23, 2017.

The official logo of The United Methodist Church—"with the cross, proclaiming Jesus Christ as its foundation, and the two flames descending to one point, celebrating its origin when two denominations became one, and affirming its readiness to go forth to the ends of the earth to all people to make disciples of Jesus Christ for the transformation of the world, as the anointing of the Holy Spirit with 'individual flames of fire' sent forth the apostles speaking the language of people wherever they went"—is maintained and protected by the *GCFA* (807.10). Though any official UM agency or *local church* may use the insignia, commercial use requires expressed written permission (807.10).

The cross and flame logo was chosen from over twenty submissions and was formally adopted by the 1968 *General Conference*. It was registered with the US Patent and Trademark Office in 1971.

70

See also: www.resourceumc.org/en/agencies/communications/brand -standards.

Curriculum—*See* Education

Daily Christian Advocate

> Greetings to General Conference delegates and subscribers to the Daily Christian Advocate! We are glad that you are reading this Advance edition of the Daily Christian Advocate as you prepare for our gathering as the General Conference in Portland, Oregon, next May. —Judi Kenaston, Chairperson of the Commission on the General Conference, "Letter from the Commission on the General Conference Chair," *Daily Christian Advocate* vol. 1 (2016), 4.

The "Advance Edition of the Daily Christian Advocate" and the "Daily Christian Advocate" are the official journals of the *General Conference* (504.2). The "Advance" edition serves as a delegate handbook (containing petitions, etc.) and the "Daily" edition records the proceedings of the *General Conference*. Both the "Advance" and "Daily Christian Advocate" are available in an online format at UMC.org and can be followed during *General Conference*. The 2020–2024 advance edition was written in four languages: English, French, Kiswahili, and Portuguese.

The original *Christian Advocate* was a weekly newssheet that went out to Methodist clergy and households. It was first printed in 1826 and had the largest circulation of any newspaper at the time. The adaptation of the name of the newssheet as a record of the General Conference is difficult to trace.

See also: www.resourceumc.org/en/content/general-conference-2020 -advance-daily-christian-advocate.

Deacon

> Quest. 2. What is the duty of a deacon? Answ. 1. To baptize, and perform the office of matrimony in the absence of the elder. 2. To assist the elder in administering the Lord's supper. 5. To appoint all the stewards and leaders, and change them. 6. To hold watch-nights and love-feasts. . . . 7. To hold quarterly meetings. 8. To take care that every society be duly supplied with books: particularly with the Saints' Rest, Instructions for Children, and the Primitive Physic. 11. To meet the men and women apart in the large societies, once a quarter. —*Discipline*, 1785, §VI, "On the constituting of Deacons, and their Duty."

Deacons "are called to ministries of Word, Service, Compassion, and Justice" (326.1). Deacons are servant ministers who "lead the *Church* in relating the gathered life of Christians to their ministries in the world." Deacons are authorized to celebrate the sacraments (328).

The requirements for being ordained a deacon include: previous election as a *provisional member*; service for at least two years under episcopal appointment; meeting all of the education requirements, including a BA or equivalent from a school listed by the University Senate; an MDiv, MS, or a specialized masters degree (approved by the Senate); or being over age thirty-five with professional certification or license. In each case, candidates must complete the basic graduate theological studies (324.4); exhibit satisfactory physical, emotional, and mental health; present a sermon, Bible study, and mission project; complete an oral and written examination; and receive recommendation by the Board of Ordained Ministry and vote of the clergy members of the annual conference (330.4).

Deacons are not guaranteed an appointment but find their own employment in the *church* or beyond. In consultation with the *bishop* and *district superintendent* a deacon may be appointed to a place of employment. Deacons are members of the *charge conference* in the *churches* where they serve. Those appointed beyond the *local church* shall designate a *charge conference* (331).

Prior to 1996, the position of deacon was the final step before being ordained as an *elder*. The relationship of the deacon to the *annual conference* evolved over the history of US Methodism, shifting from full connection to probationary status and now back to full connection.

See also: www.gbhem.org/ministry/clergy-leaders/deacons-diaconal
-ministers/.

Deaconess and Home Missioner

"I serve neither for reward nor recognition but from gratitude and love my reward is that I may serve." —Becky Dodson Louter and Myka Kennedy Stephens, "Living the Vision: How United Methodist Deaconesses and Home Missioners Understand and Embody the Lay Diaconate," 5; www.unitedmethodistwomen.org/what-we-do/service-and-advocacy/deaconess-and-home-missioner-office/news-resources/louterstephens.aspx.

Within The UMC are the offices of deaconess and home missioner, laity who are led by the Holy Spirit and express love and concern for the world through diverse kinds of service, making Jesus Christ known by alleviating suffering, eradicating injustice, facilitating and developing human potential, and building global community through the *Church* universal (1913).

Deaconesses (laywomen) and home missioners (laymen) are trained professionally, approved through the UMW process, and consecrated and commissioned by a *bishop*. Deaconesses and home missioners have a relationship with The UMC through the UMW, hold membership in a *local church*, may be appointed by the *bishop* to a full-time ministry of love, justice, and service, and are seated as full *lay members* of the *annual conference* (1913).

Formally beginning in 1888, when The MEC established the Office of Deaconess, the lay diaconate is a celebrated aspect of American Methodism. The earliest pioneers of the diakonia were laywomen who were consecrated for vocational ministry in the world. Over its history of service, this ministry has taken on many forms.

See also: /www.nadhm.org; uwfaith.org/what-we-do/deaconess-and
-home-missioner/.

Dedication—*See* Consecration

Designated Giving and Funds

> "How shall we pay the debt upon the preaching-house?" Captain Foy stood up and said, "Let everyone in the society give a penny a week, and it will easily be done." "But many of them," said one, "have not a penny to give." "True," said the Captain; "then put ten or twelve of them to me. Let each of these give what they can weekly, and I will supply what is wanting." —"Thoughts Upon Methodism," as quoted in Theodore Runyon, *The New Creation, John Wesley's Theology Today* (Nashville: Abingdon Press, 1998), 119.

Designated giving and funds are a way of funding special offerings, causes, and projects of the *local church*. Through the Advance, The UMC offers opportunities for people to make designated gifts to identified *mission* and ministry (823). *Local churches* are also encouraged to develop plans for designated giving and a list of prioritized projects to which people may give. According to the *Discipline*, "contributions designated for specific causes and objects shall be promptly forwarded according to the intent of the donor and shall not be used for any other purpose" (258.4 *f*)). Several of the official UMC *Special Sundays* have designated offerings that accompany them. Designated giving is not to be encouraged in lieu of support for the general budget of the *local church*. During the 1800s, collections were always designated for particular needs. The first collections identified in the *Discipline* were quarterly collections from the class meetings for the support of preachers, a yearly collection for building *churches*, collections at love-feasts and during *sacraments* for the poor, and an annual commitment to support Cokesbury College. Difficulties with underwriting the costs of *local churches* grew throughout the nineteenth century. By the beginning of the twentieth century, the practice of the regular Sunday morning *offering* combined with an emphasis on *tithing* helped *local churches* distinguish between the regular ongoing needs of the *church* and designated gifts to special ministries and funds.

See also: /www.umc.org/en/content/designated-giving.

Disaster—How to Prepare and Respond— *See* United Methodist Committee on Relief

Discipleship

> The mission of the Church is to make disciples of Jesus Christ for the transformation of the world. —*Discipline*, UMC, 120.

Discipleship is the process of becoming a follower of Jesus Christ, living in a relationship with God and responding to God's call to holy living in the world (135). It is, first and foremost, "a work of grace . . . marked by awakening, birth, growth, and maturation" (136). Through the intentional nurture of the *church*, profession of faith, *baptism, confirmation, worship, Holy Communion, education*, formation, and service, children are nurtured, and youth and adults are taught the meaning of the Christian faith.

Faithful discipleship is a commitment to a lifelong process of growing in the *grace* of God and witnessing to the presence of Christ in the world (216). It is expressed through both membership and participation in the corporate life of the *church* and in God's *mission* in the world (218-219).

The *GBOD* (1101-1122) and the Conference Board of Discipleship (629) support the process of growth in faithful discipleship in the *local church, district, annual conference*, and the witness of the *Church* in the world.

One of the earliest discipleship-oriented programmatic efforts of Methodism in the US was the formation of three organizations: the Bible, Sunday School, and Tract societies were formed and then endorsed by the *General Conference* of 1832. The materials developed by these agencies focused on topics such as holiness, family religion, the instruction of children, and "Sabbath schools." Materials were used for both outreach and faith formation within the societies.

See also: www.umcdiscipleship.org.

District

¶161. The duties of a Bishop are: 1. To preside in our Conferences. 2. To form the Districts according to his judgment. —*Discipline*, MEC, 1888.

Districts comprise *local churches* in a designated geographic area. The *annual conference* determines the number of districts, and the *bishop* in consultation with the *district superintendents* sets the boundaries (415.4). The *district superintendent* oversees the work of the district *clergy* and *local churches*.

Districts may organize themselves in ways that further the missional life of the *church*. Cooperative parish ministries between *local churches* are encouraged, and *churches* may be arranged in clusters (206.3). Districts are required to have the following positions and committees: District Lay Leader (660), *District Committee on Ordained Ministry* (666), District Director of Lay Servant Ministries (668), District Committee on District Superintendency (669), District Board of Trustees (2518.2), *United Methodist Women* (670), and *United Methodist Men* (671). In addition, the *district superintendent* may appoint the following: Director of Church and Society (662), Director of Ethnic Local Church Concerns (663), Director of Religion and Race (664), Coordinator of Young Adult Ministries (665), *District Committee on Lay Servant Ministries* (668), Board of Laity (667), and Council on Youth Ministries (672).

Districts first appear in the late 1870s of The MEC and were well institutionalized in their *Disciplines* of the 1880s. The MECS followed suit quickly. *Bishops* were given permission to form them, and the presiding *elders* (today's equivalent of a *district superintendent*) were responsible for presiding at *district conferences*.

See also: www.umc.org/en/content/find-district-offices.

District Board of Church Location and Building

¶91 The regular business of the district conference shall be 7. To inquire respecting opportunities for Missionary and Church Extension enterprises within the District, and to take measure for the occupation of any neglected portion of its territory. —*Discipline*, MEC, 1888.

Each *district* shall have a District Board of Church Location and Building (2519) to investigate *local church building* proposals, explore strategies for The UMC in changing neighborhoods (see 2520.2), and conduct an energy study on *local church buildings* and *parsonages* (2520.3). Membership consists of the *district superintendent* and those nominated by the *district superintendent* according to the requirements in ¶2519. The District Board of Church Location and Building works with *local churches* in "the planning and financing requirements for *local church* building" programs (2544).

Formerly known as District Boards of Church Extension, The MC established the District Board on Church Location and Buildings in 1944, expanding its responsibilities beyond that of identifying locations for new *churches* and assigning them the responsibilities for monitoring and approving *local church* decisions about their *property*.

See also: Annual conference and district office guidelines and rules.

District Committee on District Superintendency

¶289. There shall be annually, in every District, a meeting composed of one Steward from each Circuit and station, to be selected by the Quarterly Conference . . . to make an estimate of the amount necessary to furnish a comfortable support to the Presiding Elder. —*Discipline*, MEC, 1888.

Each district shall have a Committee on District Superintendency for the purpose of supporting the district superintendent in the oversight of the district. The committee has the following responsibilities: advocacy for the district budget needs, including office and secretarial support, travel, continuing education, and housing (parsonage) needs; availability for counsel; advising on relations in the district; evaluating ministry; and consulting on continuing education (669). This committee was first created by The UMC in 1976. Its responsibilities have not changed since its inception. In early Methodism, the stewards of the quarterly conferences and, later, the district stewards, would have provided such consultation to the presiding elders.

See also: Annual Conference websites

District Committee on Lay Servant Ministries

¶92 The order of business of the District Conference shall be 3. To receive Reports (4) From each Exhorter, including a statement of the Prayer-meetings he has held and other work done, especially in destitute places and among the sick and the poor. —*Discipline*, MEC, 1888.

Districts are required to have a director of lay servant ministries (266–269) who is a certified *lay servant* and are encouraged to create a Lay Servant Ministries Committee in the *district* related to the *annual conference* Lay Servant Ministries Committee. Membership includes the director of *lay servant* ministries (chair), *district superintendent*, *district lay leader*, and the instructor of *lay servant* courses. The committee will provide training and opportunities for *lay servant ministry* in the district, and report on certifications to the *charge conferences* of the certified *lay servants* (668).

When the role of *lay servant* was first conceived, it was called the "lay speaker." It was based loosely, but not fully, on the role of an "exhorter." First appearing in the 1952 MC *Discipline*, the lay speaker was certified annually by the quarterly conference of the *local church*. This responsibility moved to the district committee on lay speaking during the merger in 1968. The name of both the position and the committee was changed in 2012.

See also: www.umcdiscipleship.org/resources/lay-servant-ministries-catalog.

District Committee on Ordained Ministry (DCOM)

¶91 The regular business of the district conference shall be 2. To take Cognizance of all the Local Preachers and Exhorters in the District 3. To hear complaints against Local Preachers 4. To license Local Preachers . . . ¶92 2. To appoint Committees on the (1) Examination of Candidates for license to Preach, (2) Examination of Local Preachers in each of the four years of the Course of Study, (3) Examination of Candidates for admission into the traveling connection, (4) Examination of Candidates for Orders. —*Discipline*, MEC, 1888.

The District Committee on Ordained Ministry interviews candidates for ministry (including credit and criminal background checks and psychological assessments), supervises candidates for ordained ministry and licensed local *pastors*, recommends persons for *provisional membership* and *associate membership*, and examines certified *lay members* (666). The District Committee on Ordained Ministry functions as a subcommittee of the *Board of Ordained Ministry* (634) and is amenable to the *annual conference* through the conference *Board of Ordained Ministry* (666).

The review and credentialing of candidates for the ministry was held in the late 1700s in the *annual conference*. As the *Church* grew and administrative responsibilities of *annual conferences* became more complex, the first stages of decision-making were pushed to the quarterly conference and presiding *elder*, and then candidates were forwarded to the *annual conference*. With the formation of *districts*, these responsibilities then moved to the *district conference*, and then subsequently to established committees of the *district*. In The MC, it was named the Committee on Ministerial Qualifications. In The UMC, it became the District Committee on Ordained Ministry.

See also: www.gbhem.org/wp-content/uploads/2023/06/BOM-Handbook _complete.pdf.

District Conference

¶94. The provisions for District Conferences shall be of force and binding only in those Districts in which the Quarterly Conferences of a majority of the Circuits and Stations shall have approved the same by asking the Presiding Elder to convene a District Conference, as herein provided. —*Discipline*, MEC, 1888.

District conferences are held if directed by the *annual conference* or called by the *district superintendent* (658). Membership is determined by the *annual conference* but typically includes *clergy* of the *district* and *lay members* of *annual conference* and draws its own agenda. The district conference issues *candidacy* for ordained ministry certificates and may incorporate the *district* for the sake of *property* and handling mission funding (659).

The first attempt at a district conference took place in 1820, when local preachers protested that they were unable to be examined, licensed, and tried by their peers. Comprising all the local preachers in the area for which the presiding *elder* was responsible (not yet defined as a geographical area), solely to deal with just these issues, the district conference encountered a significant number of problems and was dissolved in 1836. The district conference and the *district*—as describing a collection of circuits, stations, and missions in a geographical area—was resurrected in a different form in the late 1870s.

District conferences were held only if the quarterly conferences within the *district* approved of turning over some of their own responsibilities to this larger body. They could be discontinued with a majority vote of the quarterly conferences in the district. According to ¶91 of the 1888 *Discipline* of The MEC, district conferences were responsible for the "general oversight of all the temporal and spiritual affairs"; cared for licensing and appointments of local preachers and exhorters; reviewed complaints against local preachers, along with trials held; and discussed the planning for new "missionary and *church* extension enterprises." The conferences were enhanced by "Religious and Literary exercises for the mutual benefit of those in attendance." Presiding *elders* were renamed "*district superintendents*" around the turn of the twentieth century, as the geographical delineations and expanding responsibilities of the presiding *elder* came into play. While the geographical region known as the *district* continues to exist today, the language about district conferences became permissive in the *Constitution* of the new MC in 1939. However, a section in the *Discipline* remained that left the decision for continuing district conferences up to the *annual conferences*. Many conferences no longer hold district conferences on an annual basis.

See also: www.umc.org/en/content/glossary-district-conference.

District Staff

> The South District Administrative Assistant is the support person for the District Superintendent (DS) and the South District, working closely with the other District Assistants and the Annual Conference staff. This person is also the resource person for South District local churches and their Administrative Assistants. The position is under the direct supervision of the DS. This person will be responsible for a great deal of varied and complex tasks, including but not limited to calendaring, coordinating of work, collaboration of work with other offices, receptionist, hospitality, administrative tasks, finance, communications, database maintenance, and event/meeting planning and support. —Job Description, Administrative Assistant, South District, Desert Southwest Conference; dscumc.org/wp-content /uploads/2017/01/Job_Description-South_AdministrativeAssistant.pdf, accessed July 15, 2017.

District staff comprise the district superintendent and office staff, which typically includes a district secretary. In addition, a variety of positions (e.g., director of lay servant ministry), both paid and not, exist as a resource for the ministry of pastors and local churches.

Historically, district superintendents maintained offices in their parsonages. As the administrative responsibilities of district superintendents and the needs of local churches for resourcing for ministry have expanded, districts have added both administrative and programmatic staff to their offices. Such decisions are usually made in conversation with the bishop and cabinet, and often as a part of a shared plan of realignment of district staff.

See also: Annual conference and district websites.

District Superintendent

> "The duty of the office . . . is as the Bishop's assistant, not in administering sacraments, but in the great business of administering every interest and province of the church in his district. A superintendent carries not only to Methodists this mean but carries it to everybody. Superintendent is a well-defined and definite term. Presiding eldership is not known in its essential

character and up-to-date meaning with our own people, for they emphasize sacrament, and we must emphasize administration." —R. A. Chase, quoted by J. Dennis Williams, "From Presiding Elder to District Superintendent: The Development of an Office in Episcopal Methodism from 1792 to 1908," Methodist History, 40:4 (July 2002): 262.

The district superintendent (often called the "DS") serves as the chief missional strategist of *districts* and assists the *bishop* in the administrative work of the *annual conference* (54. Article IX). As *elders* in *full connection*, district superintendents are appointed by the *bishop* to the *cabinet* as an extension of the *bishop's* superintending role (403.2). District superintendents serve for a term of six years but may be extended by the *bishop* to eight years and may return to the *cabinet* within certain limits (418). The district superintendent oversees "the total ministry of the clergy . . . and of the *churches*," working with the *bishop* in making *appointments* and assignments, recruiting and examining candidates, developing effective and faithful systems of ministry with *clergy*, laity, and *local churches*, leading by spiritual example, providing counsel to *clergy* (formal and informal), maintaining records, deciding questions of *church* law in the *district*, engaging in ecumenical and interreligious leadership, and serving in other capacities as assigned by the *bishop* (419). The district superintendent is also the "acting administrator" for any *local church* that has no appointed *pastor* (419).

In the MEC Annual Conference of 1785, the term "presiding *elder*" began to be used, instead of Wesley's term "assistant," for the preachers who had oversight for the other preachers on a circuit. The work of the presiding *elder* evolved over its first one hundred years from that of a presiding officer and sacramental leader to an administrative officer of the *annual conference*. The most recent change in the interpretation of the role of the district superintendent came in 2012, with the description of the officer as "chief missional strategist" of the *district*.

See also: www.gcfa.org/district-superintendent-conference-material; www.gbhem.org/sites/default/files/documents/publications/PUB_2013 DSINTHEUMC.pdf.

Ecumenical Relationships

Among other things which came up for consideration before this conference [GC 1836], was the propriety of dissolving our [MEC] Bible Society. . . . The conference, after due deliberation, recommended to the society a dissolution of its existence, . . . and our brethren and friends were advised to unite in carrying forward the objects of the American Bible Society. —Bangs, vol. 4, 233.

The UMC has covenant relationships with four ecumenical bodies: Churches Uniting in Christ, the National Council of the Churches of Christ in the USA, the World Council of Churches, and the American Bible Society. The UMC has observer status in the US National Association of Evangelicals and the World Evangelical Fellowship (434.2 c))). The *Council of Bishops* functions as the formal liaison with these bodies, through the ACEIR and the ecumenical officer of the *Council of Bishops* (436–438).

The MEC established a relationship with the American Bible Society in 1858. The Evangelical Association, a *predecessor denomination*, approved participation in the Federation of the Churches of Christ in America in 1907. The MC and EUBC were founding members of the National Council of Churches in 1950 (the Federation merged with the NCC at its founding) and the World Council of Churches in 1946.

See also: www.americanbible.org/; www.churchesunitinginchrist.org; www.oikoumene.org; www.nationalcouncilof churches.us/

Education

Quest. What shall we do for the rising generation? 7. Preach expressly on education; "But I have no gift for this." Pray earnestly for the gift, and use means to attain it. —*Discipline*, 1789, §XXVI. "On the Instruction of Children."

Education is a core value of The UMC. It is expressed in *baptism*, nurture, instruction, and *confirmation* through materials approved by The UMC (216) and the *Social Principles* (160–164). In the local church, it is found in the roles of the Sunday school, the office of church school superintendent and small-group coordinator (255), accountable discipleship (256.1 *b*)), a work area on educational ministry (254), and *lay servant ministry* (266). The Church is committed to higher education and campus ministry through the *GBHEM* (633, 1401–1417), the Ministerial Education Fund (816), requirements for *commissioning, ordination,* and licensing (318, 322, 324, 330, 335), the *continuing education* and certification of *clergy* (258.2 *g)* (8)), and observance of special days like Christian Education Sunday (262). The Curriculum Resources Committee of the *GBOD* is responsible for curriculum resources developed and used in the Christian educational ministry of The UMC (1117). Additional resources are provided by The *UMPH* (1601–1641).

Education has always had a central place in Methodist ministry, and from early on, educational resources were made available through publication and distribution. John Wesley published tracts, sermons, and commentaries to resource the spiritual lives of Methodist people. The education of both *clergy* and laity was emphasized in the earliest *Disciplines*.

One of Bishop Coke's and Bishop Asbury's first projects was to establish a school, "Cokesbury College," for the sons of Methodist preachers. Sabbath schools and sidewalk Sunday schools were designed to teach not just the faith but also basic elements of education to poor children, through the establishment of schools, seminaries, academies and colleges for boys and girls, for persons of color, indigenous populations, and speakers of languages other than English. Newly creative forms of education were lifted up at every *General Conference*. At the 1820 *General Conference*, the delegates approved a memorial to establish "literary institutions" in every *annual conference*. Throughout the 1800s, Methodism built over two hundred academies and colleges.

See also: www.umcdiscipleship.org; www.gbhem; www.cokesbury.com.

Elder

Lord, pour upon . . . the Holy Spirit for the office and work of an elder, in the name of the Father, and of the Son, and of the Holy Spirit. Take authority as an elder in the Church to preach the Word of God, and to administer the Holy Sacraments. —*BOW*, 677–78.

Elders "are ordained to a lifetime ministry of Word, Sacrament, Order, and Service" in the *church* or an *extension ministry* (332-333). The extensive responsibilities and duties of elders are framed by the "fourfold ministry" of Word, Sacrament, Order, and Service (340). As servant leaders, elders share Christ's love by ordering the fulfillment of the Church's mission in the world.

The requirements for being an elder include: previous election as a *provisional member*; service for at least two years under episcopal appointment; meeting of all the education requirements; presentation of a sermon, Bible study, and mission project; an oral and written examination; and recommendation by the *Board of Ordained Ministry* and vote of the *clergy* members of the *annual conference* after satisfying the requirements (335).

For mutual support and accountability, *elders* participate in the *Order* of Elders (306). Except for the election of *lay delegates to the General Conference*, elders in *full connection* vote on all conference matters including constitutional amendments and *clergy delegates to the General Conference* and *jurisdictional* or *central conferences*, and share with *deacons* in responsibility for clergy *ordination*, conference relations, and character (334.1, 602.1 *a)*). Elders can be elected as *clergy delegates to the General Conference* and *jurisdictional* or *central conferences* and hold office in the *annual conference* (36. Article IV). Only elders can serve as *district superintendents* and be elected as *bishops* (*bishops* remain elders even after their *consecration*).

Elders are to be "continually available for appointment." Elders itinerate and are to be continued under appointment by the *bishop* as long as they are in good standing, unless they receive a leave, retire, or have become ineligible (337). Elders are appointed primarily as *pastors* in *local churches* but also serve in a variety of *extension ministries* (337. 2, 3). Elders undergo a regular annual evaluation process as a means of demonstrating their continued effectiveness. They are also expected to serve as mentors and supervisors for candidates for ministry (334).

Through a prescribed process, elders may change orders and become *deacons* (309.2).

It was the lack of ordained Methodist elders that prompted John Wesley to ordain Thomas Coke a general superintendent and Richard Vasey an elder, to go to the new United States and ordain Francis Asbury and twelve elders. These men were then able to not only preach but also celebrate the *sacraments* with their societies. The responsibilities of the elder have expanded over the past two hundred years, but at its core, the elder's main responsibilities remain the same, Word and Sacraments, the ordering of the life of not just the *local church* but the whole *Church*, and to serve as leaders in both the *Church* and the world. Until the late 1800s, only men were permitted to be elders. Pauline Williams Martindale was the first woman ordained in a predecessor denomination, The MPC, in 1875, while in 1880, The MEC refused to ordain Anna Howard Shaw and Anna Oliver. Ella Niswonger was ordained in 1889, and Sarah Dickey in 1894, by the United Brethren Church. Minnie Jackson Goins was the first African American woman ordained by The UBC in 1904. With the reunification in 1939, The MPC gave up its practice of bestowing full clergy rights to women. In the meantime, The MEC granted rights to women as local elders and *deacons* but gave them no conference membership. This reality was perpetuated in the reunification of 1939. In 1946, women were denied ordination in the new EUBC, another compromise made this time by The UBC in the interests of merger.

In 1956, The MC finally granted full clergy rights as elders to women.

See also: www.gbhem.org/ministry/clergy-leaders/elders/; www.umc.org /en/content/timeline-of-women-in-methodism.

Endorsement

It soon became evident that these two separate efforts required separate organizational entities. On October 10, 1942, at its meeting in Washington, the Methodist Emergency unanimously adopted the following motion:

"That the present Joint Commissions be separated into two distinct bodies: the Methodist Committee on Camp Activities and the Methodist Commission on Chaplains." The commission would be responsible for recruiting, assessing, endorsing, equipping, guiding, and supporting chaplains on a denominational level. No similar office existed in any of the denominations

that merged in 1939 to become the Methodist Church. —https://milewis
.wordpress.com/2023/03/23/methodist-commission-chaplains-wwii/.

Endorsement provides the certification that demonstrates the ecclesiastical
approval of a chaplain. Related to the *GBHEM*, the endorsing agent works
with individuals and the institutions to which they aspire to be attached,
especially but not limited to the military, prisons, hospitals, nursing homes,
hospice, disaster response, and spiritual direction. An endorsement guide
provided by the United Methodist Endorsing Agency (UMEA) outlines the
requirements for a person's particular area of specialization. (See below).

The Discipline requires that endorsed ministers remain attached to the annual conference of which they are a member (344.1(4)b) and maintain their
charge conference in a congregation in that annual conference. They may
maintain an affiliate relationship to a local church in the conference in which
they are serving if they are outside the bounds of their home conference (344-
345).

Endorsement began during World War II as the church responded to the
spiritual needs of the military. After the war, the process of endorsement expanded to include other specialized contexts. This resulted in more diverse
and more professional ministries to populations who might not have access
to spiritual support.

See also: https://www.gbhem.org/ministry/chaplaincy-endorsed-ministries
/become-a-chaplain/#:~:text=Endorsement%20for%20Clergy%20
Appointed%20by%20their%20Bishop&text=Endorsement%20certifies
%20that%20a%20person,Church%20in%20a%20pluralistic%20setting.

Endowment and Planned-Giving Ministry

Endowments and planned giving are tangible expressions of faith in the
future of the Church. Webster defines endowment as "the act or process
of furnishing with an income." If the church is to remain on the frontier,
it must plan for future as well as present mission and ministry; but unless
these plans include ways of funding this mission and ministry, they may be
only empty dreams. The concept of endowment funding says to the church

and to the community that the church is here to stay and that it is both planning for and funding the future. —www.umfoundation.org/Planned GivingHandbook.pdf, 6.

Endowment and planned giving continue to be untapped resources for the *local church*. The *charge conference*, in consultation with the *Board of Trustees*, may establish an Endowment and Planned-Giving Ministry for receiving and managing major gifts (2533.5, 2534). The Endowment and Planned-Giving Ministry will invest funds in the manner prescribed by the donor and in keeping with the *Social Principles*, develop guidelines for adoption by the *charge conference*, emphasize the need for persons to have a will, stress the opportunities for persons to give through The UMC by means of wills, property, annuities, life insurance, trusts, and memorials, and educate the congregation on planned giving.

While large financial gifts have been received by *local churches* throughout their histories, the presence and importance of endowments and trusts at the *local church* level was first given recognition in the 1980 *Discipline* of The UMC with a focus on how such assets were to be handled in the event of a discontinuance or abandonment, and with encouragement to the *local church* trustees that they establish a permanent endowment and planned-giving ministry committee. In the 2016 *Discipline*, explicit guidelines for this committee were offered.

See also: naumf.org; www.umcfoundation.org.

Episcopal Area

To break up the Church by a cast-iron scheme into fixed fragments would spoil its essential unity, and we do not believe, moreover, that it would be either wise or lawful to adopt any plan which would even imply that a bishop, once elected and ordained, could be made less by any subsequent action of his colleagues or of the General Conference than a bishop of the whole Church with an intrinsic right to exercise his episcopal functions in any of the Conferences. —Bishop Collins Denny, Episcopal Address of The MECS in 1918, as quoted in James E. Kirby, *The Episcopacy in American Methodism* (Nashville: Kingswood Books, 2000), 200.

While *bishops* serve as general superintendents of the whole *Church*, episcopal areas define the region to which a *bishop* is assigned for a minimum term of four years. They are different from *annual conferences* in that they may contain more than one *annual conference* or *missionary conference*. According to the *Constitution of The United Methodist Church* regional and *jurisdictional conferences* determine the episcopal areas and boundaries of *annual conferences* (41. Article IV), upon recommendation of the respective Jurisdictional Committee on Episcopacy (524) or the Standing Committee on Central Conference Matters (404).

Until 1884, *bishops* were fully itinerant members of a general superintendency, in that they circulated through multiple *annual conferences* for the purpose of presiding at *annual conference* meetings and appointing *clergy* to their charges. They did not often live in the *annual conferences* over which they presided while conferences were in session. They were elected by the *general conferences* of their respective denominations. In 1872, The MEC *General Conference* determined that it would require *bishops* to live in certain cities in order to spread them out around the US, rather than the *bishops* self-selecting cities where they could be near one another. The MECS began the same practice ten years later. By 1884, The MEC *General Conference* determined that it would assign the *bishops* to the cities. The next step was to establish a term of office, set at four years, and by 1908, the limitations were placed on the number of terms. In 1912, the *General Conference* took the next logical step, creating areas of episcopal oversight. While The MECS *General Conference* was progressing in the same direction, The MECS *bishops* were far more reluctant to embrace the changes and continued to protest the new system in their 1930 Episcopal Address. With the establishment of the jurisdictions in the reunification of 1939, the *jurisdictional conferences* became the arena in which *bishops* would then be elected. With this dramatic change in procedures, *bishops* were assigned to episcopal areas within the jurisdictions in which they were elected.

See also: www.unitedmethodistbishops.org/about-the-council; James E. Kirby, *The Episcopacy in American Methodism* (Nashville: Kingswood Books), 2000.

Equitable Compensation

¶556. Each Annual Conference, after careful study of its needs and its sources of income for Ministerial Support, may adopt a Schedule of Minimum Support for its Pastors. This schedule shall specify the minimum financial support necessary for effective service for Clerical Members of the conference. —*Discipline*, MC, 1940.

Each *annual conference* is required to have a commission on equitable compensation or alternate structure to support full-time *clergy* serving pastoral *charges* by: recommending support standards, offering counsel, administering funds, and providing an arrearage policy to be approved by the *annual conference* (624). Ordained ministers are "entitled to receive, not less than the equitable compensation established by the *annual conference* according to the provisions of ¶ 624.3 (342).

The concept of establishing a minimum salary for conference *pastors* emerged in the 1940 *Discipline* of The MC just following reunification, and it became the Commission on Minimum Salaries, established in each *annual conference*. The name change took place with the rewrite of the *Discipline* for the merger in 1968.

See also www.gcfa.org/nacec.

Evangelism

Quest. 4. What are the directions given to the Preacher? Answ 11. You have nothing to do but to save souls. Therefore spend and be spent in this work. And go not only to those that need you, but to those that need you most. It is not your business to preach so many times, and to take care of this or that society; but to save as many souls as you can; to bring as many sinners as you possibly can to repentance. —*Discipline*, 1785, §VII. "On the Method of receiving Preachers and their Duty."

The task of evangelism is "to communicate and celebrate the redeeming and reconciling love of God as revealed in Jesus Christ to persons of every age, ethnic background, and social condition; to invite persons to commit their lives to Christ and to his *church*; and to enable persons to live as Christian disciples in the world" (629.1). The UMC resources *evangelism* in the *annual conference*, *district*, and *local church* through the Conference Board of Discipleship (629) and the *GBOD* (1111–1112).

The Methodist movement was founded in the Wesleys' deepest passion to save souls and renew the Church of England. This passion was transferred to the American colonies by lay immigrants who discovered the same need among their neighbors, and by the 1770s, implored Wesley to send preachers to help. The movement struggled but spread quickly into different parts of the expanding country once the Revolutionary War was over. It was organized as an evangelistic denomination to "reform the Continent and spread scriptural Holiness over these Lands" (The General Minutes, 1784, Question 4).

See also: www.umcdiscipleship.org; James C. Logan, *Theology and Evangelism in the Wesleyan Heritage* (Nashville: Kingswood Books, 1994).

Extension Ministry

> By contrast, if one focuses explicitly on Mr. Wesley himself, one could well argue . . . that those of us in extension ministries remain the true heirs to John Wesley. Who more than he ministered "beyond the local church"? We carry on his extension work as teacher, publisher, missionary, fundraiser, administrator of the connection, and chaplain for the people called Methodist. —Russell E. Richey, *Extension Ministers: Mr. Wesley's True Heirs* (Nashville: General Board of Higher Education and Ministry, 2008), 17.

Extension ministry refers to settings beyond the *local church* where *elders, associate members*, *provisional elders*, and persons with a *license for pastoral ministry* may be appointed to serve and witness to Christ's justice and love. *Elders* seeking this kind of *appointment* should consult with the *district superintendent* and *bishop* (343). Persons in these *appointments* are accountable to the *annual conference* and remain full participants in the *itineracy* (344). For purposes of clear distinction, categories of *appointments* apply (344). Extension ministers are evaluated in the context of their ministry, file a written report of their ministry with the *annual conference*, and hold membership in a *charge conference* (344). *Clergy* in extension ministry shall furnish to the conference secretary an annual statement of compensation for the conference journal (627). Extension ministers include but are not limited to military, hospital, and other forms of chaplaincy; *district superintendents* and *conference staff*; general evangelist, faculty and administrators at UM-related universities, colleges, and schools of theology; Wesley Foundation and college chaplains; and directors of nonprofit community organizations. The first extension ministers were the agents for the Book Concern, who worked full-time in the publishing business on behalf of the *Church*. The first "book steward" was John Dickens, who died while in the position during a cholera epidemic in Philadelphia. Until 1808 the book steward also served a station *church*. Prior to 1836, the book agent held a term of eight years. In addition, as presiding *elders* carried more and more of the sacramental and administrative burdens of collections of circuits, and were no longer appointed to one of their own, they became extension ministers. Prior to the Civil War, *appointments* emerged for developing, teaching, and administrative ministries in the schools that had been established by the various *annual conferences*. During the Civil War, a significant number of Methodist preachers volunteered as chaplains for both the Confederacy and the Union. By the 1880s, both The MEC and MECS *Disciplines* contained a long list of positions that today would qualify as extension ministers, including chaplaincies with reformatories and prisons, health institutions, and the military.

See also: Russell E. Richey, *Extension Ministers: Mr. Wesley's True Heirs* (Nashville: General Board of Higher Education and Ministry, 2008).

Fellowship of Associate Members and Local Pastors

> Your voice and source for ministry conferencing, support, encouragement, and information. —Motto of the National Fellowship of Associate Members and Local Pastors; www.nfamlp.org, accessed July 15, 2017.

Each annual conference shall have a Fellowship of Associate Members and Local Pastors, which exists for the purpose of mutual support of members and the mission of the church. The fellowship provides formational experiences, encouragement for continuing education beyond Course of Study, community, and relationships of mutual trust and support. The fellowship is convened by the bishop and coordinated by the Board of Ordained Ministry, and the elected chairperson is a member of the Board of Ordained Ministry and its executive committee (323).

The National Fellowship of Associate Members and Local Pastors was founded in 1968, at the time of the merger between The MC and EUBC.

See also: www.nfamlp.org.

Finance Committee

¶14. It shall be the duty of the stewards of each church to procure a suitable book, prepared for the purpose, and keep a financial register, in which the names of all members shall be enrolled. This book shall be ruled with columns to show opposite each name the amounts apportioned or subscripted and to give credits to each one as payments are made either weekly or monthly. It is recommended that payments be made weekly in stations, and monthly on circuits. It shall be the duty of the stewards to call on each delinquent and collect the amount due. —*Discipline*, MPC, 1936.

The committee on finance gives year-round priority to the "stewardship of financial resources" (258.4) in the *local church*. Membership includes: the chairperson of the committee on finance; *treasurer of the local church*; *financial secretary*; *church* business administrator; a *lay member of the annual conference*; the chairperson of the *Church Council*; the *lay leader*; the chairperson or representative of the *Pastor/Staff Parish Relations Committee*; a representative of the *Board of Trustees* to be selected by the trustees; the chairperson of *stewardship*; other persons as determined by the *Church Council*; and the *pastor(s)*. The *Discipline* prohibits persons in the *charge* who are immediate family members of the appointed *clergy* from serving as finance chair, treasurer, financial secretary, counter, or any paid or unpaid position on the committee and requires two unrelated people not living in the same household to count the offering (258.4).

The committee on finance "shall compile annually a complete budget for the *local church* and submit it to the *church council* for review and adoption. The committee on finance shall be charged with responsibility for developing and implementing plans that will raise sufficient income to meet the budget adopted by the *church council*. It shall administer the funds received according to instructions from the *church council* (258.4). The committee on finance also develops financial policies, makes provision for an annual audit, and ensures that designated contributions are used for their correct purposes (258.4).

An emphasis on financial accountability within the *local church* expanded dramatically during the mid-1950s in The MC. Prior to the reunification in 1939, *Disciplines* focused on general *church* and *annual conference* procedures. By 1940, *churches* were expected to implement a "Financial Plan" that included the creation of a Finance Committee and the separation of responsibilities between the *treasurer* and *financial secretary*. At that time, the basic responsibility of the Finance Committee was to work with the *pastor*, *treasurer*, and *financial secretary* on a budget, and manage an every-member canvas to raise support to fund it. By 1956, the finances of the *local church* were awarded their own complete section of The MC *Discipline*. The Finance Committee was re-created as the "Commission of Stewardship and Finance." Oversight responsibilities of the commission also now included a secretary of *stewardship* and explicit instructions that no funds could be raised through "lottery, raffle, or other game of chance" for any reason.

See also: www.cokesbury.com/search?q=guidelines+finance+2025 -2028&pagenumber=1.

Financial Records

N.B. That no ministers or preachers, traveling or local, shall receive any support either in money or other provision for their services, without the knowledge of the stewards of the circuits, and its being properly entered quarterly on the books. —Note added by Coke and Asbury to the *Discipline*, 1787, §VIII. "Of the Collections that are to be made, and how the Money is to be expended."

Financial records are kept by the *financial secretary* (258.4 *a)*). The *committee on finance* shall make plans for an annual audit, understood as "an independent evaluation" of the financial records and internal controls of the *local church* by a qualified person(s) followed by a full report to the *Church Council* (258.4 *d)*). The audit should examine reliability of reporting, safeguarding of assets, local law compliance, and procedures and policies (258.4 *d)*). The *GCAH* provides a handbook on records maintenance that includes all financial records.

In the earliest stages of the development of The MEC, the stewards worked with the deacons to create and submit reports directly to Bishops Asbury and Coke. As The MEC grew, reports were then submitted to the presiding *elders*, records were maintained by the *annual conferences*, and then eventually collated by a conference secretary, then reviewed by the *bishop* as their numbers grew and travel became more widespread. The regularization of reporting and the insistence that *local churches* keep sound financial records was established early in US Methodist history. By the end of the 1930s in The MECS and MEC, the concept of full-scale, unified approaches to financial planning in *local churches* had been introduced as a requirement in the *Disciplines*.

Financial Secretary

¶282–3 . . . Let the Stewards at the beginning of the year estimate the amount needed monthly. Then let them ascertain from each Member of the Church, and as far as practicable, from each attendant of the Congregation, what each will give as his monthly contribution Let the sums be entered by the Recording Steward in a book which he shall keep as Treasurer of the Board of Stewards. —*Discipline*, MEC, 1896.

Unlike the role of the *treasurer of the local church*, who disburses funds according to the direction of the *Church Council*, the financial secretary keeps records of *local church* contributions and payments (258.4 *a)*). These two positions should not be combined; nor should the persons who hold these two positions be related (258.4).

The position that became known as the financial secretary originated in the role of the stewards of the societies and then *local churches*. As *churches* grew, the roles of stewards became more specialized. In the late 1880s, the reception, distribution, and recording of financial information was rarely assigned to different people. This separation of powers was fully developed in all three denominations that reunified in 1939.

See also: www.cokesbury.com/search?q=guidelines&pagenumber=1/; www.gcfa.org/forms-and-assets.

Full Communion Ecumenical Partners

> We give thanks for the gift of unity that is given us through the love of Christ Jesus. We rejoice that this relationship will empower us to more authentically witness to the gospel. Charles Wesley, a priest in the Church of England and co-leader with his brother, John, in the Methodist movement in 18th Century England, wrote: "Blest be the dear uniting love that will not let us part; our bodies may far off remove, we still are one in heart." —Conclusion of A Gift to the Word: Co-Laborers for the Healing of Brokenness, The Episcopal Church and The United Methodist Church, A Proposal for Full Communion; www.ocuir.org/wp-content /uploads/2017/02/A-Gift-to-the-World-Co-Laborers-in-the-Healing-of -Brokenness-5_31_2017.pdf.

Full communion in The UMC means that two Christian *Churches*: "(1) recognize each other as constituent members of the one, holy, catholic and apostolic *church*, the body of Christ, as described in the Holy Scriptures and confessed in the *church's* historic creeds; (2) recognize the authenticity of each other's *sacraments* and welcome one another to partake in the Eucharist, (3) affirm the authenticity of each *church's* Christian ministry, and (4) recognize the validity of each other's offices of ministry" (431.1 *b*)). Full communion partners work together toward unity in mission (431.1 *c*), *d*)) and delegates from full communion partners serve on several of the *general agencies* of the *Church* (438.4, 705.3 *b*), 1006.1 *d*) (2)). Though the *Council of Bishops* can enter into *ecumenical relationships*, *General Conference* must approve and ratify full communion with other Christian bodies (431.1 *a*)).

In the spirit and legacy of John Wesley, full communion is an expression of the unity of all Christian people, something valued in Methodist tradition. On August 20, 2009, the Evangelical Lutheran Church in America adopted a full communion agreement with The UMC. Full communion was approved by the *General Conference* on Monday, April 30, 2012, between The UMC and the African Methodist Episcopal Church, the African Methodist Episcopal Zion Church, the Christian Methodist Episcopal Church, the African Union Methodist Protestant Church, and the Union American Methodist Episcopal Church. On May 17, 2016, the *General Conference* approved a full communion relationship with the Northern and Southern Provinces of the Moravian Church in North America. The *General Conference* of 2012 approved full communion with the Uniting Church in Sweden. During the postponed 2020 *General Conference* held in 2024, The UMC approved full communion with the Episcopal Church.

See also: https://www.unitedmethodistbishops.org

Full Connection Membership of Annual Conference

Observe! Taking on trial is entirely different from admitting a preacher. One on trial, may be either admitted or reject without doing any wrong. . . After two years' probation, being recommended by the Assistant and examined by the conference, he may be received into full connexion by giving him the minutes inscribed thus: "As long as you freely consent to, and earnestly endeavor to walk by these rules, we shall rejoice to acknowledge you as a fellow-labourer." —General Minutes of 1784, 6.

At the *clergy executive session* of the *annual conference*, persons who have been deemed ready for *ordination* as *elders* or *deacons* are voted on—are elected—by the body of ordained *clergy* to join them as full connection members of the conference. Requirements for full connection are the same for both *deacons* and *elders*. Full connection members have rights of voice and vote in all matters of the *annual conference* where they are members, except the election of *lay delegates to the General Conference*; they are eligible to hold office and serve on *annual conference* boards, commissions, or committees, and be *clergy delegates* to the *general, jurisdictional,* or *central conferences,* and share in the responsibility for matters of *ordination,* character, and *clergy* relations in the *annual conference.* Upon full connection membership, *elders* and *deacons* participate in their respective *orders* (329.2).

When Francis Asbury and the preachers were elected to become *elders* during the Christmas Conference of 1784, they were also given full connection in the conference, meaning that they had the full rights, privileges, and responsibilities that attained to belonging to the group. Preachers aspired to full connection, which for a few years was also bestowed upon deacons, because it provided them with access to *appointments,* the right to participate in the conference sessions, and a salary (meager as it was!). Full connection in an *annual conference* has always accompanied *ordination* as an *elder,* and since 1996, also as a deacon.

See also: www.gbhem.org/ministry/clergy-leaders/.

Funerals and Memorial Services

> Dying, Christ destroyed our death. Rising, Christ restored our life. Christ will come again in glory. —The Gathering in "A Service of Death and Resurrection," *BOW,* 141.

The time of death and the grief that ensues is a significant pastoral moment in the life of a family, *church,* or community. The *BOW* and *UMH* offer helpful commentary, *rituals,* hymnody, orders of service, and resources for ministry in situations of grief and loss. Though *pastors* typically preside at funerals and memorials services, a person leading a service does not need to have *clergy* credentials or licensing by the state to officiate.

Funerals far outnumbered weddings in the early days of Methodism and thus provided a regular context for offering a theological framework for how Methodists were to live their lives. The basic format, which has been elaborated upon over the years, began with a series of gathering statements read by the *pastor* walking in front of the coffin, and then at the grave, or in the *church* or home, offering psalms or other pertinent Scriptures, the collect, the Lord's Prayer, and a benediction. The service often focused on the "happy death" of the believer who entered a new life far better than the present. Testimonies of such "happy deaths" were circulated and shared at the funerals. The *ritual* for funerals was included in the *Discipline*, along with the *rituals* for *baptism*, new members, the *Lord's Supper*, weddings, *consecration* of *bishops*, *ordination* of *elders* and *deacons*, laying cornerstones, and dedicating *churches*.

See: "A Service of Death and Resurrection," *UMH* (870–75); "Services of Death and Resurrection," *BOW* (139–71).

General Agencies

> The essential value of these boards and agencies is that they carry out their work continually with a paid staff in their respective headquarters, and while conferences adjourn and Bishops and church executives scatter out into their several places of responsibility the boards keep steadily on, fulfilling day by day their allotted duties. —Harmon, *Understanding*, 108.

As defined by the *Discipline*, the term "agency" is used to describe boards, commissions, committees, councils, divisions, or other units (see 703 for definitions of organizational structures) at the various levels that provide both resources to ministry and connection for the *Church* (701.2). General agencies are established by the *General Conference* to provide essential structure, services, and ministries related to common ministry, vision, and mission (17.8. Article IV); the category of general agency does not include quadrennial commissions or committees created for specific purposes (701.3). General agencies are amenable to the *General Conference* (702.1) and accountable to the *Connectional Table* (702.3). General agencies exist to carry out the will of the *General Conference* between quadrennial meetings and do so by resourcing the *Church*. General agencies that serve program or advocacy functions are referred to as "program-related" (703.5), and the general agencies that primarily have administrative and service functions are designated as "administrative general agencies" (703.6).

The UMC has the following program-related general agencies:

General Board of Church and Society (GBCS), General Board of Discipleship (GBOD), General Board of Global Ministries (GBGM), General Board of Higher Education and Ministry (GBHEM), General Commission on Religion and Race (GCORR), General Commission on the Status and Role of Women (GCOSROW), General Commission on United Methodist Men (UMM), and United Methodist Women (UMW). The effectiveness of the general program-related agencies is reviewed and evaluated by the *Connectional Table* (702.3).

The administrative agencies are the *General Board of Pension and Health Benefits (GBOPHB or Wespath), The United Methodist Publishing House (UMPH)*, the *General Commission on Archives and History (GCAH)*, and the *General Commission on Communication (UMCom)*. Both the *GCAH* and *UMCom* also have program functions and are accountable to the *Connectional Table*.

The general agencies are accountable to the *GCFA* for use of the *general funds* (810.2) of the *Church* for funding, program, and mission (704). Membership on the general agencies is accomplished through nomination by the *Council of Bishops, General Conference, jurisdictional conference*, and *central conference* delegates from annual and missionary conferences in the US, along with nominations from the floor, followed by election to a jurisdictional pool (705.1). In turn, the jurisdictional nominating committees select persons for election to specified *church* bodies by a defined process (705). General agencies are staffed with the executive positions, which include a general secretary and officers (703.7). *Bishops* serve as members of the general agencies, traditionally being elected as presidents, and as a part of their responsibilities provide "general oversight" to the agencies (48. Article III).

Prior to the reunification of 1939, The MEC and MECS had a few general boards. The MEC had a Board of Education, a Board of Missions, and a Board of Managers for the Freedmen's Aid Society. The MECS had boards for both Education and Missions. It was not until the creation of The MC that an expansion in the number of programmatic and administrative boards began to happen. The directories of The MC demonstrate the expansion of the work over time; by 1952, not only were members of the boards identified but also the executive secretaries and staffs of the boards. The 1956 *Discipline* was the first to identify the boards and the agencies as distinct groups, the boards being the governing body and the staff of the agencies being the ones to lead, respond, and implement the decisions of the board. This is the model that The UMC carried into its life in 1968.

See also: www.umc.org/en/content/agencies.

General Board of Church and Society (GBCS)

Living Faith. Seeking Justice. Pursuing Peace. —www.umcjustice.org.

The purpose of the General Board of Church and Society (GBCS) is to bring the whole of human life into conformity with the will of God, by relating the gospel of Jesus Christ to the *Church*, community, and world, and addressing reconciliation and righteousness in all its personal, social, and civic dimensions (1002). By working to implement the *Social Principles* and other Christian social concerns and policies of the *General Conference*, the board provides witness and action on issues of well-being, justice, peace, and creation (1004). The GBCS develops resources to motivate, inform, and train UMs on social justice.

The GBCS consists of thirty-three members from the *jurisdictional conferences, regional conferences, Council of Bishops,* and additional representatives (one of which may be from among The UMC's *full communion ecumenical partners*) (1006).

Methodists have always been socially conscious and have organized around key social issues. Beginning with the Woman's Home Missionary Society in 1888, which worked to organize early Christian Temperance movements, the *Church's* concern over moral, social, economic, and political life eventuated into the establishment of boards and agencies with growing social interests. The 1939 merger of The MEC, MECS, and MPC saw the creation of three boards: The Board of Temperance (1940–1960), Commission on World Peace (1940-1960), and Board of Social and Economic Relations (1952-1960). The work of these three agencies was incorporated into the creation of the Board of Christian Social Concerns in the merger of The MC and EUBC in 1968. The 1972 *General Conference* changed the name to the "General Board of Church and Society" with subsequent *General Conferences* developing the agency's focus and structure.

See also: www.umcjustice.org.

General Board of Discipleship (GBOD, Discipleship Ministries)

Equipping World-Changing Disciples. —www.umcdiscipleship.org.

The General Board of Discipleship (GBOD) is the official name in the *Discipline* given to Discipleship Ministries and the Upper Room. The purpose of the GBOD is to assist in fulfilling the *mission statement of The UMC* (1101), and it does so through the work of five divisions:

(1) The Upper Room (1102.2, 1107); (2) New *church* starts through Path One; (3) Leadership ministries; (4) Young people's ministries; and (5) Discipleship Resources International. Through listening to the *Church*, research, production, and training, the GBOD delivers resources that enhance the meaning of membership (216–220), supports Christian growth, and enables congregations to accomplish their primary task (1102). The GBOD is responsible for Faith Formation, Intentional Discipleship, and Christian Education (1108-1109), *evangelism* (1111-1112), *worship* (1113), *stewardship* (1114), spiritual formation through The Upper Room (1115), and the ministry of laity (1116). It also produces *The Upper Room* devotional guide, training and consultation, representation in interdenominational and ecumenical agencies, and the incorporation of ethnic *local church* concerns (1102). The work of the GBOD also includes the Curriculum Resource Committee, which is responsible for curriculum resources (1117-1122), Young People's Connectional Network to nurture faith development and discipleship and equip leaders (1201-1202), oversight of the Youth Service Fund (1207), and grants for ministries with young people (1208).

The GBOD consists of twenty-two members from the *jurisdictional conferences, central conferences, Council of Bishops,* the Division on Ministries with Young People, and additional members based on expertise and need for representation (1105).

The GBOD was created in 1972, with the goal of developing a new structure for the similar agencies of the denominations forming The UMC. This consolidation included the former Board of Education, Board of Evangelism, Board of the Laity, and Commission on Worship.

See also: www.umcdiscipleship.org.

General Board of Global Ministries (GBGM)

"to equip and transform people and places for God's mission around the world" —www.umcmission.org.

The purpose of the General Board of Global Ministries (GBGM) is to serve as a missional instrument of The UMC (1301), connecting the *Church* in *mission* through "making disciples of Jesus Christ, strengthening, developing, and renewing Christian congregations and communities, alleviating human suffering, and seeking justice, freedom, and peace" (www.umcmission.org). Responsibilities include: discerning and witnessing to the gospel where it has not been heard, developing leadership, strengthening Christian congregations, encouraging unity, joining with other persons and faiths in common concerns, equipping women for ministry, directly addressing human need, liberating human potential amid societies and systems, imagining and engaging in new forms of *mission,* affirming Volunteers in Mission (VIM), and facilitating the assignment of *missionaries* (1302).

In 2024 the support and training for "actively resist[ing] intersecting structures of white supremacy, heterosexism, sexism, patriarchy, transphobia, xenophobia, ableism, colonialism, and classism" was added to the GBGM's list of responsibilities (1302.16). The GBGM engages in program development centered on: congregational and community development, *connectional* and ecumenical relationships, *mission education* and interpretation, *mission* service, and global health (1314). As a missional arm of the GBGM and The UMC, the *United Methodist Committee on Relief* provides direct service to persons in need (1315). The GBGM consists of members from the *jurisdictional conferences*, *central conferences*, the *UMW*, and the *Council of Bishops* (1311).

The General Board of Global Ministries embodies a rich legacy of *mission* from the history of Methodism. One of the earliest agencies, the Missionary Society of The MEC, was established in 1820, and headquartered in New York City. During the 1844 split, The MECS created its own *mission* agency with an office in Nashville. Missionary activity in both *Churches*, at home and abroad, thrived during the nineteenth century. Following the 1939 merger, The MC established the Board of Missions, which brought together eleven *mission* organizations. With the formation of The UMC in 1968, the General Board of Global Missions was formed and housed in New York City. The GBGM was restructured in 1980, and again in 1996, organizing around missional tasks and taking on more of a global ethos and perspective. Working from this global perspective, the GBGM moved its headquarters to Atlanta in 2016, while at the same time establishing a regional presence in Europe, Asia, the Middle East, and Latin America, and also maintaining the UMCOR-related field offices in Asia and Africa.

See also: www.umcmission.org.

General Board of Higher Education and Ministry (GBHEM)

> . . . to lead and connect the educational and ministerial life of The United Methodist Church. We will serve God and the worldwide Church in recruiting, nurturing, and educating lay and clergy leaders who seek wisdom and live ethically as God's peacemakers. —www.gbhem.org.

The General Board of Higher Education and Ministry (GBHEM) exists to prepare persons for licensed, diaconal, ordained, and certified ministry, and to provide oversight for institutions of higher *education*, including schools, colleges, universities, theological schools, and campus ministries (1404-1406). The work of the GBHEM maintains: educational institutions and campus ministries; the University Senate, establishing criteria for UM-affiliated schools (1410); the United Methodist Higher Education Foundation, to raise financial support (1414); the Council of Presidents of the Black Colleges, exploring the role of black colleges in higher education (1415); leading the *Church* in inviting, developing, and supporting effective and faithful spiritual leaders; and Schools of Theology of The United Methodist Church, educating lay and ordained persons, interpreting the faith, and providing prophetic leadership (1416-1417). The GBHEM is amenable to the *General Conference* and accountable to the *Connectional Table* in between sessions (1403). Membership on the GBHEM comprises representatives from *jurisdictional conferences*, *central conferences*, the *Council of Bishops*, and additional representative(s) for the sake of expertise and inclusivity and need for representation (1407).

For more than 150 years, The Methodist Church has promoted *education*. In 1816, the *Course of Study* was developed for traveling preachers. Following the expansion of schools from 1820 to 1860, in North America, The MEC created the Board of Education in 1866. Some of the celebrations of higher education and ministry have been the establishment of *college and universities*; *schools of theology*; full *clergy* rights for women in 1956; Africa University; certifications; collegiate ministry; the endorsement process for chaplaincy and pastoral care; the development of the International Association of Methodist Schools, Colleges, and Universities (IAMSCU); and the Central Conference Theological Education Fund. In 1972, the Board of Education became the Board of Higher Education and Ministry. See also: https: www.gbhem.org

General Board of Pension and Health Benefits—*See* Wespath

General Book of Discipline—*See Book of Discipline*

General Commission on Archives and History (GCAH)

> Be it resolved that the General Conference recognizes and approves the formation of the "Association of Methodist Historical Societies" and suggests the affiliation therewith of all our Historical Societies as well as those of other branches of Methodism, to the end that the writings and mementoes of the fathers be preserved, that the historical research be encouraged, and a complete survey of historical materials relating to our common Methodism may be made and become accessible to all our people. —Resolution, *Journal of the Thirty-second Delegated General Conference of the Methodist Episcopal Church* (New York: The Methodist Book Concern, 1936).

The purpose of the General Commission on Archives and History (GCAH) is to care for and promote the historical interests of The UMC by gathering, preserving, promoting, and holding title to library and archives, and disseminating resources on the Church's history (1703; 1710-1712). Membership includes two representatives from central conferences, seven elected by the general commission itself, two bishops, and the five presidents of Jurisdictional Commissions on Archives and History, one of which may be from the central conferences (1703).

Prior to the formation of The UMC, the collection and preservation of archival materials was focused in annual conference and regional historical societies. The General Conference of The MEC in 1884, in recognition of the centennial of American Methodism, found it important to catalog documents, relics, and facts that may be of historical value to the Church. In 1925, The MEC formed the "Association of Methodist Historical Societies," which in 1939 joined the regional historical societies of The MECS and MPC. Eventually, pastors were charged with the responsibility of seeing that an outline of the history of the local church was prepared. With the merger of The MC and the EUBC in 1968, the Commission on Archives and History was established as a central depository for The UMC, and in 1984, it became the General Commission on Archives and History.

See also: gcah.org.

General Commission on Communication (UMCom)

> United Methodist Communications (UMCom) seeks to be responsive to the communication needs of our denomination. That is why we are committed to communications ministries that will lead The United Methodist Church (The UMC) into a bright future. —https://www.resourceumc.org /en/content/communications-for-the-future-of-the-umc.

The theological understanding of The UMC obligates us to communicate God's grace with persons in the *Church* and world, utilizing all appropriate means (1801). The General Commission on Communication (UMCom) leads the *Church* in communication through public relations and marketing, providing resources and services, with sensitivity to racial and cultural diversity, to the *local church* and *annual conference* (1805). UMCom is accountable to the General Conference (1804). It has a consultative role with all the *general agencies* (1805). UMCom is responsible for official newsgathering and distribution; relations with public media, with attention to television; advocacy for freedom of religion and the press; public relations; resource production; oversight of the *Church*'s comprehensive communication system; education and training in communication skills; marketing of the *general funds*; research; knowledge of new technology; interpretation; the *Church*'s presence on the Internet; and UM branding (1805-1806).

The UMCom consists of seventeen members from the *jurisdictional conferences, central conferences, Council of Bishops*, persons with expertise in communications, and a designated member from each commission (1807).

Following the episcopal address of 1939, which called for a step up in publicity, The MC established the "Commission on Public Information" (also known as Methodist Information or MI). Initially, the agency worked at getting feature stories to media outlets, but as the popularity of radio increased, the *General Conference* created the Radio and Film Commission in 1948 (which, with the addition of television, became TRAFCO). The *General Conference* in 1952 created the Commission on Promotion and Cultivation (which eventually became the Office of Interpretation). In 1972, these two divisions were merged with Methodist Information to form UMCom.

See also: www.umcom.org.

General Commission on Religion and Race (GCORR)

> It's important for current generations to be aware that we have not overcome racism, we've not overcome prejudice. It's like sin: We're always a sinner no matter how good you think you are, that we're always striving to be better." —Bishop Woodie White, "'Dear Martin': Bishop Woodie W. White's Letters to MLK Trace Highs and Lows In Race Relations"; www .huffingtonpost.com/2014/01/20/bishop-woodie-w-white_n_4631658 .html, accessed July 5, 2017.

The purpose of the General Commission on Religion and Race (GCORR) is to "challenge, lead, and equip the people of The UMC to become interculturally competent, to ensure institutional equity and to facilitate vital conversations about religion, race, and culture" (2002). The GCORR empowers prophetic leadership; provides consultation, training, and resources; responds to racism around the globe; administers the GCORR Action Fund to encourage the employment of diversity; and consults for equitable and just policies (2008).

Membership includes two *bishops*, representatives from the *jurisdictional conferences* and three persons from the *central conferences* chosen by the *Council of Bishops*, and six additional persons to accomplish the work (2003). The GCORR is amenable to the *General Conference* and accountable to the *Connectional Table* between sessions (2001).

Although race and racism have been issues within Methodism leading to the withdrawal of early black Methodists in the formation of the African Methodist Episcopal Church, schism in 1844, resulting in The MEC and MECS, and organized segregation with the establishment of the Central Jurisdiction in 1939, history also reveals a growing consciousness over the issue and the *Church's* resolve to abolish it. Early efforts emphasized Christian *education*, social creed(s), Race Relations Sunday, funding for African American schools, intentional work against racial discrimination and segregation within Methodist structures, and resolutions. Though not mandated by the *General Conference*, a Department of Religion and Race was created under the Board of Christian Social Concerns in 1964, and the Board of Missions and Women's Division supported the effort. Within The EUBC, advocacy was lodged within the committee on Christian Social Action and Moral Standards. The General Commission on Religion and Race was established in The UMC in 1968 to ensure that ethnic and racial minority groups would have representation, service, and voice at all levels of the life and ministry of The UMC.

See also: www.gcorr.org.

General Commission on the Status and Role of Women (GCOSROW, COSROW)

We're helping the church recognize every person—clergy and lay, women and men, adults and children—as full and equal parts of God's human family. We believe that a fully engaged and empowered membership is vital to The United Methodist Church's mission "to make disciples of Jesus Christ for the transformation of the world." —www.gcsrw.org.

The General Commission on the Status and Role of Women (GCOSROW) exists to "challenge The UMC . . . to a continuing commitment to the full and equal responsibility and participation of women in the total life and mission of the *Church*, sharing fully in the power and in the policymaking at all levels of the *Church*'s life" (2102). Rooted in the liberating gospel of Jesus Christ, the GCOSROW serves as an advocate on behalf of women, redressing past inequities, working to prevent future inequities, and monitoring *inclusiveness* in the administrative and programmatic functions with the *Church, including the church and societies of the central conferences* (2102-2103). Membership shall include *jurisdictional conference* representatives, nine persons elected by the general commission, two *bishops*, three *central conference members*, and additional representation as needed.

Established by the *General Conference* in 1972, the General Commission on the Status and Role of Women grew out of a report given by the Women's Society of Christian Service (now United Methodist Women) requesting that a study be done of women's involvement in all aspects of the *Church*. Thelma Stevens, a Women's Caucus representative, proposed a quadrennial commission to address the inclusion of women at all levels of the *Church*. After being accepted, the new commission was charged with the responsibility of fostering awareness of the full participation of women, and became an advocate for challenging sexism, personnel policies, grievance procedures, and affirmative action, and an ally to victims of sexual harassment.

See also: www.gcsrw.org; Carolyn Oehler Henninger, *The Journey Is Our Home: A History of the General Commission on the Status and Role of Women*.

General Commission on United Methodist Men (GCUMM)

> C.C. Benscoter, Esq. of Brookville, . . . the secretary, writes: "I hope our approaching General Conference may cause the laity to feel that they have something to do in the great fields ripe for the harvest, with a corresponding responsibility to do something definite within the limitations of their respective spheres. We men long to do great things, . . . we can't . . . regard the church as an optional convenience, while our mothers, wives and sisters are up and doing the little things that are counting for time and eternity."
> —"The Laymen's Association at Erie, PA, September 6th Report to the General Convention of the Wesley Brotherhood, Louisville KY," *The Layman's Quarterly* 2:2 (New York: Charles Starr Publisher).

United Methodist Men is an official men's membership organization, with units required in every *local church* and chartered through the General Commission on United Methodist Men (GCUMM) (2301). The focus of United Methodist Men is to offer opportunities for spiritual growth and involvement in the ministry of the *Church* through the development of men as servant leaders, primarily through training and opportunities in *evangelism, mission*, and spiritual life (2302). *Clergy*, including women, are ex officio members of the local unit (256.6 *g)*).

Prior to the 1968 merger, men were involved in three types of organizations: brotherhoods, laymen's associations, and the Men's Work Program. The MEC officially gathered under the name "Methodist Brotherhood" in 1908, bringing together a variety of "brotherhoods" into a single organization; they were approved by The MECS in 1924. The EC created the Albright Brotherhood in 1930. The first *Discipline* of The MC, published in 1940, makes brief mention in ¶1213 of both the "Brotherhood Movement" and the "Men's Work Program" as falling under the General Board of Lay Activities of the denomination.

Laymen's associations are traceable to 1889, with the formation of the Philadelphia Laymen's Association of The MEC. It gathered primarily to address political concerns within the denomination, such as advocacy for lay representation in the *general* and *annual conferences*. In the decades preceding the reunification of 1939, laymen's associations were very active in advocating for and against reunification, lifting up social ills, and suggesting ways for men to deepen their faith.

See also: www.gcumm.org/files/uploads/umc_history_and_polity.pdf.

General Conference

> General Conference has become an enormous experiment in human community. —Frank, 267.

The General Conference is the main body of the *Church (9. Article I)* and has "full legislative power over all matters distinctively connectional" (17. Article IV; 501), yet it has no administrative or executive power (501). This authority is exercised by establishing the criteria for *Church* membership; defining and fixing the powers and duties of *elders, deacons, licensed local pastors, lay supply, deaconesses* and *home missioners, annual conferences,* and the *bishops*; and providing guidance for the work of The UMC outside the US, the *rituals* and hymnal, the judicial system, funding for the *mission of the Church,* and a system for the election of *bishops* (17. Article IV). The *General Conference* also initiates connectional enterprises; selects presiding officers from among the *bishops*; changes boundaries of *jurisdictional conferences*; establishes commissions; ensures the rights and privileges of membership regardless of race, gender, or status; allows *annual conferences* to structure for *mission*; and enacts necessary legislation (17. Article IV). The overall powers of the General Conference are limited by the *Restrictive Rules*.

General Conference "meets once in four years" unless a special meeting, usually comprising the delegates of the previous conference, is called by the *Council of Bishops* or the conference (15. Article II). *Bishops* preside (503) and nominate a secretary designate to be elected by the General Conference (504). The General Conference organizes and operates within the rules of order set by the previous conference, until amended at the beginning of the General Conference (505).

Petitions to General Conference may be submitted by "any organization, *clergy member*, or *lay member*" of The UMC and may address legislation and amendments to the *Constitution of The UMC* (60-62). Guidelines for writing and submitting petitions, and the process by which petitions are handled, are provided (508) and can be submitted on UMC.org. General Conference has the exclusive and official right to speak for The UMC (510), and this is done through the written legislation of conferencing as recorded in the *Discipline*.Membership in the General Conference comprises *clergy delegates to the General Conference* and *lay delegates to the General Conference*, according to the ratio for representation set by the General Conference (16. Article III; 502). Four delegates are from the British Methodist Church (14. Article I; 502.1 *b*)).

As the Methodist movement grew in North America, the practice of conferencing expanded through quarterly meetings on circuits, followed by *annual conferences*, then multiple sessions of a single *annual conference*, and then finally a quadrennial General Conference that was first held in 1792. In 1800, only preachers who had traveled for at least four years were allowed to participate in the General Conference, and in 1804, participation was limited to full connection traveling elders. With the development of the first *Constitution* in 1808, plans were made for a delegated General Conference to balance participation among the *annual conferences*, and this met for the first time in

1812. Though the 1824 General Conference voted against a proposal for lay representation, and in 1828, The MPC later split over lay representation—resulting in The MPC—the seeds were sown for eventual lay participation and *inclusivity*. In 1870, The MEC first seated laymen in General Conference, and in 1900, full laity rights were given to women. By 1932, laypeople had become voting delegates in all conferences. In 1939, the number of laity was based on charge (appointed *clergy*), and in 1976, the number was based on all *clergy* (including retired).

See also: www.umc.org/en/content/ask-the-umc-how-does-the-general-conference-work.

General Council on Finance and Administration (GCFA)

"We are Better Together" —www.umcgiving.org.

"Our Ministry Is to Support Your Ministry" —www.gcfa.org.

The purpose of the General Council on Finance and Administration (GCFA) is to manage the finances of The UMC, serving as the general treasurer of the *Church*. The GCFA oversees the General Funds (810-818), the Episcopal Fund (819), and Financial Appeals beyond the General Funds, and attends to matters of audit and review, personnel policies, legal responsibilities, and corporate governance (805). The GCFA is amenable to the *General Conference* for the receiving, disbursing, and reporting of all contributed funds (804), and works with the *Connectional Table* in budgeting with program agencies (804). *General agencies* are to be fiscally accountable to the GCFA (806.4-5).

The GCFA consists of twenty-one members from the *Council of Bishops, jurisdictional conferences, central conferences*, and persons with special knowledge, diversity, and experience (805).

General Funds

Quest. How may we raise a general Fund for carrying on the whole "Work of God"? Answ. By a yearly Collection, and, if need be, a quarterly one, to be raised by every Assistant in every principle Congregation in his Circuit. . . . "How shall we send Labourers into those Parts where they are most of all wanted? Many are willing to hear, but not to bear the Expense. Nor can it as yet be expected of them." —*Discipline*, 1785, §XXVIII. "On raising a general Fund for the Propagation of the Gospel."

General funds, also designated by the terms "general *Church* fund(s)," is the way in which The UMC supports the ministry and *mission* of the *Church*. The general funds include the *apportionments*, and a range of special emphases related to the *Church's mission*, which are received through *Special Sunday offerings* and initiatives.

In 1761, the conference in England established a "General Fund" to build Methodist preaching houses, with the expectation that all Methodists in England would contribute. Again in 1763, the conference created a "Preacher's Fund" to pay pensions to preachers who were "worn out" and their families. These practices, and many other initiatives, have forged the way in which UMs give to support vital ministry and *mission* around the world. In the US, the General Fund was the first churchwide collection taken, established in 1784, to help pay for sending preachers out to frontier communities.

See also: www.gcfa.org/search?q=budget+apportion+funds+2025 &type=blogs.

General Rules of Methodism

There are three simple rules that have the power to change the world. While they are ancient, they have seldom been fully put to the test. But when and where practiced, the world of things as they were was shaken until a new formation, a new world was formed. The Wesleyan movement is a prime example of this new creation that is formed when these three simple rules are adopted as a way of living. —Rueben P. Job, *Three Simple Rules: A Wesleyan Way of Living* (Nashville: Abingdon Press, 2007), 7.

The General Rules are part of the Doctrinal Standards of The UMC (104), and the following questions regarding them are asked of all candidates for *ordination* during the Historic Examination for Admission into Full Connection: Question 6 "Do you know the General Rules of our *Church*?" and Question 7 "Will you keep them?" (336). In their simplest configuration, they are first, "Do no harm," second "Do good " and third, "Attend upon the Ordinances of God" (104).

Because of how they help Methodists think about how faith meets life, the General Rules are considered to be a forerunner of the *Social Principles*. However, based in Scripture, these rules also stand in their own right as a time-tested guide to Christian faith and life.

Since 1808, the General Rules have appeared in the *Book of Discipline* and are protected by *the Restrictive Rules* (22. Article V). John Wesley originally penned the "General Rules for the United Societies" in 1743, as a way of bringing discipline to a growing movement and a means by which persons could be held accountable. Though some criticized the use of rules as being legalistic or akin to works righteousness, Wesley saw them as a means of helping persons grow into Christlikeness. Participation in the societies was contingent upon a person's willingness to abide by these rules, and they were later included by Wesley as a part of the foundational documents of The MEC in 1784.

See also: Rueben P. Job, *Three Simple Rules: A Wesleyan Way of Living* (Nashville: Abingdon Press, 2007); www.umc.org/what-we-believe/the-general-rules-of-the-methodist-church.

General Secretary

The proposal honored professionalism—election of agency staff by its own board was, as one proponent put it, in accordance with "the usual practice when you are seeking experts as these boards will require to perform an expert job." —MEA I, 386.

In the organizational structure of The UMC, a general secretary is the title given to "the chief staff officer of a *general agency*," who functions as its chief administrative officer (703.7 *a)*). Under the general secretary are the deputy general secretaries, with administrative and programmatic over particular units (703.7 *b)*). Associate general secretaries are the chief staff officers over a department or division of a *general agency* unit (703.7 *c)*), and assistant general secretaries are assistant staff officers in a *general agency* (703.7 *d)*).

Prior to the emergence of the *general agencies* in 1956, the general boards were staffed by an executive secretary (MEC) or general secretary (MECS) and perhaps a few staff, depending on the scope of their work.

See also: Website and directory of each general agency.

Grace—*See* Wesleyan Way of Salvation (*Via Salutis*)

Historical Statement

> Quest. 2. What was the Rise of Methodism, so called, in America? Answ. During the Space of thirty Years past, certain Persons, Members of the Society, emigrated from England and Ireland, and settled in various Parts of this Country. About twenty Years ago, Philip Embury, a local Preacher from Ireland, began to preach in the City of New-York and formed a Society of his own Countrymen and Citizens. —*Discipline*, 1785, §I. "Of the Rise of Methodism (so called) in Europe and America."

The last major revision of the historical statement titled, "A Brief History of The United Methodist Church" was approved in 1992. It is intended to be not a comprehensive history of the denomination, but an outline of key events in the development of The UMC. Through this text, readers are introduced to major themes and crucial events that have shaped and formed The UMC.

Beginning in 1785, The MEC began the *Discipline* with a historical state-ment, "On the Rise of Methodism (so called) in Europe and America." The MPC followed suit, the historical statement having the clear intent of casting their expulsion from The MEC in 1828 in a positive light. The MECS did not include a historical statement. With the reunification of 1939, the his-torical statement was introduced, glossing over the significant issues that the three *Churches* had faced with one another in the past. In 1968, a "Historical Statement" was introduced that focused on tying the Methodist and EUBC traditions together and of addressing the issue of racial inclusion as a key theme. Appearing first in 1968, a "Historical Statement" has been included in every edition of *The Book of Discipline of The UMC*.

See also: Richard P. Heitzenrater, *Wesley and the People Called Methodists* (Nashville: Abingdon Press, 1995); Russell E. Richey, Kenneth E. Rowe, and Jean Miller Schmidt, *Methodist Experience in America*, Vol. 1 (Nashville: Abingdon Press), 2010.

Historically Black Colleges, Universities, and Schools of Theology (HBCUs)

Your Committee on "Freedmen's Aid" has had under consideration the duty of the Methodist Episcopal Church to aid in the relief and education of the freedmen, and the means for the prosecution of this twofold and very necessary work. The following facts have been ascertained; namely: 1. Ev-erywhere in the South the freedmen are eager to have schools among them for their children and for themselves; but coming forth from the house of their bondage in deep poverty, they are not able, as yet, to support the teachers they need and desire. 2. Among the freedmen is found the most inviting and promising field of missionary efforts; and every denomination in our country, imbued with the aggressive spirit of the Gospel, is turning with interest and hope toward them. —Resolution to establish an MEC Freedmen's Aid Society as an auxiliary to the original, www.drbronsontours .com/bronsonfreedmensaidsociety methodistepiscopalchurchhistory.html, accessed July 14, 2017.

Eleven of the 107 historically black colleges and universities open today were either founded by, or soon adopted for support by, one of The UMC's *predecessor denominations*, The MEC.

These institutions include: Bennett University, Greensboro, NC; Bethune-Cookman University, Daytona Beach, FL; Claflin University, Orangeburg, SC; Clark Atlanta University, Atlanta, GA; Dillard University, New Orleans, LA; Huston-Tillotson University, Austin, TX; Meharry Medical College, Nashville, TN; Paine College, Augusta, GA; Philander Smith College, Little Rock, AR; Rust College, Holly Springs, MS; and Wiley College, Marshall, TX. They receive partial support today through the Black College Fund apportionment.

Gammon Theological Seminary was founded by The MEC in 1883. It receives support along with the other twelve official *schools of theology* through the *GBHEM*.

A total of eighteen schools were founded by the Freedman's Aid Society, a post–Civil War *general agency* of The MEC, in an effort to rapidly expand educational and missionary opportunities among "freedmen."

See also: www.gbhem.org/sites/default/files/documents/publications /FACTBOOK HBCU_0.pdf; www.gbhem.org/education/bcf-for-schools /list-of-bcf-schools/.

Holy Communion—*See* Lord's Supper, The

Housing Allowance (for Pastors)

Pros: A housing allowance allows the pastor to select housing which best meets the needs of the family; the pastor has the opportunity to build up financial equity in a house; the church is free of the responsibility of owning/maintaining a parsonage.

Cons: Over time, a housing allowance is more expensive for a local church than parsonage ownership; in some communities, housing which meets parsonage standards is not available or not in the price range which clergy can afford; some clergy are not able to afford a down payment for a home; at the time of a move, it may be difficult for the clergy to sell a home; time spent on home maintenance may reduce time available to spend on ministry. —Clergy Housing Frequently Asked Questions (FAQS), Iowa Annual Conference Parsonage Task Force, 2013; www.northcentral.iaumc.org/files /fileslibrary/Clergy_Housing_FAQ.pdf, accessed July 12, 2017.

The *Pastor/Staff Parish Relations Committee* shall consult with the *pastor* on housing, which may be a *church*-owned parsonage, or in lieu of a parsonage a housing allowance where the *annual conference* policy permits (258.2 *g)* (16)). Housing allowances should take into consideration *annual conference* policy and the cost of housing in the community surrounding the *church*. This amount paid to the *pastor*, in addition to the base compensation, shall be reported by the *local church* to the *annual conference* (626 (2)). Clergy couples should consult the district superintendent and conference policy regarding housing allowances and parsonages.

Housing allowances are a more recent development in UM practice and dependent upon *annual conference* policy.

See also: www.gcfa.org/resource/clergy-housing-allowance-explained.

Hymnal—*See United Methodist Hymnal*

Inclusivity

The United Methodist Church is a part of the church universal, which is one Body in Christ. The United Methodist Church acknowledges that all persons are of sacred worth. All persons without regard to race, color, national origin, status, or economic condition, shall be eligible to attend its worship services, participate in its programs, receive the sacraments, upon baptism be admitted as baptized members, and upon taking vows declaring the Christian faith, become professing members in any local church in the connection. In The United Methodist Church no conference or other organizational unit of the Church shall be structured so as to exclude any member or any constituent body of the Church because of race, color, national origin, status or economic condition. —*Discipline*, 2016, ¶4, Article IV.

119

Inclusivity is one of the highest values of The UMC. Written into the core of the *Constitution of The UMC* is the statement, "The UMC is a part of the *church* universal, which is one Body in Christ. The UMC acknowledges that all persons are of sacred worth. All persons without regard to race, color, national origin, status, or economic condition, shall be eligible to attend its *worship* services, participate in its programs, receive the *sacraments*, upon *baptism* be admitted as baptized members, and upon taking vows declaring the Christian faith, become *professing members* in any *local church* in the connection" (4. Article IV). Because of the example of Jesus's ministry with all persons, we embrace the diversity of all people in their special giftedness, and deny any manner of discrimination. *Worship* services are open to all. The *Church* works to enable the full participation of all people in the life of the *church*, community, and world, and to work toward full *accessibility* for persons with disabilities.

The *Church* works for the total involvement of all persons who meet the requirements of the *Discipline* in membership and leadership. Throughout the *BOD* the inclusion of diverse persons is emphasized as an important dynamic of committee and church membership. The value of inclusivity has been a contested issue throughout the history of the *Church* in the US. Prior to the Civil War, the most contentious issues were the inclusion of lay representatives, the racial integration of class meetings and societies, and slavery. In addition to other less serious schisms, the *Church* split in 1828–30 over lay representation, when The MPC was established. It split again in 1844, over slavery. The reunification of 1939 required two moral compromises: the establishment of the racially segregated Central Jurisdiction and The MPC's willingness to revoke their previous commitment to full *clergy* rights for women. The late 1800s witnessed the emergence of the issue of including women in both lay and *clergy* roles. This issue was not finally settled until 1956, when, in The MC, women finally received full *clergy* rights. The Central Jurisdiction was not dismantled until the merger of 1968 between The MC and The EUBC. At that point, the principle of *inclusivity* was written into the *Constitution of The United Methodist Church* as a way of ensuring that segregated structures would never exist in the *Church* again. At the postponed 2020 general conference, held in 2024, all references to the exclusion of LGBTIA persons from ordination, the performance of weddings, and any other kind of church leadership were removed from the *BOD*. In addition, people with disabilities were added to the listing of groups included by The UMC.

Incorporation of the Local Church

Under the law, a corporation is a separate legal entity from its officers, directors and incorporators, with the power to enter into contracts and agreements in its own name. The corporate form provides a continuous entity for the ownership and management of property and for the carrying out of the business and programs of the local church. If proven, assertions of liability for acts undertaken by the corporation may be satisfied only by corporate assets, not by the personal assets of the corporate directors, except in cases of fraud against the corporation by a director or when corporate formalities are not followed. —GCFA Legal Manual, 16; www.gcfa.org/legal-manual, accessed May 20, 2017.

Subject to the *Discipline*, the *charge conference* may "direct the *board of trustees* to incorporate the *local church*... in accordance with the pertinent local laws" (2529.1 *a)*) and in a manner that will fully protect members and officials, jointly and as individuals, from liability, and free them from *local church* obligations and debts (2529.1 *a)*). *Local church* articles of incorporation must reflect connection to The UMC and must be approved by the *district superintendent* (2529.1 *c)*). Some local laws require the incorporation of *local churches*. The *GCFA Legal Manual* is an excellent guide for incorporation.

While the *Discipline* increasingly identified a wide range of Methodist organizations that needed to be incorporated through the 1930s and early 1940s, the strong encouragement that *local churches* be incorporated was included in 1948.

See also: www.gcfa.org/resource/legal-manual.

Itinerancy (or Itineracy)

And in all his subsequent history, in his expulsion from the Established Church, in his out-door and field preaching, in the origin of class-meetings,

121

the employment of lay preachers, the settlement of the poll deed, securing the chapels forever to the itinerancy of Methodism, thus perpetuating the system, binding it equally upon preachers and people, we see not the wisdom and policy of man, but the wisdom and power of God. —George G. Cookman, "George C. Cookman Celebrates Achievements at Centennial," *Speeches Delivered on Various Occasions* (New York: George Lane for the MEC, 1840), 127.

The word "itinerant" simply means "traveling." The itinerant system is one of the primary characteristics of Methodist *polity*, the "accepted method of The UMC by which ordained *elders*, *provisional elders*, and *associate members* are appointed by the *bishop* to fields of labor" and the covenant that these *clergy* agree to uphold (338). The UMC practices open itinerancy (often spelled itineracy), which means "*appointments* are made without regard to race, ethnicity, gender, color, disability, marital status, sexual orientation, or age, except for the provision of mandatory retirement" (425.1). This is done through the work of *bishops* and *district superintendents*, and through *annual conferences* educating and training *pastor/staff parish relations committees* to the open nature of itinerancy. Sensitivity is also exercised in the *appointments* of *clergy* with physical challenges (425.1). Elders in good standing who identify as LGBTQ may be appointed across annual conferences out of concern for their safety (425.2).

Full-time service is the norm (338.1); however, itinerant *clergy* may be granted less than full-time service on occasion, which may vary according to constraints and type of service (e.g., quarter-time, half-time, three-quarter-time), and which are initiated by the *bishop* or *clergy* (338. 2).

Itinerancy was always and continues to be a key characteristic of Wesley's and historic Methodism's *missional* strategy for *evangelization* and *discipleship* formation. The itinerancy undergirds the Methodist understanding of the work of *elders*, in particular, as those who were "sent" to the places where they were needed. Wesley began the Methodist movement by sending out lay preachers on circuits to *evangelize* in communities desperate for words of hope in the face of resignation and poverty and then to shape class meetings and societies. Virtually the same model was used by Bishop Asbury and later *bishops*, in consultation with presiding *elders*, once The MEC was established and well into the 1800s. Prior to the Civil War, the *General Conference* lengthened the maximum number of years for serving in the same place from two to four years. In the later 1800s, the work of the presiding *elder* included the identification of locations where there was no society and to which men would be sent to *evangelize* and start new ones. While historically, the maximum length of *appointments* was set by the *General Conference*, today's *clergy* make fewer moves during their time of service due to longer *appointments*.

See also: www.resourceumc.org/en/content/to-be-united-methodist-what-is-itineracy.

Judicial Council

"Is that resolution by General Conference in accord with The United Methodist Constitution of The United Methodist Church?" "Was due process followed in that clergy trial?" "Did the bishop rule correctly on a point of law?" Deciding questions like these is the work of nine men and women who sit on the United Methodist Judicial Council, sometimes referred to as our "Supreme Court." —www.umc.org/who-we-are/about-the-judicial-council, accessed June 14, 2017.

The Judicial Council is "the highest judicial body" in The UMC (2601). As such, it has authority: (1) to determine the constitutionality of acts of the *General Conference*, *jurisdictional conference*, or *central conferences*; (2) to determine any appeal of a *bishop*'s decision on a matter of law in the *annual conference*; (3) to validate decisions of law made by a *bishop* in the *annual conference*; (4) to determine the legality of actions taken by the *General Conference*, *jurisdictional conferences*, or *central conferences* bodies or boards; (5) to have other duties conferred by the *General Conference*; and (6) to provide its own methods of procedure and organization (57. Article II). Decisions of the Judicial Council are final (58. Article III; 2609.11) and are posted on The UMC website (2612.1).

The Judicial Council may be called upon to make a declaratory decision from specified groups within the *Church* (2610.2) regarding the *constitutionality*—application, meaning, or effect of the *Discipline* on any act or legislation of the *General Conference, jurisdictional conferences, central conferences,* and *annual conferences,* or by bodies created by the *general conferences, jurisdictional conferences,* or *central conferences* (2610.1).

Membership consists of nine members reflecting the diversity of The UMC, who are nominated by the *Council of Bishops* as well as from the floor of a given plenary session at the General Conference. They are then *elected* via a series of ballots by the *General Conference.* The members include a five to four ratio of *clergy* and laity, which shifts each *quadrennium* (2602).

Prior to the formation of the Judicial Council in 1939, the three denominations handled issues of law in different ways. In The MECS, the College of Bishops originally ruled on matters of law. Their decisions were included as a part of the *Discipline.* By 1930, a Judiciary Committee for general boards and committees existed. In 1938, a Judicial Council had taken its place, its members nominated by the College of Bishops. In The MPC a request for a judicial decision on a rule or act of the *General Conference* required a majority vote of all the *annual conferences,* which would then send two delegates back to the location of the previous *General Conference* and evaluate the decision. Decisions were then recorded and published. The MEC had a Judicial Conference that addressed appeals of *clergy* who had been tried for misconduct, and a Judiciary Committee of the *General Conference* to address decisions of law. The current Judicial Council, established in 1939, is independent of both the *Council of Bishops* and the *General Conference.*

See also: www.umc.org/en/who-we-are/structure/judicial-council.

Jurisdiction

At some point during the 1924–1928 quadrennium the probability became apparent that the Southern ME Church would accept the inclusion of Blacks in a reunited Methodist denomination under one condition: The Blacks would have to be confined to a separated, "racially"-defined organizational structure of the reunited denomination. Within eight years of this development the joint commissions completed a Plan of Union and presented it to their parent church bodies. —W. Astor Kirk, *Desegregation of the Methodist Church Polity* (Pittsburgh: RoseDog Books, 2005), 7.

A jurisdiction is an administrative unit of The UMC, encompassing *annual conferences* within a given geographical area in the USA. There are five *jurisdictional conferences* in the US: Northeastern, Southeastern, North Central, South Central, and Western. Conference boundaries and mergers are determined by the jurisdictions. (Paragraph 28, Article V.4)

The jurisdictional system was created during the 1939 merger of The MEC, MPC, and MECS, as a solution to the impasse between The MEC and MECS over how African Americans were to be included in a reunified denomination. The resulting MC was divided into six jurisdictions. Five jurisdictions were divided into geographical regions in the US and consisted of white churches. The sixth jurisdiction was national in geographical scope and segregated on the basis of race, to include the African American *churches* and newly formed segregated *annual conferences*. At the time of the 1968 merger of The MC and The EUBC, the central jurisdiction was eliminated and its *churches* integrated into *annual conferences* of the other five jurisdictions. Paragraph 10, Article II was written into the *Constitution of The United Methodist Church*, stating "that in The UMC there shall be no *jurisdictional* or *central conference* based on any ground other than geographical and regional division."

See also: www.umc.org/en/content/jurisdictions.

Jurisdictional Conference

By legitimating, indeed, equating the connection of annual conference with region, by dividing conferences jurisdictionally, by locking conferences into space, they made it difficult to reclaim the notion of conferences as provisional and missional expression of a collective Methodist ministerium. It would be henceforth unthinkable to imagine redrawing conference lines to cross jurisdictions. —Russell E. Richey, *The Methodist Conference in America: A History* (Nashville: Abingdon Press, 1996), 184.

A jurisdictional conference has the responsibility to: (1) promote within its boundaries the *evangelistic*, missionary, *educational*, and benevolent interests and institutions of The UMC; (2) elect and help support *bishops*; (3) establish jurisdictional conference boards that are auxiliary to the general boards of the

Church; (4) determine the boundaries of *annual conferences* within their area; (5) administer the work of the *Church* within the *jurisdiction*; and (6) appoint a committee of appeals for trials. Jurisdictional conferences also have authority to elect or appoint the necessary agencies to accomplish its work (28. Article V). In each *jurisdiction*, there shall be: an Interjurisdictional Committee on Episcopacy (513), a Commission on Archives and History—auxiliary to the *GCAH* (533), a Jurisdictional Young People's Ministry (534), *UMW* (537), *UMM* (538), and an Administrative Review Committee (540). Jurisdictions may have a United Methodist Volunteers in Mission team (539). Through the Jurisdictional Nominating Committee and the jurisdictional pool of candidates nominated by delegates to *General Conference* and jurisdictional conference, persons are selected for election to The UMC boards and agencies (705.1).

Jurisdictional conferences meet at the time determined by the *Council of Bishops* and convene at the same time (27. Article IV; 518), or a special session may be called for a single specific purpose (522). Membership comprises *clergy* and *lay delegates to general, jurisdictional, or regional conferences where jurisdictions exist* (24. Article I; 26. Article III; 515). The *bishops* preside (523).

Jurisdictional conferences were first held following the creation of the *jurisdictions* by the uniting *General Conference* of 1939. They became the new location for the election of *bishops* in the US.

See also: www.umc.org/en/content#tag=jurisdictional conference.

Law(s)

The unanimous decisions of the Supreme Court of the United States declaring varying types of segregation by law unconstitutional express in legal form the ethical principles which national and international church bodies have set forth as demanded by the Gospel. We deplore official and unofficial efforts and movements to circumvent the clear intent of these decisions.
—"Resolution of the Assembly of the Division of Home Missions (UBC),"
World Evangel 75/3 (March 1956): 84.

UM entities are expected to comply with local, state, and national laws unless otherwise prohibited by the sections of the *Discipline* that constitute *Church* law. For example, regarding *property*, civil laws take precedence over the *Discipline* unless they put the *church* at risk for losing the possibility of ministry in that location without having any due process (2506). When the *local church* incorporates, it must do so in accordance with the local laws (2529.1 *a)*). The *GCFA* maintains an easily accessible *Legal Manual* on its website that provides counsel to *local churches* and the denomination regarding common legal concerns.

The doctrinal statements from the two predecessor traditions of The UMC bear within them a contradictory tone regarding a UM understanding of civil law. The *Articles of Religion* have an attachment adopted by the Uniting *General Conference* of 1939. It reads "it is the duty of all Christians . . . to observe and obey the laws and commands of the governing or supreme authority of the country of which they are citizens or subjects or in which they reside, and to use all laudable means to encourage and enjoin obedience to the powers that be" (Article XXV; page 72). Article XVI of the *Confession of Faith* makes a different statement: "civil government derives its just powers from the sovereign God," and "as Christians we recognize the governments under whose protection we reside and believe such governments should be based on, and be responsible for, the recognition of human rights under God. We believe war and bloodshed are contrary to the gospel and spirit of Christ. We believe it is the duty of Christian citizens to give moral strength and purpose to their respective governments through sober, righteous and godly living" (104; page 77).

Methodists have always both respected the law and sought to change laws they believed to be unethical. In its earliest years, The MEC struggled with the issue of slavery, reinforced in the South by laws that did not permit owners to free their slaves. Laws abolishing slavery in the northern states emerged as they developed their state constitutions following the Revolutionary War. Abolitionist movements arose in the North, directing their attention toward the southern states. The South simply tightened their laws in response. The *Discipline*, from 1785 until 1844, reflected the dissension between northern and southern *clergy*, resulting finally in the split between The MEC and MECS in 1844. Both sides struggled with the question of the role of the *Church* in relationship to the current law of the land in their particular regions.

Following the Civil War, predecessor denominations participated in temperance movements to change laws regarding criminalization of the use and distribution of liquor as well as social movements, such as the establishment of the eight-hour workday, anti-lynching, and eventually civil rights.

See also: www.gcfa.org/resource/legal-manual.

Lay Delegate to General, Jurisdictional, and Central Conferences

> . . . to resist the claim of the laity to participate in the general administration of the Church . . . a resistance of the whole tendency of the Christian life in this our age. In all the Protestant Churches of the world—unless our own be the sole exception—a more perfect association of the ministry with the laity in the administration of the interests of the kingdom of Christ is forming. —"Address of the Laymen's Convention," *Journal of the Methodist Episcopal Church General Conference* (1864), 409.

Lay delegates are elected to participate in *General Conference*, the *Regional Conference*, and the *Jurisdictional Conference* in numbers equal to the *clergy*. Lay delegates are elected by the *lay members* attending the *annual conference* session either one or two years prior to the *General Conference*. For instance, a youth may not have been elected a *lay member of the annual conference* from the *local church* but is able to be elected as a delegate. Lay delegates do not have to be *lay members* of the *annual conference*. Lay delegates must be *professing members* of a *local church* within the bounds of the *annual conference* electing them. They must have been *professing members* for at least two years and active in their *churches* for at least four years (14. Article I; 26. Article III; 37. Article V).

Lay representation at *general conferences* of The MEC and MECS did not occur until the early 1870s. The MECS seated voting male lay delegates, equal to the numbers of *clergy*, in 1870. In 1872, The MEC seated two male lay delegates from each *annual conference*. In the 1890s, The MEC still limited lay delegates to two per *annual conference* unless an *annual conference* was so small that it had only one *clergy* delegate. It was finally changed in 1900, after being approved as a constitutional amendment in 1896. The UBC seated lay members in equal numbers in 1893, and the EA, in the early 1900s.

Meanwhile The MPC and UBC were already seating women as lay delegates. In 1888, The MEC refused to seat five women who had been elected by their *annual conference*. Women were finally given laity rights in The MEC in 1900 and in The MECS in 1918.

See also: www.umc.org/en/content/ask-the-umc-how-are-general -conference-delegates-chosen.

Lay Leader

> Quest. 2. What is the duty of stewards? . . . to attend the quarterly meetings of their circuit; to give advice, if asked, in planning the circuit; to attend committees for the application of money to churches; to give counsel in matters of arbitration; to provide elements for the Lord's Supper; to write circular letters to the societies to be more liberal, if need be; as also to let them know the state of the temporalities at the last quarterly meeting.
> —*Discipline*, 1789, §XXXIV. "On the Qualification and Duty of Stewards."

The lay leader is a position held by a *layperson* in a *local church*, a *district*, or an *annual conference*. In a *local church*, the lay leader is elected by the *charge conference* or, in mid-year situations, by the *Church Council* when approved by the *district superintendent* (249.5, 251). When needs warrant, an associate lay leader may be elected. In a circuit, a lay leader is elected for each *church* (251.1).

The lay leader is a *professing member* who is the "primary lay representative of the laity" in a *local church*. The lay leader is, first and foremost, a bridge builder, serving as an interpreter of the laity and their engagement in ministry to others and informing the laity of the *annual conference* and *church* (e.g., interpreting *apportionments* [247.14, 251.1 *a)c)*]). The lay leader meets regularly with the *pastor*; serves on the committees on *finance, nominations and leadership*, and *pastor/staff parish relations*; advises the *Church Council*; and participates in and encourages other laity to attend training events sponsored by the *district* and *annual conference* (251.1).

The *local church* lay leader is sometimes, but not automatically, elected to be a *lay member of the annual conference* (251.2). This decision is made by the *pastor* and the *Committee on Nominations and Leadership Development* based on the needs of the *church*. *District* lay leaders and the *annual conference* lay leader are elected by their respective bodies and oversee the boards of lay ministry and sit on various committees and boards for those bodies (419.4, 602.4, 605.2, 607, 630, 636, 648, 649, 660, 667, 1116.2, 5).

Wesley's original "Rules, &c. of the United Societies" makes first mention of lay class leaders and stewards of the societies. The earliest *Disciplines* provide details about the leadership of these laity. Laypersons led class and band meetings, outlined in the 1785 *Discipline*, and served as stewards, a position not clearly defined until the 1789 *Discipline*. A committee of laity would also be chosen by the deacon to determine how the collections would be distributed. The position of lay leader emerged from the singular "Steward of the Quarterly Conference" and was first found in The MECS *Discipline* of 1910. The position was identified at the *charge*, *district*, and *annual conference* settings in the *Discipline* of the reunified Methodist Church in 1939.

See also: www.cokesbury.com/Guidelines-Lay-LeaderLay
-Member-2025-2028; www.umcdiscipleship.org/resources/lay-leader.

Lay Member of Annual Conference

Question 1. Who shall compose an Annual Conference, and what are the regulations and powers belonging to it? ¶44 Ans. 1. All the traveling preachers in full connection with it, and four lay representatives—one of whom may be a local preacher—from each Presiding Elder's District . . . chosen annually by the district Conferences: provided, that no one shall be a representative who is not twenty-five years of age, and who has not been for six years, next preceding his election, a member of the church. —*Discipline*, MECS, 1890, §II. "Of the Annual Conferences."

The lay member of annual conference represents the charge at regular and special-called sessions for the year or quadrennium for which they are elected, unless they are no longer a member of the charge or are unable to serve. The number of lay members who represent a particular charge is determined by the number of clergy appointed by the bishop to that charge. So, it is common for a circuit to have more than one lay leader for each charge, but to have only one lay member of the annual conference. Alternate lay members should also be elected by the charge conference. (See 252.2.)

The lay member votes on all matters of the annual conference except those pertaining to clergy relationships and unless that lay member also serves on the conference Board of Ordained Ministry or Committee on Investigation (34. Article II). The lay member is required to report to the Church Council within three months of an annual conference session (251.2).

Total lay membership in an annual conference is based on a complex formula that ensures inclusive representation of many different organizations and people, as well as district at-large members. The goal is to achieve an equal number of laypersons and active/retired clergy (33. Article I; 602.4-7). Because retired clergy often cannot attend sessions of the annual conference, it is common for the laity to actually outnumber clergy at any given time in the annual conference.

One of the early schisms in Methodism took place in 1828, over the question of the inclusion of laity in decision-making in The MEC. The resulting denomination, The MPC, began with equal representation of white laymen from the local church to the General Conference and annual conferences. The MPC eventually reunified with The MEC and MECS in 1939. The MEC began considering lay representation in the annual conferences in 1888, as a constitutional amendment. It was reintroduced at every General Conference thereafter, but not ratified until 1932, and included seating women. Beginning in the 1880s, MECS lay representation stood at four laymen per district of each presiding elder; it rose to eight lay representatives in 1918, was expanded again in 1926 and 1930, and reached full representation in 1938. By contrast, The UBC established mandatory equal lay representation in annual conferences in 1889.

See also: www.cokesbury.com/Guidelines-Lay-LeaderLay
-Member-2025-2028.

Lay Minister, Certified

> Could God be calling you as a layperson to be a part of a ministry team using gifts given to you? Could you serve God faithfully as a CLM in the congregation in which you are currently a member or a nearby congregation in need of lay leadership? Are you willing to explore this form of leadership in The United Methodist Church? If you can answer "yes" to any of these questions, consider becoming a Certified Lay Minister and experience what it is like to be faithfully alive to the possibilities of leading the mission and ministry of a church today as part of a ministry team. —www.umcdiscipleship.org, accessed May 15, 2017.

A position of leadership created for laypersons serving in a variety of pastoral roles, most often in small congregations, a certified lay minister is already a certified lay servant or lay missioner, who has also completed an additional track of study as defined by the GBOD and annual conference (268.1-2). A certified lay minister has been trained and equipped to preach and to provide pastoral, worship, and program leadership in a congregation to which one is assigned by the district superintendent (419.2). A certified lay minister is not credentialed to celebrate sacraments or perform weddings.

The Conference Committee on Lay Servant Ministries recognizes the certified lay minister and renews this certification every two years as long as a person submits reports, participates in continuing education through advanced Lay Servant Ministries courses, and is recommended by the district superintendent (268.3-4). Certification is transferrable between districts or annual conferences (268.5). If a certified lay minister receives any compensation, the person is paid as a layperson and taxes must be paid accordingly (268.6).

Established by the 2004 General Conference, the certified lay minister is an alternative to the position of what used to be called lay supply. In contrast to lay supply, it provides a viable and accessible process of training for laity who serve in churches or positions that cannot be served by clergy.

See also: www.umcdiscipleship.org/leadership-resources/certified-lay
-minister; www.umcdiscipleship.org/articles/clm-resources.

Lay Missioner, Certified

Believing that "el pueblo," the people themselves are the best resource the
church can count on, the NPHLM has trained thousands of laypersons for
Hispanic/Latino ministry, enabling them to exercise the priesthood of all
believers. These lay missioners working together with mentor pastors have
caused a movement that has planted new communities of faith throughout
the connection and extended ministries of compassion and justice to communities throughout the United States. —The National Plan for Hispanic/
Latino Ministries 2012–2016, 10; National-Plan-for-Hispanic-and-Latino
-Ministry, accessed May 15, 2017.

Equipped through training and certified by the Plan for Hispanic/Latino
Ministry, a certified lay missioner is a *layperson* who works, in complementary
ways, with a pastor-mentor as part of a leadership team to extend and develop
ministry out into the community (269). Some lay missioners may become
part of the Lay Missionary Planting Network that has training programs in
both Spanish and English. Developed in the 1990s by the Plan for Hispanic/
Latino Ministry, the *Discipline* now provides for this position to lead to the
position of *certified lay minister* (269). It was found in the *Discipline* for the
first time in 1992.

See also: www.umcdiscipleship.org/new-church-starts/floating10;
www.umcmission.org/national-plan-for-hispanic-latino-ministry/.

Layperson

There is one only condition previously required, in those who desire admission into these societies, "a desire to flee from the Wrath to come, to be
saved from their Sins. But, wherever this is really fixed in the soul, it will
be shown by its fruits. It is therefore expected of all who continue therein,
that they should continue to evidence their desire of salvation." —"General
Rules of The United Societies," John Wesley, *Works*, vol. IX, 70.

A layperson is either a baptized or *professing member* of a *local church*. Called, by virtue of one's *baptism*, to ministry that extends Christ's love out into the world, a layperson lives out the Great Commission found in Matthew 28:18-20, in "service for the *mission* of God in the world" (133). This ministry is expressed in diverse and complementary ways but is always grounded in the interdependent *connection* of Methodism (126–132).

A layperson may serve in almost every aspect of Methodist ministry with the exception of presiding at *sacraments* and *weddings*, for which credentialing by either the *annual conference* or the state is required. A layperson may also, through the conference committee on lay servant ministries, become a *certified lay servant*, lay speaker, or *lay minister*. *Lay missioner*s are trained through the National Plan for Hispanic Ministry. In addition, the *GBHEM* offers ministry certifications in twelve professional areas in which laypersons may be employed.

The first Methodist laypersons became so by joining a weekly class meeting that then joined regularly with other class meetings to constitute a society. The only requirement as described by Wesley in the "Rules &c. of the United Societies" was the desire to "flee the Wrath to come, to be saved from their Sins." He described the purpose of these groups as "seeking the Power of Godliness, united in order to pray together, to receive the Word of Exhortation, and to watch over one another in Love, that they may help each other to work out their Salvation." The fruit of their salvation was demonstrated by their willingness to follow the *General Rules*.

While laymen were identified to hold various positions in the early societies, e.g. stewards, the role of laywomen was restricted to particular positions. Full laity rights for women in the *annual conference* were established in The UBC in 1893. Women gained full laity rights in The MEC in 1904, and in the MECS in 1918, when they were finally seated in the *General Conference* in 1922.

See also: www.umc.org/content/rediscover-wesleys-vision-of-a-lay-led -church.

Lay Servant, Certified

Till last Sunday for the sake of privacy we always met up two pairs of stairs. The room was so excessive hot and for convenience I ventured on Sunday evening in the lower room but when I rose up from prayer and saw the room full of people, the enemy buffeted . . . immediately I found power to look up to him and cast my care upon him and he gave me utterance more than an hour. I exhorted them to repentance and to come to the knowledge of God by the remission of sins. A solemn awe was over them and though some came for the purpose to make game, the Lord prevented and we departed in peace. —Gareth Lloyd, "Sarah Perrin (1721–1787): Early Methodist Exhorter," *Methodist History* 41, no. 3 (April 2003): 85.

A certified lay servant offers *discipleship* ministries of witness, leadership, and service to and through the *local church*. Certification is the result of: (a) the recommendation of the *pastor* and *Church Council* or *charge conference*, (b) the completion of the Lay Servant Ministries BASIC course and at least one advanced course, and (c) review by the *District Committee on Lay Servant Ministries*. Certification is renewed annually (266.)

A certified lay speaker is a certified lay servant who is eligible to preach upon request of a *pastor*, *district superintendent*, or committee on Lay Servant Ministries, having taken a track of courses that focuses on *worship* and preaching in addition to the entire set of Lay Servant Ministries courses (267).

Lay servants were first identified as "exhorters" in the early Methodist societies, approved and licensed by their quarterly conferences to preach and offer testimony and encouragement to the work of God in the lives of the people, but to do so without basing their preaching on a particular biblical text. By the late 1800s, the work of exhorters was detailed in the *Disciplines* of The MEC, MECS, and the reunified MC. Exhorters were renamed "certified lay speakers" in the 1948 *Discipline* of The MC. The name of the position changed again to "certified lay servant" in 2012. The exhorters and lay speakers were available to conduct *worship*, lead laity in prayer meetings, and offer exhortation, under the direction of the *pastor* and, like the early exhorters, were amenable to the quarterly conference of the charge. Today, the role of lay speaker is a track within the broader role of the certified lay servant.

See also: www.umcdiscipleship.org/resources/getting-started-lay-servant
-ministries.

Lay Supply

> Quest. 1. What can be done to supply the Circuits, during the Sitting of
> the Conference? Answ. 2. Engage as many Local preachers and Exhorters as
> will supply them; and let them be paid for their Time. —*Discipline*, 1785,
> §XVII. "How to provide for the Circuits in the Time of Conference, and to
> preserve and increase the Work of God."

"Lay supply" is a term still in common use, but no longer used in the *Discipline,* to define a *layperson* who has been assigned (not appointed) by the *district superintendent* with the approval of the *bishop* to lead ministry in a *charge*. A lay-supply person is not *clergy* and is not approved for celebrating *sacraments* or performing *weddings*.

Lay-supply ministry is directly accountable to the *district superintendent* or a *mentor* assigned by the *district superintendent*. A rule change took place in 2016 *General Conference*: If it is presumed that the *layperson* is to serve longer than a year, the person must begin either *candidacy* or training to become a *certified lay minister* (268). Hence, while a lay-supply person may have completed the certification of *lay servant minister* and *lay speaker*, these are not preparation courses for long-term service as *pastors*. *Laypersons* who "supply pulpits" are neither *clergy* nor *pastors* by definition of the *Discipline* (339), as they are not licensed and appointed to fulfill the responsibilities of a *pastor* (340).

Given the different ways in which laypersons may now be trained for servant ministries in the church, the term "supply pastor" continues to fall out of use. It is a historic phrase previously used by *cabinets* to identify *laypersons* serving in charges, who have not yet received a *license for pastoral ministry*. In early Methodism, exhorters and local preachers might be considered parallel positions to the supply pastor. These persons were used to preach in the circuits when the *elders* were attending conference. They were amenable to the quarterly conference and expected to begin pursuing credentials. Confusion regarding the phrase "lay supply pastor" is reflected in a 1958 Judicial Council Decision, No. 156, which stated that the *General Conference* would have to define the phrase. This resulted in a convoluted addition to the 1960 MC *Discipline* that added a section on "Approved Supply Pastors," thus confusing the terminology to an even greater extent. In the 1968 UMC *Discipline*, the term is dropped and replaced with the term "lay pastor," only to then be replaced by the term "local pastor" in 1976.

See also example: https://vaumc.org/lay-supply/.

Lectionary

> Quest. 2. Are there any smaller Advices relative to Preaching, which might be of Use to us? Answ 4. Always suit your Subject to your Audience.
>
> Chuse the plainest Texts you can. 6. Take care not to ramble, but keep to your Text let your young Preachers often exhort without taking a Text. 11. Always avail yourself of the great Festivals by preaching on the Occasion. —*Discipline*, 1785, §XV. "On the Matter and Manner of Preaching and other Public Exercises."

The Revised Common Lectionary (RCL) is a three-year cycle of biblical texts assigned to the Sundays and holy days of the Christian year. Each set consists of texts from the Hebrew Bible, Psalms, New Testament Epistles, and Gospels. The lectionary is a helpful tool for maintaining a systematic approach to devotional reading and methodical preaching. Each cycle begins with the first Sunday in Advent and ends with the celebration of Christ the King Sunday. The UMC strongly encourages the use of the lectionary for preaching.

The lectionary is rooted in the ancient Jewish practice of reading specific texts each week in order to complete the full reading of the Torah in a year. Christian traditions developed lectionary cycles in the early medieval ages. The Revised Common Lectionary is designed for Protestant *churches*. The *GBOD* is responsible for participating in the Consultation on Common Texts that develops the Revised Common Lectionary and for providing resources for creating *worship* services that frame the lectionary texts (1113.5-6).

The recovery of the use of the lectionary is a late twentieth-century practice. As the earliest preachers traveled their circuits, preaching was not limited to Sundays. Preachers were expected to identify daily preaching locations, preaching in both the morning and evening of each day. There is little evidence of their use of the lectionary during this phase of Methodism's history. As an Anglican priest, Wesley would surely have been familiar with the lectionary and seasons of the Christian year, reinforced through his use of and support for the *Book of Common Prayer*. While several researchers have looked at the possible connections between Wesley's sermons and the occasions when he preached them, there is no real evidence that points to his use of the lectionary.

See also: www.umcdiscipleship.org/worship-planning.

Legal Manual

> He has no right at all to be independent or governed only by himself; but is in duty bound to be governed by the powers that be, according to the laws of the country. And he that is thus governed, not by himself; but the laws, is, in the general sense of mankind, a free man. —John Wesley, "Some Observations on Liberty. Occasioned by a Late Tract (1776)," in Graham Maddox, *Political Writings of John Wesley* (London: Thoemmes Press, 1998), 54.

The Legal Manual is published by the *GCFA*. It contains detailed legal information regarding a wide range of topics common to organizations throughout The UMC. It focuses on (1) *Church* Structure, (2) *Local Church*, (3) Personnel, (4) *Property* and Estate Planning, including *copyright laws* for video, audio, and music; the use of the *name "United Methodist"*; and use of the *cross and flame* logo, and (5) Risk Management. *The Legal Manual* does not in any way replace the role of professional legal advice when one is involved in a difficult situation. It does not provide information on clergy taxes.

John Wesley reflected in his writing an absolute commitment to the rule of civil law and the expectation of every person to follow it. In his tract "Some Observations on Liberty," he posed the strong distinction between liberty on the one hand and independence on the other hand. Civil liberty was the right to make decisions about one's own "lives, persons, and fortunes," but only in accordance with the "*laws* of our country." Violation of the law led, justifiably in Wesley's mind, to "fines, imprisonment, or death."

He did, however, speak out against laws he believed to be immoral, including bribery laws, unequal representation in Parliament, growing legal bureaucracy, and most notably, slavery. Francis Asbury and Thomas Coke, in the "General Minutes of the Conferences of the Methodist Episcopal Church forming the *Constitution* of the said *Church*," aligned the "cause of religion in America" with the "political interests of these States." Shortly thereafter, they mentioned the "civil affairs" through which the young country had passed due to the revolution and the changing structure of civil law in the American environment that required the formation of the new *Church*. From these earliest days, Methodists have always taken their relationship to state and federal law very seriously.

See also: www.gcfa.org/legal-manual.

License for Pastoral Ministry

Before any person shall be licensed to preach as a local preacher among us, he shall bring a recommendation from the society or class of which he is a member, and be personally examined before the quarterly meeting conference by the presiding elder, . . . touching his acquaintance with the doctrines of our Church, to which he shall declare his assent, together with his gifts and grace for preaching; . . . and they believe he will be generally acceptable and useful as a preacher, he shall then receive a license, signed by the presiding elder . . . which license it shall be the duty of such local preacher to have annually renewed. —Resolution, 1816 General Conference, Bangs, vol. 3, 52.

The License for Pastoral Ministry provides a person with the credentials necessary for *appointment* to a *local church* as a *pastor*. Any person, other than an ordained *elder*, who receives an *appointment* to carry out the duties of a *pastor*, must have a license for pastoral ministry. This includes certified candidates who have projected *appointment* as a *licensed local pastor* (311), provisional *elders*, *associate members*, ordained *deacons* who are changing to the *order of elder*, and licensed or ordained *clergy* from other denominations whose education is not equivalent to an MDiv.

This license is obtained by attending *Licensing School for Pastoral Ministry*, which is sponsored by the *annual conference*, and being approved by the *Board of Ordained Ministry*. The license is valid only while under *appointment*. The license for pastoral ministry provides credentials different than those of a *certified lay servant* or lay speaker, *certified lay minister, lay missioner*, or a *lay supply* person. The license provides the credentials necessary to celebrate the *sacraments* and to preside at *weddings* in the location where one serves.

Licensing began as a provision of the Act of Toleration in 1689 in England, which allowed dissenters from the Church of England to meet and set apart *clergy* for the work of their *churches*. John Wesley licensed both the Methodist chapels and preachers in England. Such licensing may have been required in the colonies as well, as is evidenced in Francis Asbury's *Journal* when he was challenged by a "*church* minister" opposed to his preaching in his parish as to whether or not he was licensed (Bangs, vol. 1, 71).

See also: www.gbhem.org.Bom-Handbook_complete.pdf.

Licensed Local Pastor

> N.B. Let none who are local, preach or exhort in any of our societies without a note of permission from the Deacon: let every local Preacher or Exhorter take care to have this renewed yearly: And let every Elder insist upon it. —*Discipline*, 1789, §VII. "On the Method of receiving Preachers, and their Duty."

"Licensed local pastor" is a category of *clergy* within The UMC. A licensed local pastor has completed *candidacy* (310) and the *Licensing School for Pastoral Ministry* ("License to Preach School"), been approved by the *Board of Ordained Ministry* and *clergy executive session* of the *annual conference* and received an *appointment* to a *charge* or *extension ministry* (316.2, 3). Licensed local pastors are required to complete the five-year *Course of Study* (COS) while they are serving a *local church*, unless they are matriculated with or have graduated from an approved *school of theology*.

The license grants the local pastor the authority to perform the responsibilities of a *pastor* only in the community or *extension ministry* to which one is appointed (317.1, 340). Local pastors are responsible to the *clergy session* of the *annual conference*, supervised by the *district superintendent*, and assigned a *mentor* while in *Course of Study* (317.3, 4).

Local pastors hold membership in and "shall attend the sessions of the *annual conference*" (317.5, 33. Article I, 370.1, 602.1). They also belong to the *Fellowship of Local Pastors and Associate Members* (323). They may serve on *annual conference* boards, commissions, and committees. They may vote on everything except amendments to the *Constitution*, the election of, or service as, *clergy delegates to General Conference, jurisdictional conferences*, or *central conferences*, and *clergy* relationships with the *annual conference* (317.6). Local pastors may upon retirement request a license to serve, at the request of the appointed *pastor*, in a *local church* where they hold membership (320.5 *d*).

There are three categories of local pastors: full-time, part-time, and students (318.1-3). Under very particular circumstances as determined by the *Board of Ordained Ministry*, part-time years of service may equate to full-time years of service (322.2). Local pastors may apply to become *associate members* in the *annual conference*. As such, they join the itinerant ministry with security of *appointment* (322).

Local pastors are held to the same expectations as *deacons* and *elders* with regard to *continuing education* (351); standards of conduct (605.7); chargeable offenses (2702.1); and right to due process through the *complaint* and investigation process (2704.2). They also have the same access to maternity/paternity and medical leaves (356, 357), but not sabbatical, personal, family, or voluntary or involuntary leaves (352, 353, 354). They are recognized but are no longer licensed to do sacraments and weddings.

Conditions for discontinuing or retiring from licensed local pastor status are specific to this category of *clergy* (320). Regardless of one's means of exiting ministry, the local pastor's license is surrendered to the *district superintendent* (320.1-4). Only local pastors with significant progress in the *Course of Study* are eligible to retain recognition as a retired local pastor with limited provision for participation in the *annual conference* (320.5). They may retain their license for service (but not an appointment) in the local church where they hold membership for the purpose of providing weddings and funerals and only with the request of the appointed pastor. A retired local pastor may also continue to serve under appointment with the permission of the district superintendent (319.5).

Today's licensed local pastor has its precedent in the original position of "local preacher." By the late 1800s, local preachers were reviewed and licensed by the district conference and supervised by the presiding *elder*. In the earliest decades of The MEC, local preachers were identified, licensed, and appointed by the traveling *elders*.

See also: www.gbhem.org/ministry/clergy-leaders/local-pastors.

Licensing School

Be diligent. Never be unemployed. . . . Which of you spends as many hours a day in God's work, as you did formerly in man's work? We talk, talk,—or read what comes next to hand 1. Read the most useful books, and that regularly and constantly. 2. Steadily spend all the morning in this employment, or at least five hours in four and twenty. "But I have no taste for reading." Contract a state for it by use, or return to your former employment. "But I have no books." Be diligent to spread the books, and you will have the use of them. —*Discipline*, 1789. §XVII. "Of employing our Time profitably, when we are not travelling, or engaged in public Exercises."

Licensing School is an eighty-hour course carried out by *annual conferences* as a prerequisite for anyone being appointed to a *local church* as a *provisional elder, licensed local pastor, associate member,* ordained *deacon* who is transitioning to *elder*, or a transfer from another denomination (315.2 *a*)(3)). The curriculum is designed by the Division of Ministry of the *GBHEM*. A person must be projected for an *appointment* to attend. It is also a prerequisite for the *licensed local pastors' Course of Study.*

John Wesley was deeply concerned about the *education* of his preachers and assigned lists of texts to them to read. Likewise, in the early US, texts were published by The MEC Book Concern, with the expectation that the preachers would read and distribute them. These lists of expected readings eventually grew into the *Course of Study*. Originally called "License to Preach School," this intensive training was designed to jump-start the educational process for local preachers as an entry-level training process for persons seeking to become *clergy*. By the 1880s, *district conferences* were responsible for ensuring that their local preachers were completing a curriculum assigned to them in order to receive the license. Eventually *annual conferences* took over the License to Preach School, and ultimately the *GBHEM* was given responsibility for shaping the full curriculum.

See also: www.gbhem.org/bom-library/.

Liturgies—*See* Ritual

Local Church

> Quest. 1. Is any thing adviseable in regard to building? Answ. Let all our churches be built plain and decent; but not more expensively than is absolutely unavoidable: Otherwise the necessity or raising money will make rich men necessary to us. But if so, we must be dependent on them, yea, and governed by them. And then farewell to the Methodist-discipline, if not doctrine too. —*Discipline*, 1789, §XXII. "On building Churches, and on the Order to be observed therein."

The *Discipline* defines a local church, along with *extension ministry*, as "the most significant arena through which disciple-making occurs" (201, 120). Disciple-making includes preaching the Word of God, administering the *sacraments*, ongoing *worship*, forming believers, and "redeem[ing] the world" (201).

It is the "strategic base" from which ministry into the community and world is extended. The function of a local church is "to help people to accept and confess Jesus Christ as Lord and Savior and to live out their daily lives in light of their relationship with God." This function is carried out by ministering to people in the community, providing training and nurture to all, cooperating with other local churches in ministry, defending God's creation and living as an ecologically responsible community, and participating in the worldwide *mission* of the *Church* (202). This work of *evangelism* and *mission* (outreach), nurture, and witness frames the life of the local church (204).

Each local church exists as a part of the Methodist *connection* and is a part of the "*church* universal" as declared in the Apostles' Creed (203). One or more local churches make up a *charge*. When more than one local church is included in a pastoral charge, it will be structured as part of a circuit, as a cooperative parish, or as an ecumenical shared ministry (205, 206, 207-211).

In the early days of US Methodism, groups of classes made up a society that formed a circuit traveled by one or two preachers appointed for a year. The society met in quarterly conferences. By the first decade of the 1800s, when a large society was located in a city or town, it became a "station" and was appointed a preacher of its own. In the earliest *Disciplines*, the word "*church*" referred to the physical building—also called a meeting house, house of *worship*, and chapel. The word "*church*" as applied to local communities of faith first emerged in The MEC *Discipline* in 1816, when the terms "connection" and "society" were increasingly replaced with the word "*church*," referring to both the denomination and to the building that would house the community of faith for *worship*. The MECS *Discipline* of 1858 changed every reference to "society" and "societies" to the word "*church*," except in the *General Rules*. According to Tom Frank the term "local church" became popular in the 1920s, and in 1928, the bishops of The MEC identified the "local church" as the location for "test[ing] the value of our organization and *polity*" (Frank, 175).

See also: John Wigger, *American Saint: Francis Asbury and the Methodists* (New York: Oxford University Press, 2009).

Local Church Administrative Responsibilities

> Quest. 2. What is the duty of Stewards? Answ. To take an exact account of all the money, or other provision made for and received by any travelling or local Preacher in the circuit; . . . to inform the Preachers of any sick or disorderly persons; to tell the Preachers what they think wrong in them; to attend the quarterly meetings of their circuit; to give advice if asked, in planning the circuit; to attend committees for the application of money to churches; to give counsel in matters of arbitration; to provide elements for the Lord's Supper; to write circular letters to the societies in the circuit to be more liberal, if need be; as also to let them know the state of the temporalities at the last quarterly meeting; to register the marriages and baptisms.
> —*Discipline*, 1789, §XXXIV. "On the Qualification and Duty of Stewards."

The administrative responsibilities of a local church exist for the purpose of starting, supporting, financing, and protecting its ministries—those activities that fulfill its primary task to reach out to people and support them in their discovery of and commitment to God's love for them in Jesus Christ (243).

The *pastor* is the administrative officer of the *local church* and is responsible for ensuring that the *local church* fulfills its organizational responsibilities and manages its temporal affairs (340.2 *c*)(1)-(2)). As the administrative officer, the *pastor* is an ex officio member of every group in the *church*—every conference, board, council, commission, committee, and task force, "unless otherwise restricted by the *Discipline*" (244.3; see Judicial Council Decision 500). Two are restricted: the *Pastor/Staff Relations Committee* (258.2 *a*)) and the *Board of Trustees* (2525).

Administrative committees fulfill responsibilities for managing the *church's* resources, its personnel, finances, buildings, and leadership. They report to the *Church Council* and *charge conference*. The main committees are the *Pastor/Staff Parish Relations Committee*, the *Committee on Finance*, the *Board of Trustees*, and the *Nominations and Leadership Committee* (244).

Other committees may be established as needed. For example, a *church* is required to establish a study or *building committee* when remodeling or building a new building (2533.1, 2544.1 *c*), 4 *a*)). An *endowment committee* may be needed if a *church* has received a major bequest that requires monitoring and management of its funds (2534). The administrative responsibilities of societies and *local churches* were carried out originally by *laypersons* called "stewards," roles identified in the earliest *Disciplines*. Formed into a board of stewards, this structure moved through various stages of expansion and change as new positions were created to empower *laypersons* to take on greater responsibilities for ministry areas, such as *education* and *mission*. By the twentieth century, *clergy* were better trained to understand the legal and administrative matters of *local churches* and thus became responsible for ensuring that these matters were carried out in accordance with the *law*. Ultimately, the *Discipline* defined one of the roles of the *pastor* as the "administrative officer" of the *local church*.

See also: www.cokesbury.com/forms/DynamicContent .aspx?id=283&pageid=1081.

Local Church Historian

> But though the materials for furnishing a very particular history of the early days of Methodism in these United States are comparatively sparse. . . . yet when carefully collected and put together in consecutive order, they cannot fail to form an interesting and instructive medium of information; and more especially to those whose spiritual welfare is identified with this humble branch of the church of Jesus Christ. —Bangs, Preface to vol. 1, 5.

The *Discipline* strongly encourages every *local church* to have a church historian. The church historian may also chair a committee on records and history. Along with the preservation and maintenance of records and historical materials, the church historian should also lead the *church's* work to preserve and update a written narrative of the *local church* history (247.5 *a*)).

The earliest known histories of US Methodism were *The History of Methodism in America*, published by Jesse Lee in 1807, and Nathan Bangs's four-volume set, *The History of the Methodist Episcopal Church*, originally published between 1838 and 1841. Historic documentation of *local church* life tended to coincide with significant anniversaries of the *church*. For example, the fiftieth or one hundredth anniversary would prompt interested persons to collate and compose a story of the *church*. The position of church historian was inherited from our EUBC tradition and was integrated into the 1976 *Discipline* of The UMC.

See also: www.gcah.org/resources/how-to-write-a-local-church-history; www.cokesbury.com/product/9781501830334/guidelines-church -historian/; www.umc.org/how-we-serve/pro-tips-for-preserving-local -church-history.

Local Church Ministry Responsibilities

It was manifest to all that the increased duties of preachers, in consequence of the introduction of Sabbath schools, the organization of the Missionary and Tract Societies, and the increase of members in the larger towns and villages, rendered it expedient, that every part of the work might be duly and seasonably be performed, that the circuits should be shortened, and that each thriving village should be privileged with preaching every Sabbath, otherwise it was impossible to establish a permanent congregation. —Bangs, Discussion at the 1824 General Conference, vol. 3, 279.

In order to carry out effective ministry, the *Church Council* organizes and oversees a variety of committees, groups, positions, and boards. The way in which these responsibilities are organized depends on the size of the *local church*. Ministry responsibilities are designed to fulfill the *local church's* primary task (243) and include nurture, outreach, and witness (244, 252). Nurturing ministries include *education, worship*, formation, membership care, small groups, and *stewardship*, with special attention to age-level ministry (252.2 *a*)). Outreach ministries include local community and global ministries of compassion, justice, and advocacy (252.2 *b*)). Witness ministries focus on developing approaches to *evangelism* and Lay Servant Ministries (252.2 *c*)).

Prior to the Civil War, *clergy* were, by *Discipline*, responsible for the *education* of children and the promotion of *mission* and *evangelism*. They had created the Tract Society in 1817, and the Missionary Society in 1819. By the time that Methodists were trying to regain their energy and focus on expansion following the Civil War, the need for the increase in the number and specialization in the role of stewards in a *local church* or circuit had become evident. In the late 1800s, stewards fulfilled roles in the areas of *mission* and *education* within their stations and circuits.

See also: www.cokesbury.com/forms/DynamicContent .aspx?id=283&pageid=1081.

Local Church Policies

> In the relationship that exists between a pastor and his own particular parish, pastor and congregation should clearly understand their mutual rights under both church and civil law. Church laws differ in different places, and legal relationships and rights also vary under different charters. Often it takes a factional fight to bring out the exact legal status of mutual rights. So ministerial prerogatives and oversight, trustees' control and property rights, membership rights, and the like ought to be understood very thoroughly by all parties concerned. —Harmon, EE, 116.

Local church policies provide a basis for the healthy *stewardship* of a *local church*'s resources and are designed to provide a common understanding and expectation of personal behavior by members, *volunteers*, *staff*, and *clergy*. *Local churches* are expected to have written and approved policies that are designed to clarify expectations in the arenas in which people work and protect both individuals and the *local church* from mismanagement and immorality, especially in the areas of finances, *staff* behavior, the use of computers and *church media*, the use of *copyrighted materials*, and the protection of children, youth, and at-risk adults. *Churches* may also develop policies for other areas, such as but not limited to *weddings*, earth care and recycling, *endowments*, *cemeteries*, use of the *buildings* by members and non–church-related groups, and *mission* teams.

The *Discipline* and *Book of Resolutions* are the first sources for policy development. *Annual conferences* may mandate that *churches* have specific policies (such as *Safe Sanctuary* policies) and provide policy templates to be used by *local churches*. If so, they should be easily accessible on the *annual conference* website. The *charge conference* and *Church Council* may develop additional policies unique to that specific *charge*. The internet is a great source for examples of local church policies that a *church* may adapt. Permission to adapt the policy should be requested in writing of the *local church* that posted the policy.

In addition, several *general agencies* provide templates for a variety of policies on their websites. For example, the *GBOD* provides training and templates for *Safe Sanctuaries*® and *local church* staff policies, and a host of additional ministry areas. The *GCFA* provides policy guidelines for handling money, *property*, and the *trust clause*. The *GCFA* has also posted a copy of the *Legal Manual* for *local churches*. The *GBGM* has a copy of policies for *mission* teams.

The *local church* must publicize their policies and implement them. A location on the *local church* website is a great place for them. *Clergy, staff,* and *volunteers* should sign a copy of the policies pertinent to their areas to give witness to the fact that they know the policies. When a *local church* has a policy such as one concerning *Safe Sanctuaries*®, but does not implement it, the *church* may be liable for legal action when a person is harmed. When a *local church* has clear staff policies, they provide the basis for disciplinary action when a staff member behaves in a manner contradictory to the policy.

In Wesley's era, the policies for membership in the classes, bands, and societies were very strict, and resulted in expulsion if persons were unable to maintain them. Wesley's model deed was the first official policy for local meeting houses and chapels. Policies for the original MEC were embedded in the *Discipline* itself. For example, the agent for the Book Concern served a term of office limited by the *Constitution*. Members of *boards of trustees* of the early schools and seminaries (comparable to high schools) were required to be active members of a class meeting in their local society and not burdened by debt. The early *Disciplines* describe the job descriptions of the *elders, deacons*, local preachers, assistants, helpers, and stewards. As legal requirements for nonprofit organizations, such as *churches*, were enacted by both state and federal governments, the need for policies in both the *Discipline* and additional local church policies became necessary.

See also: www.umcdiscipleship.org/resources/what-to-include-in-a-policy -manual-for-congregational-staff1.

Local Church Structure—How to Change It

It may sound hard to believe, but a growing number of congregations across the conference are bidding "goodbye" to committee-heavy church structures and saying "hello" to a single board model. Dr. Jesse Brannen, Director of the TAC Center for Congregational Excellence and Vibrant Church Initiative Director Rev. Mike Tyson are seeing churches experience new levels of success in their mission. —www.txcumc.org/newsdetail /single-board-model-of-governance-brings-benefits-to-congregations-of -all-sizes-3860130, accessed June 15, 2017.

A *local church* may develop an alternative structure to the regular *Church Council* as long as the new structure follows specific disciplinary rules (244.2). This decision may come about in response to A Process for *Assessment of Local Church Potential* (212-213).

The responsibility for the organization and administration of the *pastoral charge* and *churches* rests with the *charge conference*, the *district superintendent*, and the *pastor*. Such changes by a *charge conference* require the approval of the *district superintendent*. The decision to change a church structure should be based on circumstances including, but not limited to, the size of *church* membership, *missional* opportunities in the community, and *church* resources. Alternative forms may include a wide range of creative locations for services (247.2).

Variations in the size of the *Church Council* are acceptable as long as these changes come about in alignment with the circumstances described above. The *Church Council* must include a minimum of eleven persons filling the positions outlined in the *Discipline* (252.5). If reduced to this size, this core group remains responsible for ensuring that the ministry areas of nurture, outreach, and witness are fulfilled. These responsibilities may be carried out by various coordinators and ministry groups as elected by the *charge conference* (253-256).

Throughout the history of Methodism, the structure of a *local church* has evolved from being totally *clergy*-centric to having a strong lay-led structure that encompasses a wide range of both administrative and ministry-oriented responsibilities. Early circuits in the US were led by *clergy*, but managed by stewards, *laypersons* chosen by the traveling or presiding *elders* for specific responsibilities detailed in the *Discipline* of 1785. The structure of the society was based in the quarterly conference when the clergy and stewards gathered to review the status of the circuit, receive collections, bring *laypersons* to trial and/or expulsion, identify exhorters, license local preachers, and identify potential candidates to be considered for pursuing ordained ministry. In the early twentieth century, the structures of *local churches* began to increase in complexity and the term "steward" was replaced by a variety of more specialized positions. By the 1968 merger, the local church structure reflected the organization and nomenclature of secular organizations.

See also: www.umcdiscipleship.org/leadership-resources/local-church-officer-job-descriptions.

Lord's Supper

> It was the judgment of many of the ancient Fathers, that we are here to understand the sacramental bread also; daily received in the beginning by the whole church of Christ, and highly esteemed, till the love of many waxed cold, as the grand channel whereby the grace of his Spirit was conveyed to the souls of all the children of God. —Sermon 26, "Upon Our Lord's Sermon on the Mount: Discourse VI," in John Wesley, *Works*, vol. 1, 584–85.

The Lord's Supper (Holy Communion), as it was commonly referred to by John Wesley, is one of two *sacraments* in The UMC, which are "ordained by Christ" and serve as signs of grace, reminding us of how God works invisibly in us to quicken, strengthen, and confirm our faith (*Articles of Religion*, Article XVI—Of the Sacraments). United Methodists do not believe in the Roman Catholic doctrine of transubstantiation, but receive the body and blood of Jesus "in a spiritual manner" through "faith" (*Articles of Religion*, Article XVIII—Of The Lord's Supper). The Lord's Supper is a "means of grace" and regarded as "a token of love and union which Christians have with Christ and one another" (*Confession of Faith*, Article VI).

Unlike *baptism*, which is a once-and-for-all observance, celebrating the entry point into the Christian faith, The Lord's Supper is a continual observance, offering the opportunity for repentance, forgiveness, healing, sanctification, and growth in love.

One of the unique aspects of the Lord's Supper in The UMC is the practice of open table. Because the table belongs to the Lord Jesus Christ, it is open to all who respond to Christ's love regardless of *church* membership, age, or physical, neurological, mental, psychological, developmental conditions or abilities (162.I). Furthermore, John Wesley regarded The Lord's Supper as a "converting *sacrament*," a point at which people could experience spiritual birth. Following Wesley's spirit, the Lord's Supper is celebrated as an occasion for the reception of preventing, justifying, or sanctifying grace in a believer's life.

Elders, Deacons, and *licensed local pastors* (in the *churches* to which they are appointed) are to administer Holy Communion according to Christ's ordinance, explaining the meaning and encouraging regular participation, and recruiting and training *laity* in serving the consecrated elements (340).

Along with prayer and searching the Scriptures, Wesley regarded the Lord's Supper (Holy Communion) as one of the "chief" means of grace. Based first upon the command of Christ to receive the bread and wine, and second on the benefits of forgiveness and strength and refreshment for the soul, Wesley encouraged Methodist people to commune as often as possible. This was difficult for his English Methodist followers because of the tenuous relationship between the Wesleyan movement and the Church of England; Anglican priests were either unwilling to receive communicants or could not accommodate the numbers of people seeking the *sacrament*. It was equally challenging for the North American Methodists, as there were not enough ordained preachers, and so the Lord's Supper became a quarterly occasion. Though Wesley intended Holy Communion to be a regular part of the regular Sunday service, The MEC, during the revivalist movement, deemed Holy Communion as more solemn than lively, and preaching took precedence.

Throughout periods of Methodist history there have been calls for return to the *sacrament*, and in the latter part of the twentieth century, The UMC has seen liturgical reform through the development of services and the *United Methodist Hymnal*. In 2004, the *General Conference* adopted "This Holy Mystery" as an official statement and resource on the UM theology and practice of Holy Communion.

See also: www.umc.org/what-we-believe/communion-this-holy-mystery; blog.umc discipleship.org/three-communion-practices-to-quit-doing/; "Services of Word and Table," *UMH*, 6–31; "An Order for Holy," *BOW*, 152.

Media

METHODIST PAMPHLETS FOR THE PEOPLE

Series I. On Church Economy. 12 pamphlets, 25 cents.

On Doctrinal Points. 12 pamphlets, 25 cents.

On Romanism. 24 pamphlets, 30 cents.

On Temperance. 12 pamphlets, 15 cents.

—Advertisement for "Publications of the M. E. Church, South," Methodist Pamphlets for the People, Volume 4 (Nashville: E. Stevenson and F.A. Owens, agents for the Methodist Episcopal Church, South, 1857).

"Media" is a broad term that encompasses a wide range of communications approaches to information dissemination, marketing plans, and the use of online, web-based, email, television, print, and social media. The invention of the Internet revolutionized communications and the meaning of the term "media." Guidance and resources for *local churches* on the use of media for marketing, community access, and communications among members are found at the *UMCom* website (1806). *Churches* must think broadly about their relationships with local media outlets for making positive impressions in the community, but more important, for crisis communications. *UMCom* offers webinars and seminars in these vital aspects of *local church*, *district*, and *annual conference* communications.

In addition, every *church* should have a coordinator of communications (255[3]) and *local church policies* regarding use of *copyrighted materials*, social media, and online communications to prevent misuse by and maintain accountability with *church staff, clergy*, leaders, and *volunteers. Annual conferences* should provide guidelines to *local churches* regarding the maintenance of computer information and data (245). *Local churches* also have access to the *Legal Manual* through the *GCFA* that provides a guide for upholding the *law.*

The original "media" of Methodism included pamphlets, tracts, sermons, and letters written primarily by John Wesley. Similarly, when the US *church* was established, the same tools were used to communicate among preachers. The first magazine, the "Methodist Magazine," was published from 1798 to 1799, but it was not successful. The "Christian Advocate" was established in 1826 as a weekly newssheet available to *clergy* and members alike. Versions of the "Advocate" continued throughout the history of US Methodism, adopted by related denominations and *annual conferences*. It ended circulation in 1973, to be replaced by a variety of affiliated news sources, including newspaper. The MC established the first communications *general agency* in 1940, which grew to include oversight and production of radio, print, television, and film resources. Today, various boards, agencies, and groups have their own *publications* and media. For example, *UMW* publishes a monthly magazine, "response," available in both print and online. The *GBHEM* published *Interpreter Magazine* for both clergy and lay leaders. The UMC branched out into several television formats beginning in 1956. Its most popular program, "Catch the Spirit," ran for eight seasons and 208 episodes. With the rapid development of the Internet and website technology, virtually every aspect of church-related communication is now found on online media with websites, Facebook pages, and Twitter.

Membership Records and Removal

Q. 60. What is the Business of an Assistant? . . . To take exact Lists of his Societies and bring them to the Conference. 9. To send an Account of his Circuit every half Year to one of the Superintendents. —General Minutes of 1784.

Every *church* must maintain accurate membership records for each *baptized member* and *professing member*. The data required in these records is found in the *Discipline* (230.1). In addition, a Constituency Roll, an Affiliate Membership Roll, and an Associate Membership Roll should be maintained that contains data on others who are involved in the *church* (230.3-5).

The acceptable formats for maintaining the membership rolls are found in the *Discipline*. If in paper form, it must be in a book prepared specifically for this purpose, produced by the *UMPH* (233.1). Alternative systems, including electronic membership records, are now acceptable, but back-up paper-based systems are required (233.2-3). Membership records are maintained by a Membership Secretary, elected by the *charge conference*, who, as directed by the *pastor*, keeps accurate membership records and reports them annually to the *Church Council* (234).

Every year, the *pastor* is expected to report to the *charge conference* the names of persons who have been baptized, joined the charge, and/or been removed during the previous year. The *charge conference* is also responsible for removing the names of persons who have been unresponsive to inquiries about their inactivity or who cannot be found. The names of *baptized members* are permanent records (233).

The process for removing names from the membership roll is very specific. Upon identifying a *professing member's* inactivity, the *pastor* and members should attempt contact with the member for the purpose of reconnecting the person with the congregation. If the person lives in the community, but does not want to remain a member, then the person should be encouraged to request transfer to another *church* or request withdrawal. If the member resides outside the community and contact is made, then the person should be encouraged to join another *church* or withdraw (228.2 *b)* (1)(2)).

When a *charge* has either lost all contact with a *professing member* or the member refuses to respond over a two-year period, the person's name may be removed from the roll. The *Discipline* prescribes the procedures for removing names from the roll. The list of *professing members* removed from the roll must also be maintained. A *professing member* may be restored to the roll by reaffirmation of faith or transfer (228.2 *b*) (3)(4)(10)).

The *GCFA* oversees the record-keeping for membership. The website provides the form for the maintenance of *charge conference* membership records, called "The Report of the Pastor."

In the original Methodist classes and bands, leaders held their members accountable for their deepening *discipleship* through weekly meetings during which they reflected upon a series of questions provided to them by John Wesley. The goal was to ensure that members were convinced that they were progressing in the *Wesleyan Way of Salvation*. Members who did not follow the rules of the classes and bands were either expelled from membership or left of their own accord. Once the Methodists became a denomination in the US, records of conversions, *baptisms*, sanctifications, attendance at quarterly meetings, and ultimately membership and attendance in *local churches* became a regular administrative responsibility of the *clergy* and *lay leaders*. Throughout the nineteenth and early twentieth century, it was fairly common for inactive or misbehaving laity to be remanded for a *church trial* and expelled from the *church*.

See also: www.gcfa.org; www.umcdiscipleship.org.

Mentors

Quest. 2. What is his duty? . . . Answ. 3. In the absence of a Bishop, to take charge of all the Deacons, travelling and local Preachers, and exhorters.

To change, receive or suspend Preachers. —*Discipline*, 1789, §V. "On the constituting of Elders, and their Duty."

Mentoring is an integral part of the process of moving toward licensing, *commissioning*, and/or *ordination* (349). All *elders* are expected to be willing to offer mentoring to others (334, 349). Official mentors include, first, *elders* and *deacons* assigned to persons in *candidacy* and/or residency stages of progress toward becoming a *licensed local pastor* or *ordination*. *Candidacy* mentoring takes place either in groups or in a one-to-one relationship, and is required for all persons seeking certified *candidacy* (310.1 *b*), 2 *a*); 349.2 *a*)).

In addition, once a person is certified as a candidate for licensing as a local *pastor*, one is supposed to receive a mentor until one has completed the *Course of Study* (349.2 *b*), 317.4). When certified as a candidate for *provisional membership*, a person is supposed to receive a *clergy* mentor until commissioned (311; 349.2. *b*)). Once someone is commissioned, mentoring takes place in the "Residence in Ministry" groups, which, depending on the *annual conference*, may also include *licensed local pastors*. One may also continue to work directly with a mentor during this stage (318.2, 326, 327.4).

Contrary to the image of the lonely circuit rider traveling by himself into the frontier, traveling preachers were rarely assigned to circuits by themselves. They were usually accompanied by assistants of various statuses, most often *deacons* and traveling preachers, men "on trial" who were early in the process of being approved for *ordination*, and who worked under the supervision of and were mentored by the traveling preacher.

Merger with Another Church

> "They're already moving to the next level to do everything that they can to make this work," he said. "They've put personalities aside to work for the common good . . . it's a very mature body of Christ." . . . In late July 2015, the Southold church was sold for just over $1 million. They were also able to "come off of life support," MacLeod said. "No more equitable compensation. We're paying our apportionments and our bills. We hope to ride that excitement into the new building." —www.nyac.com/newsdetail/4-churches -merge-to-build-north-fork-umc-8053950, accessed May 15, 2017.

Merger is a process that *local churches* may use to combine two or more congregations into one *pastoral charge*. The purpose of a merger is to assist congregations with becoming more effective in *mission* to their community. In addition to a traditional merger, in which two *churches* dissolve and are re-created as a single *church*, the *Discipline* defines several other structures into which *churches* may be merged. These include a circuit (205.2), a cooperative parish (206), and an ecumenical shared ministry (207). The decision to merge into a different structure should be made in conjunction with a process for *Assessment of Local Church Potential* (213). A plan of merger is developed based on the findings of the assessment.

The steps for proceeding with the merger begin with a proposal to the *charge conference* of each of the merging *churches*. It must then be approved by the *district superintendent*. The process must meet the requirements of the *laws* of the state or states in which the *churches* are located. Finally, all archives and records of merging *churches* must be cared for by the newly merged *church*. Mergers can take place with *churches* of other denominations (2546-2548).

In the early days of American Methodism, the primary organization of pastoral leadership was a circuit through which one or two preachers would rotate among a group of classes and societies in a specified geographical area. With the establishment of strong and stable communities, "stations" were developed where preachers were appointed to a charge consisting of a single *church*. The process for merging *churches* came about when, in response to major population shifts and easily accessible transportation, older *churches* that no longer functioned as neighborhood *churches* could unite and become more effective in ministry, realign resources, and reduce the costs for being in ministry. In the South, where many MEC and MECS *churches* literally overlapped neighborhoods, mergers between these *churches*, often located just blocks from each other, began to take place following the reunification of 1939. Directions for such mergers were included in the 1940 *Discipline*.

See also: www.umcdiscipleship.org.

Ministry Certifications for Lay and Clergy

South Atlanta, Georgia, December 18, 1902.

DEAR FRIENDS: It is now a little more than a year since I began my work here, and varied indeed have been my experiences. During the winter the cry of the poor is constantly heard. With money furnished from various sources I have been able to relieve many. Into many poor homes where there was illness I have gone with simple remedies. As I have charge of our sewing class, and am thus brought into contact with the children, the pastor decided that I would well with the Sunday school, so I was elected superintendent. —Anna E. Hall, "An Interesting Letter from Our First Colored Deaconess," *Woman's Home Missions* 20, no. 2 (February 1903): 37, in MEA II, 458.

The *GBHEM* provides a process by which both lay and *clergy* may be certified in twelve different areas of ministry. There are three tracks: professional, undergraduate, and paraprofessional, appealing to a wide range of educational backgrounds. The twelve ministry areas include: Camp/ Retreats, Children's Ministry, Christian *Education*, *Evangelism*, People with Disabilities, Ministry with the Poor, Music Ministry, Older Adults, Parish Nursing, Spiritual Formation, Urban Ministry, and Youth Ministry. Information about these certifications is found at the *GBHEM* website.

Specialization in ministry began with the missionary movements, initiated by both the *Church*, as it focused on sending out men as missionaries to the frontier to work especially with Native Americans, and the women's missionary movements in the late 1800s. The *deaconess* movement became a means by which women could serve in ministry, while still denied the right to licensing and *ordination*. The *deaconess* movement was defined as a specialized ministry that required a specific training program, as women were trained in ministry with the poor, healthcare, and *education*, and then deployed to ministries in the expanding US and as *missionaries* to other parts of the world.

See also: www.gbhem.org/.

Mission

Believing it will be pleasing to many . . . to know of the progress of the mission among the Indians at Sandusky . . . John Steward, a coloured man, but born free, and raised in the state of Virginia, Powhattan county, having been brought to the knowledge of salvation by the remission of sins, and become a member of the Methodist Episcopal Church, at Marietta, Ohio, being divinely impressed . . . the latter end of the year 1815, went among these people, with a view to impart to them a knowledge of the true God. —James B. Finley, Ridgeville, August 30, 1820, "Account of the Work of God Among the Wyandot Indians at Upper Sandusky," *Methodist Magazine* 3, no. 11 (November 1820): 431–37.

The term "mission" is used in four ways in The UMC. It is used to describe: (1) God's call upon the *Church* (120–125) or any organization to its particular work in the world; (2) an organization that develops ministry with a particular group or region or a first step in moving toward becoming a *local church* (259.1 *a*)) or a provisional *annual conference* (590); (3) an outreach ministry that addresses the need of the community beyond a *local church* (256.1 *c*)); and (4) the essential nature of Methodist ministry as a "sent" ministry to which people are called to affirm God's presence in the world and join in the work God is already doing in the world to "reclaim, restore, and redeem the life of all creation to its divine intention" through Jesus Christ (1301). The *GBGM* is the *general agency* responsible for oversight and management of the missional work of the denomination (1301-1315).

Wesley was involved in mission to and with the poor and working classes of England, from field preaching to the establishment of the Foundery in London, and then, later in life, speaking out on social issues. Thomas Coke, an early American bishop, returned to England to assist with establishing and strengthening missional outreach in the West Indies and Europe and died on a trip to establish Methodist work in the country now known as Sri Lanka (Ceylon). In the American colonies, Methodists began their mission through the establishment of small groups known as class meetings and societies, as men called to preach followed the expansion of the frontier west and south, and then throughout the world.

See also: www.umcmission.org;

Missionary

I wish not to move a step out of his way . . . but I sometimes almost fear that I have mistaken the path of duty, and done wrong in coming here this time; and yet I see the wonderful goodness of the Lord in his preservation of my life where many others die. Already one of the dear young ladies who accompanied us out the last voyage is dead—two of the Presbyterian Missionaries down the coast, and the wife of one of them has died since our arrival. —Ann Wilkins papers from Millsburgh, Liberia, June 20, 1842, Missionary Correspondence United Methodist Archives, Madison N.J., in MEA II, 261.

Missionaries are *laypersons* and *clergypersons*, who are called and sent forth to live all or part of their lives in service to peoples of other races, cultures, and nations for the purpose of proclaiming the gospel and expressing the mission of the *Church*. The *GBGM* is responsible for the recruitment, sending, receiving, and assigning of missionaries throughout the world (1302.3, 15).

Clergy retain membership in their home conferences. *Laypersons* retain membership in their home *churches* but may become associate members in a *local church* where they are assigned (237).

The *GBGM* provides training and a wide range of opportunities for short- and long-term missionary service within and beyond countries of origin. Service includes pastoring *churches*, teaching in schools, a wide range of healing ministries, social work, new *church* development, and *evangelism*, in both United Methodist and ecumenical settings.

Methodism began as a missionary movement, as Wesley sent out *clergy* and *laypersons* to evangelize people with no relationship to Jesus Christ. Methodism spread to the American colonies, the US frontier, and other parts of the world, primarily through lay Methodists who may not have thought of themselves as missionaries, but who were certainly involved in the work. Missionary work expanded to other parts of the world from the US during the second half of the nineteenth century from a number of predecessor denominations and organizations, especially women's organizations.

See also: www.umcmission.org/Get-Involved/Missionary-Service.

Missionary Conference

The Creeks in Council, again in 1844, made a law prohibiting any of its citizens from preaching, under penalty of fifty lashes on the bare back for each violation. The Indians regarded preaching as belonging to white folks alone. . . . Many fled from their homes in order to escape . . . , and I was one of that number. I was admitted into the Indian Mission Conference in 1852 on the superannuated list for the past two years.

> . . . I think the cause of Christ is still prospering among us notwithstanding the hindrances occasioned by our domestic troubles. —Chief Samuel Checote, Okmulgee, Indian Territory, "Letter from Chief Checote," *Our Brother in Red* 1, no. 10 (June 1883): 2, in MEA II, 411.

A missionary conference functions similarly to an *annual conference* but is defined by its distinctive cultural identity, limited resources, and different leadership needs. Missionary conferences are linked to the *GBGM* for administrative guidance and financial support (585).

Because a missionary conference may overlap one or more *annual conferences*, the *College of Bishops* of the *jurisdiction* determines which *bishop* oversees the missionary conference. The *bishop* appoints a conference superintendent and/or *district superintendents*. The missionary conference is able to elect *clergy* and *lay delegates* to the *General Conference* and *jurisdictional conferences* in the same way as *annual conferences*. The creation or change of status of a missionary conference can take place only at *General Conference*. They have the same rights and limitations as *central conferences* to make changes in the way they carry out ministry and *ordination* (586-588).

The UMC has had four missionary conferences. The Red Bird Missionary Conference, whose name was changed to the Central Appalachian Missionary Conference in 2022, was established in southeastern Kentucky in 1968, in response to MEC, UBC, and EC missions that began in 1921 to address the needs of Appalachian families. Currently, the *bishop* of the Tennessee-Western Kentucky Episcopal Area oversees the Central Appalachian Missionary Conference. The Alaska Missionary Conference was officially established as the Alaska Mission of The MEC in 1904, in response to mission work begun there in the early 1880s. The *bishop* of the Greater Northwest Episcopal Area oversees the Alaska Missionary Conference. The Oklahoma Indian Missionary Conference was established in 1972, in response to a long history of mission by The MECS, MEC, MPC, and UBC, begun in the mid-1800s, with the tribes that were relocated to Oklahoma from the East along the Trail of Tears. It is located primarily in Oklahoma but also has *churches* in Texas and Kansas. It is overseen by the *bishop* of the Oklahoma Episcopal Area. The current Rio Texas Conference is the result of a merger in 2016 between the former Rio Grande Missionary Conference and the Southwest Texas Conference. The Rio Grande Conference was founded, first, as a *mission district* in response to *mission* by The MECS with Mexican immigrants in 1858. It became a conference in the 1939 merger.

See also: alaskaumc.org; www.umc-oimc.org; www.centralappalachian umc.org.

Mission Statement of The UMC

Q. 4. What may we reasonably believe to be God's Design in raising up the Preachers called Methodists?

A. To reform the Continent, and to spread scriptural Holiness over these Lands. —General Minutes of 1784.

The mission statement of The United Methodist Church is "to make disciples of Jesus Christ for the transformation of the world" (120). The mission statement helps to frame the attention of UMs on the work of "proclaiming the good news of God's grace and by exemplifying Jesus' command to love God and neighbor, thus seeking the fulfillment of God's reign and realm in the world" (121). The mission statement is grounded in the understanding of our various founders that, when focused on the mission, "God has used our Church to save persons, heal relationships, transform social structures, and spread scriptural holiness, thereby changing the world" (121).

The General Conference of 1996 approved the first version of the mission statement "to make disciples of Jesus Christ." Eventually, the Council of Bishops grew to believe that the mission statement needed to state more clearly the end toward which the making of disciples was focused. The Council and the Task Force to Study the Episcopacy recommended the addition to the mission statement, "for the transformation of the world," at the 2008 General Conference, and it was approved.

See also: www.umc.org/news-and-media/united-methodist-mission -statement-revised.

Mission Statement of a Local Church

> Such a Society is no other than "a company of men 'having the form, and seeking the power of godliness,' united in order to pray together, to receive the word of exhortation, and to watch over one another in Love, that they may help each other to work out their salvation." —"General Rules of the United Societies," in Wesley, *Works*, vol. 9, 69.

The second sentence of the *mission statement of the denomination* reads: "*Local churches* and *extension ministries* of the *Church* provide the most significant arenas through which disciple-making occurs" (120, 201). Every *local church* is expected to understand how it fits into the *mission* of the denomination. Some *churches* simply adopt the denominational mission statement as their *local church* mission statement. Others will go through a process of identifying their vision and mission and arrive at a more customized mission statement that reflects the congregation's self-understanding of its *mission* to its local community and the world.

The *Book of Discipline* does not require that each *local church* and *extension ministry* have its own mission statement. However, a mission statement can be very helpful for *local church* members when it comes to identifying, planning, carrying out, and evaluating their ministry. *Local church* mission statements and processes for how to create them are easy to research online.

The development of mission statements for *local churches* is a relatively new idea. Mission statements for organizations emerged in the 1980s, and today, it is expected that *churches*, agencies, and organizations of the denomination will be able to define their *mission* succinctly, as a way to provide focus for attention, time, and resources.

See also: "local church mission statements" on Google.

Music

> Above all, sing spiritually. Have an eye to God in every word you sing. —John Wesley, 1761, in *UMH*, vii.

Instrumental music and singing are welcomed aspects of *worship* and *discipleship* in The UMC. Most children are taught Christian children's songs at an early age. *Church* school classes and small groups will often sing together. Many *church*es have choirs and bands for virtually every age group. Music is encouraged for every type of *worship* service; some *worship* services are actually based on the type of music that is played. *Worship* music must, however, be understood as a support to the overall *worship* experience, not as performance or entertainment.

People often have strong musical preferences, and so it is important for a *church* to either vary music in its services or offer different services using different styles of music in order to appeal to the range of tastes of the congregation. Regardless, congregants should be taught new hymns and songs prior to the beginning of a *worship* service.

Choirs are a great addition to *worship*. Choir music should be integrated with the themes of the *worship* services. The choir director(s) should always be in regular conversation with the *pastor* about plans for *worship* and preaching and/or be a member of the *worship* planning team. The choir director is directly amenable to the *pastor* and the *Pastor/Staff Parish Relations Committee*.

The United Methodist Hymnal (UMH) is a great source of historic, traditional hymns. The traditional hymns were an indispensable tool for teaching sound doctrine and helping people commit the doctrines to ministry. The UMC also has supplemental hymnals, including *The Faith We Sing*, *Songs of Zion*, and the *Upper Room Worshipbook*.

The Methodists, as well as members of The United Brethren and Evangelical Church, sang without instruments up until the second half of the nineteenth century. Singing was led by a leader who would line out the words of the hymns. They used hymnals that were updated and approved by the *general conferences* about every thirty years. The original Methodist hymnal was altered first in 1808, and then again in 1820, with a tune book added to it. By the late 1800s, choirs and instruments, especially organs, were introduced into *local churches* for *worship*. The most recent *UM Hymnal* was published in 1989, and the 2016 General Conference approved the publishing of a new one.

See also: www.umcdiscipleship.org/worship/music.

Name of "United Methodist"

Lord of the Church, we are united in Thee, in Thy Church and now in The United Methodist Church. —Prayer recited by Bishop Reuben H. Mueller, EUBC, and Bishop Lloyd C. Wicke, MC, at the Uniting Conference, April 23, 1968; http://www.umc.org/who-we-are/formation-of-the-united -methodist-church, accessed April 24, 2017.

The only organizations that can use the name "United Methodist" are *churches*, *general agencies*, and institutions registered with the *GCFA*. It cannot be used in any trade name, trademark, or part of the name of any other kind of business firm or organization (2502). The *Legal Manual* of the *GCFA* addresses this issue directly, in Section 4—Property and Estate Planning.

The name of the denomination, "The United Methodist Church," was approved in the 1968 merger between The MC and The EUBC. Conversations about merger between The Evangelical United Brethren and Methodist Church began in the early 1950s. One of the greatest stumbling blocks to merger was the existence of the segregated Central Jurisdiction in The MC. As conversations picked up steam in the early 1960s, The EUBC insisted that the Central Jurisdiction be dismantled if merger was going to happen. The other consideration was that The MC was a much larger church than The EUBC, so in order to give each denomination equal footing in the merger they took the word "United" from The Evangelical United Brethren Church and "Methodist" from The Methodist Church.

See also: www.gcfa.org; umc.org.

Nominations and Leadership Development, Committee on

¶98: The regular business of the Quarterly Conference is 3. To elect Trustees, where the laws of the State permit, and also Stewards, for the Circuit or Station to elect one a District Steward and one a Recording Steward to confirm Sunday-School Superintendents upon the nomination of the Sunday-School Board, and also, as Members of the Quarterly Conference. —*Discipline*, MEC, 1888.

The Committee on Nominations and Leadership Development is a required committee of the *local church*. The *pastor* is the chairperson. A vice-chairperson is elected from the lay members of the committee. Its members must be *professing members* of the *church*, divided into rotating, three-year classes. They shall neither succeed themselves nor be members of immediate families (258.1, 258.1 *d*)).

This committee works throughout the year to address the spiritual and leadership development and congregational needs for leaders who serve in voluntary and elected roles in the *local church*. The responsibilities are threefold: (1) it assesses the need for, recruits, and nurtures leaders; (2) it assists the *Church Council* with filling vacancies of leadership between *charge conferences*; (3) it recommends, through the nominations process, persons to be elected as officers and ministry leaders of the *local church* at the annual *charge conference* (258.1 *a*),*b*)).

Following the Civil War, The MEC and MECS began to give new shape to lay leadership in the *local church*. New structures and organizations such as Sunday schools, probationers' classes, and *mission* societies emerged to provide *discipleship* formation. The old forms of class meetings, leadership of stewards, and quarterly conferences began to slip away, and did not carry the same authority as before. New lay positions were developed to provide leadership, including the Sunday school superintendent, trustees, and *mission* secretaries.

In the late 1880s, The MEC was progressing toward the idea of an Official Board but still held on to the "leaders and stewards meeting." Leaders of the *churches* and circuits were elected at the fourth quarterly conference, by nomination of the *pastor*, and their committee members were appointed. Until the formation of The MC in 1939, the *pastor* nominated the lay stewards, who were then confirmed by the quarterly conference of the station or charge and who elected their own leaders. In the 1944 *Discipline* of The MC, a mention of a nominating committee, along with other lay committees that together would form the Official Board, was first found. By 1964, a full slate of both elected stewards and specific positions was found.

See also: www.cokesbury.com/product/9781501829543/guidelines
-nominations-leadership-development/.

Non-United Methodist Resources

> An old rule of the Discipline prohibited a traveling preacher from publish-
> ing anything without first obtaining the leave of his conference. Under this
> rule the Genesee Conference, at its first session, provided a weighty com-
> mittee . . . "to examine all compositions prepared by any of its members
> for publication, and that those compositions shall or shall not be published
> according to the resolution of the committee." —George Peck, ch. 6: Pro-
> ceedings of the Genesee Conference, Early Methodism within the bounds
> of the old Genesee Conference from 1788 to 1828 (New York: Carlton and
> Porter, 1860), 496.

United Methodist *local churches* and organizations are strongly dissuaded
from using non-UM resources, especially for *discipleship* development. Using
materials from other denominations tends to confuse both young persons
and new Christians as to what UMs believe. It is the responsibility of the
pastor and lay teachers in the congregation to teach from a UM perspective.

Two of the main objectives of The *UMPH* are to create materials useful to
the cause of Christ and Christian *education* from a UM perspective (1613).

John Wesley started his own printing office in 1778 and prescribed specific
reading lists of both his own writings and other texts for his preachers and
members who sought a deeper relationship with Christ or clarity about their
salvation, sanctification, and ministry. Through the use of the model deed, he
prohibited the teaching of non-Methodist views. Wesley's own works, including sermons and notes on the New Testament, became the essential core set
of resources for early training of Methodist preachers. In 1804, The MEC
General Conference passed a rule that restricted preachers from "improper
publications" and required that they be reviewed by the book committee of
the Book Concern or their own *annual conference*. Throughout Methodist,
EUBC, and EA history, publishers have vetted and produced materials that
reflect Methodist doctrine.

See also: www.umcdiscipleship.org.

Offering

Quest. 1. How many Collections are to be made in a Year?

Answ. 1. A Quarterly Collection from the Members of the Society, to supply the Preachers 2. A Yearly Collection from all our Members that are of Ability, for the building of convenient Churches. 3. A Collection at Love-Feasts, and on sacramental Occasions, for the Poor of our own Society. 4. An Annual Collection or Subscription for the College. —*Discipline*, 1787, §VIII. "Of the Collections that are made, and how the Money is to be expended."

The offering in a worship service is a communal act of worship through which members return to God a tithe of their income and offerings (gifts beyond the tithe) to be used for the ministry of the church. The offering is collected by ushers and blessed by the pastor or worship leader. Technology has now made it easy to give electronically. Special Sunday offerings have been established by the General Conference during which congregations have the opportunity to contribute through designated giving to the work of the whole Church.

According to Dr. L. Edward Phillips, in his article "Eucharist and Money" in *A Wesleyan Theology of the Eucharist*, it was not a regular practice to have an offering as a part of the preaching service in early Methodism. Offerings were called "collections" and taken up most often in the class meetings and quarterly conferences and then for designated purposes. Alms for the poor were collected at Holy Communion. As churches grew, some moved to the practice of renting pews, while others sought a means for voluntary giving to underwrite the increasing costs of ministry. Pew renting was outlawed by several of our predecessor denominations. The MEC added the "collection" to the official order of worship in 1888. During the first four decades of the 1900s, "the collection" was reframed theologically as "the offering" of both tithes and offerings, and included as an act of worship in the weekly orders of worship. In many churches, the practice of leaving a small offering for the poor on the altar rail during Communion still continues.

See also: www.umcgiving.org/; www.umcdiscipleship.org/resources/; www.umcdiscipleship.org/search/results?q=electronic%20giving; L. Edward Phillips, "Eucharist and Money," in *A Wesleyan Theology of the Eucharist: The*

Presence of God for Christian Life and Ministry, ed. Jason E. Vickers (Nashville: General Board of Higher Education and Ministry, 2016), 223–38.

Office of Christian Unity and Interreligious Relationships—*See* Bishop

Orders

> Baltimore, Friday, Dec 24-Jan. 2, 1785: On Christmas-eve we opened our conference: which was continued ten days. I admire the body of American preachers. We had had near sixty of them present. The whole number is 81. They are indeed a body of devoted, disinterested men, but most of them young. The spirit in which they conducted themselves in chusing [*sic*] the elders was most pleasing. I believe they acted without being at all influenced either by friendship, or resentments, or prejudice, both in chusing and rejecting. They also elected three deacons. —Vickers, 42.

An order is a community of *clergy* who are in covenant with one another, connected by the distinctive character of the vows that set them apart for particular types of work in the *Church*. Ordained UM *clergy* belong to either the order of *deacon* or the order of *elder*. As a member of an order, *clergy* are expected to support, care for, and hold one another accountable. The *Board of Ordained Ministry*, in consultation with the *bishop*, nominates the chairpersons of the orders. It is possible to transition from one order to the other (305-309).

Prior to 1996, the order of *deacon* was a provisional status to which one was ordained prior to being ordained a second time as an *elder*. This historic pattern followed the Anglican-Episcopal tradition to which John Wesley belonged. For example, when Francis Asbury was ordained, after years of leadership in the Methodist movement in the colonies, he was ordained a *deacon*, then an *elder*, and then a general superintendent (the early term for a *bishop*) on consecutive days during the Christmas Conference of 1784.

See also: www.gbhem.org/clergy.

170

Ordinances—Means of Grace

These are the General Rules of our societies; all which we are taught of God to observe, even in his written Word, the only rule, and the sufficient rule both of our Faith and Practice. And all these we know his Spirit writes on every truly awakened heart. —*The Nature, Design, and General Rules of the United Societies*, 1742, in Wesley, *Works*, vol. 9, 73.

An ordinance is a rule or practice to be carried out by followers of the one who establishes the ordinance. Based upon his reading of Scripture and the ministry of Jesus, John Wesley identified ordinances of God in the third part of the *General Rules* (104). Complementary to *sacraments*, ordinances are spiritual practices that are instituted means of grace, exercised on a regular, disciplined basis, to aid a disciple with growing and strengthening relationship with God. Methodists are called upon to be attentive to and participate in all the ordinances of God, most specifically: public *worship* of God, reading and expounding on the Word (i.e., Bible study), the *Lord's Supper*, family and private prayer, searching the Scriptures, and fasting or abstinence (104).

Members of societies were expected to participate in the ordinances as regular practices of their *discipleship*. They were identified by Wesley, from the earliest days of the class meetings, as rules of the societies designed specifically to help disciples monitor their progress. Persons who refused to participate to the levels expected by the leaders were admonished, and if they did not improve, were expelled from the society.

Ordination

Baltimore, Friday, Dec. 24-Jan. 2, 1785: On Christmas-eve we opened our conference: which was continued ten days. The Lord, I think, was peculiarly present whilst I was preaching my two pastoral sermons; the first when I ordained brother Asbury a bishop. The second when we ordained the elders. —Thomas Coke, "The Journal of Thomas Coke, Bishop of the Methodist Episcopal Church, from September 18th, 1784, to June 3, 1785," *Arminian Magazine* 1, no. 6 (Philadelphia: June 1789): 237–44, 290–93, in MEA II, 77.

The UMC understands ordination as a process of being called by God through the Holy Spirit and confirmed by the authority of the *Church* to be set apart through "the laying on of hands" for specific sacramental and leadership responsibilities in the life of the *Church*. Ordained ministry is patterned after the ministry of the apostles in the early *Church* (301-302).

All persons are called first into *discipleship* and general ministry through their *baptism*. Although never "separate from the ministry of the whole people of God," some persons receive a call from God for the ministries of service by representing God's love to others, proclamation through preaching and teaching, ordering the life of the *Church*, administration of the *sacraments*, extension of compassion, and search for justice in the community. These responsibilities are carried out by two distinct *orders* of ministry, *deacons* and *elders*. The UMC does not "re-ordain" persons when they transfer from another denomination (302-303).

Persons who want to explore their call to ministry go through a process of *candidacy* during which they explore whether their sense of call fits with UM ordination. One must be a member of The UMC for a year before beginning *candidacy*. This process leads to certification as a candidate for ministry. As a certified candidate, a process that includes completion of the MDiv degree— or, in the case of some *deacon* candidates, the Basic Graduate Theological Studies core curriculum—must be completed before one is *commissioned* and receives *provisional membership* in an *annual conference*. After two or three years in a residency process within the *annual conference*, a person then applies for *ordination*, and, if approved, is ordained at a session of the *annual conference* (310-314, 324-327).

The denomination has an alternate process that can also lead to ordination. A person may receive a *License for Pastoral Ministry*, receive an *appointment* to a *local church*, and proceed through both the *Course of Study* and Advanced Course of Study. Although it can take many years to complete, this is an appropriate path for persons for whom a full-time, three-year seminary education is not an option. These persons must still fulfill the requirements for *provisional membership* and *commissioning* (315-320). The *GBHEM* provides leadership to the denomination on all matters related to ordination (1401-1417).

United Methodist ordination was grounded first in the understanding of ordination from the Church of England. After the American colonies won the Revolutionary War, John Wesley, who remained a priest of the Church of England, had to determine how the Methodists in the new country were going to receive the *sacraments*. The Church of England had withdrawn from the country, and early Methodists, who were still meeting in small classes and societies for accountability and preaching, were left without priests. In addition, few priests in the newly formed Protestant Episcopal Church were sympathetic to the plight of the Methodists.

Wesley, without the presence of a *bishop*, performed an "extraordinary ordination" of Thomas Coke as a general superintendent and Richard Vasey as a priest, and sent them to the US to ordain Francis Asbury as a *deacon*, then *elder* and general superintendent. They then ordained a core group of the current traveling Methodist preachers in order for the Methodists to have access to the *sacraments*. Methodist *clergy* were first ordained *deacons and* then *elders*. Until 1940, *bishops* were ordained to the episcopal position. In 1940, The MC changed the process to *consecration*, so *bishops* now remain members of the *order* of *elders*. They do not, however, hold membership in an *annual conference*. At the 1996 *General Conference*, the two distinct *orders* of *deacon* and *elder* were established.

See also: www.gbhem.org.

Other Methodist Churches

II. 1. "If it be, give me thine hand." I do not mean, "Be of my opinion." You need not: I do not expect or desire it. Neither do I mean, "I will be of your opinion." I cannot. It does not depend on my choice. I can no more think, than I can see or hear, as I will. Keep you your opinion; I mine; and that as steadily as ever. You need not even endeavour to come over to me, or bring me over to you. I do not desire you to dispute those points, or to hear or speak one word concerning them. Let all opinions alone on one side and the other: only "give me thine hand." —Sermon 39, "On Catholic Spirit," Wesley, *Works*, vol. II, 89.

There are many Methodist *churches* in addition to The UMC throughout the world. The *World Methodist Council* includes eighty Methodist *churches* that trace their lineage back to John Wesley. The UMC has official relationships with a number of these *churches*: through an Act of Covenanting (570.4, 573), a concordat agreement (570.5, 574), or by having entered into *Full Communion* (442) with the *churches* of the *Pan-Methodist Commission*, as the *General Conference* approved in 2012.

These *churches* are divided into autonomous Methodist *churches*, affiliated autonomous Methodist *churches*, and affiliated united *churches*. Each is self-governing. Autonomous Methodist *churches* were not founded by The UMC or one of its predecessor bodies. Affiliated autonomous *churches* were founded by The UMC or a predecessor body. Affiliated united *churches* are denominations in which a former MC, which was historically related to The UMC or a predecessor body, is now a member (570.1-3).

The late 1800s witnessed a movement toward strengthening relationships among Methodist bodies, especially between British and US Methodism. To this end, a series of ecumenical conferences began in 1881, the first held at City Road Wesleyan Chapel in London, on September 7, 1881. At this first event, ten Methodist denominations related to British Methodism, thirteen denominations from the US, and five from Canada participated. By the 1880s, Methodist denominations were moving into establishing missionary work in Asia, South America, and Africa, as well as expanding beyond France into Europe. These *missionary* endeavors were eventually designated *central conferences* by the US Methodists, a number of which were spun off as autonomous, nationally based denominations in the early to mid-1900s. Those established by British Methodist *missionary* work were often organized to become their own nationally based denominations. It is, therefore, quite common to discover multiple Methodist denominations in any given country.

See also: umc.org.

Our Theological Task

The question is, of the Office and Operation of the Holy Spirit; with which the doctrine of the New-Birth, and indeed, the whole of real religion, is connected. On a subject of so deep concern, I desire to be serious as death. But at the same time, your lordship will permit me to use great plainness. And this I am the more emboldened to do, because by naming my name, your lordship, as it were, condescends to me on even ground. I shall consider, first what your lordship advances concerning me; and then what is advanced concerning the Operations of the Holy Spirit. —"A Letter to the Rt. Rev. The Lord Bishop of Gloucester, Occasioned by His Tract on the Office and Operations of the Holy Spirit," in *The Works of the Rev. John Wesley*, vol. IX, First American Edition (New York: J & J Harper, 1827), 69.

The section of the *Discipline* titled "Our Theological Task" speaks to how UMs think about and interpret "the world's needs and challenges to the *Church*" and "the gospel to the world" through the doctrinal lens of Wesleyan theology. The theological task is one of "testing, renewal, elaboration, and application of our doctrinal perspectives in carrying out our calling 'to spread scriptural holiness over these lands'" (105, Section 4).

While our doctrines are preserved in the *Articles of Religion* and *Confession of Faith*, and protected by the *Constitution of The United Methodist Church*, UMs are expected to apply this theology to issues in their widespread and rapidly changing contexts. In the section's assertion that UMs are called to take this task of theological reflection seriously, it describes the nature of this task in four ways: (1) it is critical and constructive, (2) it is both individual and communal, (3) it is contextual and incarnational, and (4) it is practical. The guidelines for how UMs go about this task are found in the four "Sources and Criteria" for theological reflection—what has come to be known as the *quadrilateral*. This task is identified as crucially important to the work of speaking into the major controversies of the day and of grounding our shared *mission* while affirming our diversity as a gift of God (105, Section 4).

Introduced in the *Discipline* in 1972, Section 4 was originally expected to fall under the *Restrictive Rules* as an extension of the *Constitution*. This understanding was overturned by a ruling of the *Judicial Council*, making it instead subject to the legislative processes of the *General Conference*. Until the merger of 1968, there was no entry in the *Discipline* to explain either our doctrinal heritage or theology beyond the inclusion of the *Articles of Religion* or *Confession of Faith*.

See also: www.umc.org/what-we-believe/section-3-our-doctrinal-standards -and-general-rules; www.umc.org/what-we-believe/reflecting-on-our-faith.

Pan-Methodist Commission

That They May Be One. —The Pan-Methodist Commission Mission Statement, www.panmethodist.org, accessed April 13, 2017.

The Commission on Pan-Methodist Cooperation and Union works to establish closer relationships between The UMC and five historic African American Methodist denominations in the US The African Methodist Episcopal Church, the African Methodist Episcopal Zion Church, The African Union Methodist Protestant Church, The Christian Methodist Episcopal Church, and The Union American Methodist Episcopal Church. The commission is made up of nine people from each denomination: three bishops, three clergy, and three lay members. It holds a quadrennial Consultation of Methodist Bishops (433.2). The most prominent project of the commission is the Pan-Methodist Campaign for Children in Poverty.

Methodism splintered along racial lines with the walkout of Richard Allen and his followers from St. George Chapel in Philadelphia in 1792. The African Methodist Episcopal Church was established in 1816. Other historic black denominations soon followed. The Christian Methodist Episcopal Church was the last to separate from The MECS in 1870. Inheriting the work that was begun in 1985, with the Commission on Pan-Methodist Cooperation, and in 1996, with the Commission on Union, the Pan-Methodist Commission was founded in 2000, to explore the possibilities of a merger among the member denominations. Rather than merger, the conversation resulted in a relationship of *full communion* with all five denominations in 2012.

See also: www.panmethodist.org/; www.pmcforchildren.org.

Parsonage

> Those preachers who refuse to occupy the houses which may be provided
> for them on the stations and circuits where they are from time to time
> appointed, shall be allowed nothing for house-rent, nor receive any thing
> more than their simple quarterage for themselves, wives, and children, and
> their traveling expenses. —Resolution, 1816 General Conference, Bangs,
> vol. 3, 46.

It is the responsibility of a charge to provide living accommodations for a clergyperson and immediate family. This responsibility can be carried out by providing either a parsonage or a housing allowance. A parsonage is a domicile, purchased and maintained by the local church(es). Each annual conference has a housing policy and parsonage standards with which both the charge and parsonage family are expected to comply. This is the case for both single and multiple church charges. (See 247.18-19.)

The Pastor/Staff Parish Relations Committee is responsible for ensuring that the housing arrangements are in accordance with annual conference policies. The Pastor/Staff Parish Relations Committee and Board of Trustees chairpersons are required to review the parsonage annually in order to address any maintenance and health issues (258.2 *g*) (16)). The Church Council reviews Pastor/Staff Parish Relations Committee recommendations regarding housing of clergy families in compliance with annual conference policies and parsonage standards (252.4 *e*)). These policies should be found in the Journal of the annual conference and are often posted on the website.

The requirements of design and procedures for purchase, inclusion of the trust clause in deeds, building codes and maintenance, and sale of a parsonage are subject to the same disciplinary and legal requirements as any other property purchased and used by the charge (2503.3, 2508, 2520.3, 2521, 2528.1, 2528.4, 2536-2544). The *Discipline* also identifies specific accessibility requirements (2544.4 *b*)).

In the earliest days of Methodism in the US, circuit riders were housed in rooms attached to members' houses. These rooms would have an exterior door so that the preacher could arrive at any time of the day or night without disturbing the family. When preachers began to be assigned to single-church charges, the local Methodist society was responsible for providing a house for the preacher and his family, because the length of their appointments was limited to a maximum of three, one-year renewable appointments. As appointments have lengthened, housing allowances have become an attractive option for clergy. Some annual conferences do not allow housing allowances.

See also: Annual conference bylaws and journals.

Pastor

PASTOR. See In-charge, Preacher. —*Discipline*, MECS, 1930, index.

There are two qualifications for a person to be called a "pastor." First, one must be approved by the *clergy* session of the *annual conference* as an *ordained* or *provisional elder or deacon, associate member*, or *licensed local pastor*. Second, a pastor is usually under *appointment* to a ministry—most to a *local church*—by the *bishop* (339). These appointed *clergy* may serve as senior pastors, co-pastors, or associate pastors (258.2 *g*) (7)). The term "assistant pastor" should be used to identify non-ordained *clergy* and especially those of another denomination who have been hired by the *local church*.

Provisional *elders* and local pastors are licensed to perform all the duties of a pastor "within and while appointed to a particular *charge* or *extension ministry*" (317). The extensive responsibilities and duties of *elders* and local pastors are framed by the "fourfold ministry" of Word, *Sacrament*, Order, and Service (340). Provisional *deacons* are licensed and called to ministries of "Word, Service, Compassion, and Justice," leading the church to ministry in the world (328-329) and may be referred to as pastors given their particular context.

In the Bible, the term "pastor" is associated with the word "shepherd" (Eph. 4:11; Acts 20:28; 1 Pet. 5:2). The term points to the care-giving and nurturing roles of a minister.

"Unauthorized Conduct" by pastors includes engaging an unapproved evangelist without the consent of the *district superintendent*, discontinuing services without the consent of the *district superintendent*, arbitrarily organizing a new pastoral *charge*, holding religious services within the bounds of another pastoral *charge* without the consent of the pastor of the *charge* or *district superintendent* or re-baptizing people. Additional unauthorized conduct includes betraying *confidentiality*, except in those instances required by *law* to report or if it is believed that a person has the potential to hurt another person or him- or herself. (See 341.)

Historically, Methodist *clergy* were called preachers, defined by their essential task of saving souls and leading members in their *discipleship* and by the policy of *itinerancy*. The term "pastor" did not occur in the early *Disciplines*, except in reference to "pastoral visiting" from house to house. The term did not emerge in various *Disciplines* as a synonym for preachers until the early twentieth century. Histories of the early EUBC traditions make a clear distinction between William Otterbein as a pastor of *churches*, and Martin Boehm and Jacob Albright as itinerant preachers who circulated throughout different regions without ever serving as the leader of a specific congregation.

See also: Annual conference bylaws and journals.

Pastor's Compensation and Benefits

Quest. 2. What is the regular annual Salary of the Bishops, Elders, Deacons and Preacher?

Answ. Twenty-four Pounds Pennsylvania Currency, and their travelling Expences. —*Discipline*, 1785, §VIII. "Of the Collections that are made, and how the Money is to be expended."

United Methodist *clergy* are self-employed for Social Security purposes and employees for FICA. *Local churches* must give clergy a W-2 tax form. There are some unique characteristics to *clergy* compensation and benefits. "Compensation" refers to the actual salary and housing allowance (if there is not a parsonage) earned by a *clergyperson*. Compensation is subject to federal and state income tax laws. *Clergy* are considered self-employed for purposes of Social Security/Medicare. A housing allowance is not taxable for income tax purposes but it is subject to the full Social Security/Medicare tax. *Clergy* are expected to submit quarterly payments to ensure payment of taxes in the year they are earned.

"Benefits" refers to the insurance, pension, vacation time, leave-time opportunities, and *continuing education* funds available to the clergy. *Annual conferences* establish minimum requirements for these particular funds; they are not taxable. Reimbursement accounts are not considered a benefit for *clergy work expenses and reimbursements.*

In consultation with the district superintendent and by recommendation of the *pastor/staff parish relations committee,* the *charge conference* sets the pastor's compensation (247.13). Local *charges* are obligated to pay the compensation and provide the benefits for their *pastor(s)* as established by the *charge conference,* in accordance with *annual conference* policies, and to report these expenditures to the *annual conference* (626). Base compensation for full-time *pastors* is established by the conference's *Commission on Equitable Compensation* (622-624). Part-time compensation is usually provided on a pro rata basis, depending on the agreed-upon amount of time committed to the *charge.* Clergy serving in *extension ministries* are to provide to the conference a statement of their compensation (627).

Salaries of the *clergy* were originally set by the *General Conference* and included in the *Discipline.* All *clergy* received the same salary. The first record of a common salary was in the General Minutes of the second regular *annual conference* in 1774. It was set at "Six Pounds Pennsylvania currency per quarter." The salary set for all preachers in the 1785 *Discipline* was "Twenty-four Pounds Pennsylvania Currency, and their travelling Expenses." If one was married, the wife also received the same amount "if they are in want of it." By 1812, the *annual conferences* were responsible for figuring out how they were going to raise the "supplies for ministers." By the late 1800s, salaries were established by the quarterly conference in all three Methodist predecessor *churches,* identified in the specific questions outlined for this meeting in each of the *Disciplines.*

See also: gcfa.org.

Pastor/Staff Parish Relations Committee

> Quest. 2. What is the duty of Stewards? Answ to inform the Preachers of any sick or disorderly persons; to tell the Preachers what they think wrong in them; —*Discipline*, 1789, §XXXIV. "On the Qualification and Duty of Stewards."

The Pastor/Staff Parish Relations Committee functions as the personnel committee of a *local church*. It is responsible for all matters related to appointed *clergy* and hired *staff* (258.2 *g*)). This committee is responsible for the process of evaluation of *clergy* and consultation with the *district superintendent* regarding the *appointment* of *clergy*. It is responsible for the hiring and termination of hired staff.

The five–nine, rotating members must be spiritually mature, *professing members* of the *charge*. The committee also includes the *lay leader*, the *lay member of the annual conference*, and a young adult. Technically speaking, the *pastor* is not a member, but functions in the role of consultant (258.2 *a)-d*)).

The committee meets, at a minimum, on a quarterly basis. It meets only with the knowledge of the *pastor* and/or the *district superintendent* and with the *pastor* in attendance, unless the *pastor* excuses herself or himself. If the committee is meeting with the *district superintendent*, conversation with the *district superintendent* may occur without the *pastor* present. However, the *pastor* must be brought into the conversation immediately thereafter. The committee meets in closed sessions. All discussion is confidential (258.2 *e)-f*)).

The responsibilities now assigned to the Pastor/Staff Parish Relations Committee were originally carried out by a board of stewards, a team of lay members responsible for all of the administrative responsibilities of the society. Following the merger of 1939, The MC established both a Pastor Relations Committee and a Lay Personnel Committee, which were then merged to become the Pastor Parish Relations Committee or the Pastor/Staff Relations Committee in The UMC.

See also: www.awfumc.org/expectationsforpastoralleadership.

Periodicals

> This year marks a favorable epoch in the history of our Church, by the re-commencement of the Methodist Magazine, the first number of which was published by J. Soule and T. Mason, in January, 1818. —Bangs, vol. 3, 73.

There are thirteen official UM magazines, sponsored by *general agencies* and available through UMC.org.

John Wesley published the "Arminian Magazine," founded in 1778 for the Methodists in England. The "Methodist Magazine" was first published in 1797 and lasted for only a few years. The *General Conference* of 1812 ordered the publication of a monthly magazine, but this was not actually published until 1818.

See also: www.umc.org; www.gbhem.org.

Plans for Ethnic and Language-Based Plans

> It is a thing plainly repugnant to the Word of God, and the custom of the primitive church, to have public prayers in church, or to minister the Sacraments, in a tongue not understood by the people. —Articles of Religion, Article XV, Discipline, 2016, ¶104.

There are six ethnic and language-based plans in The UMC. Four are administered by the *GBGM*: (a) The Asian American Language Ministry, whose caucus is the New Federation of Asian American United Methodists; (b) Plan for Hispanic and Latino Ministry, whose caucus is Methodists Associated Representing the Cause of Hispanic/Latinx Americans, MARCHA; (c) The Pacific Islander Ministry Plan, whose caucus is the Pacific Islander Caucus; and (d) the Korean Ministry Plan. The *GBOD* administers the Native American International Caucus and Strengthening the Black Church for the 21st Century (SBC21). The different plans seek to strengthen and expand ministry with and by persons of these populations with strategies that honor their distinctive cultures. The caucuses are made up of members who advocate for the plans and issues related to their various populations.

Missions to German-speaking communities in the Ohio Conference began in the 1830s, to Indian tribes in the US about the same time, and to Spanish speakers in the Southwest following the end of the Mexican-American War in 1848. Work was organized by both indigenous and appointed *missionaries*. The work grew considerably in the German-speaking areas. The Indian Missionary Conference was created in 1844. The work in the Southwest received little support from distant conferences. Even so, The MECS established the Rio Grande Missionary Conference in 1858. Interest waned in domestic *mission* in proportion to a skyrocketing fascination and expansion with international *missionary* work. MEC work expanded among Chinese and Japanese immigrants in California in the late 1800s, and in The MECS with Koreans in the early 1900s. As a part of the merger that eliminated the Central Jurisdiction, the General Conferences of 1968 established the Commission on Religion and Race, and became increasingly aware of the importance of focusing on ethnic congregations as a source of connection and growth in light of the growing diversity of the US. The 1976 and 1980 General Conferences established "the Ethnic Minority Local Church" as one of The UMC's highest priorities. The Ethnic and Languages caucuses and plans began development starting with BMCR in 1967.

See also: umcmission.org/racial-and-ethnic-ministry-plans/; www.sbc21 .org/; www.naicumc.com; www.umcdiscipleship.org/equipping-leaders /native-american; www.umcdiscipleship.org/equipping-leaders/african -american.

Polity

Polity is a living process because the church is a living, continuous, yet ever-changing community. One generation's verities are the next generation's straitjacket. In each era the church has to work out the political arrangements that will structure the people of God for effective witness to the gospel. Frank, 44.

"Polity" is an inclusive term that encompasses all of the ways in which we order the life of, not just the *local church*, but the entire UMC.

Thomas E. Frank, in his seminal work, *Polity, Practice, and the Mission of The United Methodist Church*, describes how polity includes structure and the ways organizations and communities govern themselves. These include everything from the *Constitution of The United Methodist Church*, which assigns and limits powers to the various offices and lines of authority and processes established to ensure representation. It also covers how The UMC defines and organizes its membership, how the *local church* is organized, how persons are prepared for ministry, ordained, and appointed to *churches* and ministries, how we organize for *mission*, and how we structure our *connection* (Frank, 44).

While polity includes the rules, procedures, and practices of the *Church*, it is so much more. Polity is grounded in our history and doctrine and has evolved in response to the changing environments in which The UMC has lived.

Theologically speaking, polity is both a ministry and a practice defined as "Order." Grounded in the ministry of Word and *Sacrament*, Order is the *stewardship* of the household of faith that serves and organizes the *church* for *mission* and ministry. *Elders* are called and ordained to the ministry of Order in the life of the whole *Church*. This is one reason why *district superintendents* and *bishops* are required to be *elders*. Local *pastors* are responsible for ordering the life of the *local church* to which they are appointed. (See Frank, 45.)

Ecclesiastically speaking, polity is expressed in the disciplines and connections that are inherent to Methodism. It is the process of human practice, interaction, reflection, and new action (Frank, 42).

A comparison is often made between the three branches of US government—the executive (president), legislative (Congress), and judicial (the court system and Supreme Court)—and parallel structures in The UMC. The *Council of Bishops* embodies the executive branch; the *General Conference* is the legislative branch; and the *Judicial Council*, established later in 1939, fulfills the judicial functions. In reality, while we have three parallel structures that fulfill these roles, the Church structures and their powers are very different from those of the secular government.

See also: Thomas E. Frank, *Polity, Practice, and the Mission of The United Methodist Church* (Nashville: Abingdon Press, 2006).

Predecessor Denominations

In December 1784, the famous Christmas Conference of preachers was held in Baltimore at Lovely Lane Chapel. At this gathering the movement became organized as The Methodist Episcopal Church in America.

. . . Two other churches were forming in America, which, in their earliest years were composed almost entirely of German-speaking people. The first was founded by Philip William Otterbein (1726–1813) and Martin Boehm (1725–1812). A second church, The Evangelical Association, was begun by Jacob Albright (1759–1808). —*Discipline*, UMC, 2016. "A Brief History of The United Methodist Church."

The original Methodist Church in the US was The Methodist Episcopal Church (MEC) founded in 1784. Two churches combined to create The Evangelical United Brethren Church (EUBC). They were The United Brethren Church (UBC) and Evangelical Church (EC). The United Methodist Church is the result of the 1968 merger of The Methodist Church—established in the reunification of 1939—and The Evangelical United Brethren Church—a merger of The UBC and EC in 1946. Prior to the merger, both traditions moved through what, at times, were tumultuous schisms and re-unifications.

The first event that had significant impact on The UMC today began in 1792, when Richard Allen led the walkout of African Americans from St. George's Chapel in Philadelphia. This group would become the African Methodist Episcopal Church in 1816. The reason for this walkout was the mistreatment of black members, which escalated to the point that they were consigned to a small part of the balcony of the sanctuary.

The second event was in 1796, when James O'Kelly led a schismatic group out of The MEC over the issue of the power of the *bishops*. It would become the short-lived Republican Methodist Church (RMC). The RMC would soon join with the Campbell-Stone Movement to become the Disciples/Christ Christian Church.

The third event took place in 1828–30, with the expulsion of members and *clergy* advocating for lay participation in decision-making. This group became The Methodist Protestant Church (MPC) that eventually took part in the reunification of 1939.

The year 1844 witnessed the most significant schism in the US Methodist tradition as the northern and southern conferences split over slavery. This action resulted in the formation of The Methodist Episcopal Church, South (MECS) and a much smaller MEC, primarily in the northern states. The MPC, MEC, and MECS reunited in 1939, and became The Methodist Church (MC) and included the formation of the segregated Central Jurisdiction for black members. The MC is the *Church* that merged with The EUBC in 1968.

The EUBC tradition was not without its own controversies. The UBC emerged out of the Mennonite and German Reformed traditions. It faced its greatest schism in 1889, over issues of freemasonry, procedures on changing the Constitution, and social issues. The Church of the United Brethren in Christ (Old Constitution) and Church of the United Brethren in Christ (New Constitution) were the result.

Founded in 1800, the Evangelical Association named itself in 1816. It also passed through a couple of controversies, most notably the exit of the United Evangelical Church in 1891. These two groups reunited in 1921 to become the Evangelical Church (EC).

See also: Russell E. Richey, Kenneth E. Rowe, and Jean Miller Schmidt, *The Methodist Experience in America: Sourcebook*, Vol. 2 (Nashville: Abingdon Press, 2009).

Professing Member

Lastly: the true members of the Church of Christ "endeavor," with all possible diligence, with all care and pains, with unwearied patience, (and all will be little enough) to "keep the unity of the Spirit in the bond of peace;" to preserve inviolate the same spirit of lowliness and meekness, of long-suffering, mutual forbearance, and love; and all these cemented and knit together by that sacred tie, —the peace of God filling the heart. Thus only can we be and continue living members of that Church which is the body of Christ. —Sermon 74, II.8, "Of the Church," Wesley, *Works*, vol. 3, 55.

A professing member is a person who has been baptized and who has also professed faith in Jesus Christ through the services of the baptismal covenant *ritual* or by transfer from another *church*. Professing members are those who comprise the "membership of the *church*" for statistical purposes (215.2-3). Assisting persons to become professing members, including children through *confirmation* classes, and the *discipleship* formation of adults, is a major responsibility of the *pastor* (216.2-3).

The services for transitioning a person from baptized to professing member are found in *The UMH* (38, 43). These services include an essential set of questions that call a person to a full profession of faith in Jesus Christ, loyalty to Christ through The UMC, and commitment to the *local church* through which the person becomes a member by taking vows of support through prayers, presence, gifts, service, and witness. A professing member, through personal disciplines, participation in accountability groups, and participation in the ministries of the *local* and universal *church*, is responsible for growing in faithfulness (217-221).

An affiliate member is a professing member of another UM *church*, an affiliated autonomous Methodist *church*, a united *church*, or a concordat Methodist *church*, who is living for an extended time in an area far from her or his home *church*. Affiliate members may hold leadership positions within the *local church*, while associate members may not hold any position that gives them a vote on the *Church Council*. Affiliate members are reported and counted on the roll of their home church only. An associate member is a professing member of another denomination. Associate members are not counted in membership statistics (227).

Historically, Methodist membership could be fluid. While still an evangelical movement in the eighteenth and early nineteenth century, persons would join the classes, bands, and societies. If they did not fulfill their responsibilities, they were expelled, were invited to leave, or left of their own accord. Diligent recordkeeping was maintained because these numbers represented persons who had experienced conversion and were, hopefully, growing in grace. As societies developed into *churches*, and the movement settled into becoming a denomination, membership expanded to include the management of the *local church* and an expanding number of lay volunteer positions.

See also: www.umc.org; www.umcdiscipleship.org/.

Program Ministries

> The "Tract Society of the Methodist Episcopal Church" was formed this year (1817), by some members of our Church, with a view to furnish the poorer class of the community with religious reading. It has gone on from that time to the present (1840) and has done much good by diffusing abroad the truths of the gospel, by issuing doctrinal, experimental, and practical illustrations of the Holy Scriptures. —Bangs, vol. 3, 55.

Program ministries are created to provide systems for "nurture, outreach, and witness" in the life of a local church (243-244). The Church Council is responsible for planning, implementing, and overseeing these ministries (252.1-2). The charge conference determines how these ministries are represented on the Church Council (252.5). The programs are led by coordinators (253-254).

Program ministries are designed to assist persons with deepening their relationship with Jesus Christ and to discover ways in which they can live out their faith as Christians in the world. These usually take the form of small groups created by the Church Council, emerging as a need from a group of people, or as an ongoing part of the historic structures of the denomination (256).

Program ministries include, but are not limited to, the church school, discipleship groups, mission and ministry groups, support groups, age-level ministries especially for children, youth, and young adults, United Methodist Women, and United Methodist Men (256.1-6). General agencies of the

Church provide a wide range of ideas and resources for the development of program ministries.

The earliest program-like ministries that emerged in Methodism were efforts in evangelism, mission, and education that were quickly formalized into societies between 1817 and 1832, such as: the Bible Society, Sunday School Society, Tract Society, and the Mission Society.

See also: www.umc.org/who-we-are/agencies.

Property

> Quest. 1. Is any thing adviseable in regard to building? Answ. Let all our churches be built plain and decent; but not more expensively than is absolutely unavoidable: Otherwise the necessity of raising money will make rich men necessary to us. But if so, we just be dependent on them, yea, and governed by them. And then farewell to the Methodist-discipline, if not doctrine too. —*Discipline*, 1789, §XXVII. "On building Churches, and on the Order to be observed therein."

Property includes land, buildings, equipment, and assets. United Methodist churches, agencies, and institutions may "acquire, hold, maintain, improve, and sell" property as long as its uses align with the mission of The UMC (2501.3). Properties, whether belonging to a local church, conference, agency, or institution, are managed by a Board of Trustees serving under the direction of the appropriate body.

Requirements for Buildings: The *Discipline* contains the following requirements for the development and maintenance of church property: (1) Accessibility—an annual accessibility audit shall be conducted by the Board of Trustees (2533.6); (2) Building—churches considering remodeling, renovating, or construction—requires the election of a building committee (2544); (3) Energy efficiency—the Board of Church Location and Building shall explore the best way to make church or parsonage buildings energy efficient (2520.3); (4) Incorporation of the Local Church—for the sake of protection and obligation, local churches may incorporate (2529.1); (5) Leases—churches may lease property as long as it does not interfere with the mission of the church (2540, 2541, 2505) (see Property Taxes); (6) Policies for building use—local church policies should be developed for the healthy stewardship and legal protection of church property.

Purchasing Property: When a local church wants to purchase land and buildings, a resolution must be passed by a majority of members present and voting at an official charge conference called for that purpose. In addition, the District Board of Church Location and Building must evaluate and approve the project as to its appropriateness as a building site, its potential for remodeling, and its fit into the district strategy for new, relocated, and discontinued faith communities (2519). When purchased by an unincorporated local church, the property is conveyed to the members of the Board of Trustees and its designated representatives. When purchased by an incorporated church, the property is conveyed to the local church, in its corporate name. Both must include the trust clause (2501, 2503, 2536, 2538).

Sales, Transfers, Leases, and Mortgages: When a local church sells, transfers, leases, or mortgages property, the process begins with several steps that take place in the district among the pastor, the district superintendent, and the District Board of Church Location and Building, who evaluate the missional needs of the community, conformity to the *Discipline*, and the determination of the future of the congregation after the action (e.g., discontinuance or relocation). The district superintendent must certify that the sale conforms to the *Discipline*. These actions also require a resolution that must be passed by a charge conference called specifically for this purpose. In addition, however, the pastor of the local church and the district superintendent must give their consent to the action in writing and attach them to the legal documents of the action. If the property belongs to an unincorporated church, the resolution passed by the charge conference may be carried out by any two duly authorized officers of the Board of Trustees. If belonging to an incorporated church, then the charge conference will also pass a resolution that directs and authorizes the corporation's board of directors (i.e., the Board of Trustees) to carry out the process. Proceeds from a sale or mortgage are managed by the Board of Trustees of either an unincorporated or incorporated church (2540-2542).

Title and Deeds: All property is "held, *in trust*, for the benefit of the entire denomination, and ownership and usage of church property is subject to the *Discipline*." The trust clause is required in every deed (2501, 2503). All property deeds and conveyances are required to conform to the local, state, and national laws where the property is located. Local law takes precedence over the *Discipline*, unless the laws point to depriving The UMC of the use of property without due process or violate the US constitutional guarantee of freedom of religion. (See 2506, 2508.)

Restrictions on Proceeds: There are restrictions and permissions on the use of the proceeds of a sale or mortgage. A local church shall not use such proceeds for current budgeted expenses. They may be used for capital improvements beyond the operating budget with the written approval of the pastor and the district superintendent. The church may use the proceeds as security for a loan to be used for construction of a new church. With the permission of the annual conference, the bishop, and the cabinet, the proceeds may be used for congregational redevelopment that includes program ministries and staff (2543).

When an annual conference closes a church (see Closure/Discontinuance of a Local Church), title to the property goes to the Conference Board of Trustees, who will hold it in trust, and then determine its disposition or future use (2549).

Review of Parsonage: The Board of Trustees, or Parsonage Committee if one exists, shall do an annual review of the parsonage (2533.4).

Usage of Facilities by Outside Groups: Use of church facilities shall be in keeping with the Social Principles (160-164) and at the discretion of the pastor and/or Board of Trustees (2533.3).

As Methodism spread in England and the colonies, meeting houses and chapels were built to house class meetings and, eventually, societies. As societies grew and became stable, they were often renovated into larger church buildings. Wesley's model deed and what became known in the US as the trust

191

clause helped control who preached and what doctrines they espoused. Lay trustees were held personally responsible for the buildings.

See also: gcfa.org/legal services.

Property Taxes

> As Christians, we are called by God to be good stewards of the resources with which we have been entrusted. In the context of allowing third parties to use church property, this means analyzing the risks and rewards of the proposed use and how the proposed use will impact the broader ministry of the church now and in the future. —"What to Consider Before Allowing a Third Party to Use Real Property," GCFA; s3.amazonaws.com /Website_GCFA/Leasing_Third_Party_Church_Prop.pdf.

When a *local church* leases space or use of land for commercial purposes unrelated to the *mission* of the *church* or for other nonprofit activities, the *church* is obligated to pay annual property taxes on the *property*. For example, if a *church* rents a house to a person or family, then it is required to pay property taxes on the house. If the same *church* uses the house as partial compensation for a *staff* person or for a program of the church (e.g., a *Scout* program), then it does not. It cannot, however, receive rent from either the *staff* person or the *Scout* program, and in the case of a program, it must be documented that the program is actually sponsored and supported by the *local church*. It is always incumbent upon *local church* leaders to ensure that the *church* is in compliance with local and federal *laws*.

The earliest *Disciplines* of 1785 and 1789, in Section XXV on "guarding against those Sins that are so common to Professors (persons who profess the faith)," were clear that the practice of "buying or selling goods that have not paid the duty laid upon them by government" was to be rooted out and abolished, and that anyone who was not willing to comply with the law about such "duties" was to be expelled. This sin ranked equally with the sin of bribery and the unwillingness to discharge one's personal debts.

See also: gcfa.org.

Provisional Membership

Quest. 1. How shall we try those who profess to be moved by the Holy Ghost to preach? Answ. 1. Let them be asked the following questions, viz. Do they know God as a pardoning God? Have they the love of God abiding in them? Do they desire and seek nothing but God? 2. Have they gifts (as well as grace) for the work? 3. Have they fruit? Are any truly convinced of sin and converted to God by their preaching? —*Disciplines*, 1789, §XII. "Of the Trial of Those who think they are moved by the Holy Ghost to preach."

When persons are *commissioned*, the intermediate step between being a *certified candidate* for ministry and getting ordained, they also receive provisional membership in the *annual conference* by a vote of the *clergy executive session* and then the *annual conference*. These two actions take place at the same time, but are not the same thing.

Provisional membership provides for a period of testing out one's call, character, leadership, and effectiveness in ministry. One may hold provisional membership for a minimum of two or three years (depending on the *annual conference*) and a maximum of eight years. The provisional member is required to participate in a two- or three-year *residency program* designed and carried out by the *annual conference*. Accommodations can be made by the *Board of Ordained Ministry* to not require actual physical residency within the geographical boundaries of the *annual conference* (325-326). The *residency program* will, however, require a number of face-to-face activities to which a provisional member will have to travel in order to participate. Following the fulfillment of this *residency program*, it is expected that the provisional member will apply to the *Board of Ordained Ministry* for *ordination* to the *order* of either *deacon* or *elder* and *full connection membership* in the *annual conference* (326, 327).

Provisional membership to become an *elder* provides the person with a *license for pastoral ministry* which provides the right to be appointed by a *bishop* to a *charge* (315). Provisional members seeking *elder's* orders are eligible for *appointment* to *extension ministry* and work in graduate degree programs as well (326).

If one is seeking *deacon's* orders, a person is licensed for ministry to perform the duties of a *deacon*. The person finds a ministry in which to work, and then the *bishop* appoints the person to that ministry (326.1). While a provisional member, one may choose to change one's *ordination* track (326.4). Both the person and the *Board of Ordained Ministry* have the right to discontinue the relationship of provisional membership. This process requires the surrender of *commissioning* credentials to the *district superintendent* (327.6). Provisional members who reach mandatory retirement age will either automatically be discontinued, or may be classified as a retired local *pastor* (327.7, 320.5). Provisional members have the right to vote in an *annual conference* on all matters except Constitutional amendments and matters pertaining to *clergy*–conference relationships (327.2). They may serve on any conference organizations except the *Board of Ordained Ministry* (327. 3). They are not eligible to be elected as a *delegate to General Conference* (327.2, 3).

The historic terms for provisional membership emphasize this stage of progress toward *ordination* as a time of testing out the gifts, graces, and skills of a person seeking *ordination*. Originally, the term for provisional members was "on trial." These men were given the role of "assistants" to the traveling *elders*. This term was then preempted by the term "probationary" or "on probation." The term "provisional" replaced these when major changes in the United Methodist understanding of ministry were approved at the *General Conference* of 1996.

See also: www.gbhem.org.

Quadrennium

> Before the conference adjourned, they passed a resolution to have another General Conference at the end of four years, to be convened in the city of Baltimore, November 1, 1796, and that it should be composed of all the traveling preachers who should be in full connection at the time it was to be held. —Bangs, vol. 1, 351.

A quadrennium is a four-year time span that begins on January 1, following a regular *General Conference* (722.2). Thus, regular *general conferences* and *juris-*

dictional conferences are held toward the end of a quadrennium. *Central conferences* meet at various times, but usually during the first year of a quadrennium. Sometimes the *General Conference* will establish quadrennial programs requiring extra financial support for that time period. Official publications are often printed for the current quadrennium.

The first *General Conference* to be held on a quadrennial basis was in 1792. From this date forward, each of our predecessor *churches* met on a quadrennial basis.

Quadrilateral

> Let us each seriously examine himself. Have I, (1) Such a knowledge of Scripture as becomes him who undertakes to explain it to others . . . Do I understand Greek and Hebrew . . . (3) Do I understand my own office . . . (4) Do I understand so much of profane history as tends to confirm and illustrate the Sacred . . . (5) Am I a tolerable master of the sciences . . . (6) Am I acquainted with the Fathers . . . (7) Have I any knowledge of the word. —"An Address to the Clergy" (February 16, 1756), *Wesley's Works* (Jackson, 1872), vol. 10, 490–92.

The term "quadrilateral" refers to a fourfold way of approaching, understanding, evaluating, and living out our faith, through processes of discernment and analysis using Scripture, tradition, reason, and experience. The *Discipline* defines the components of the quadrilateral as "Sources and Criteria" of Methodist theology in the section *Our Theological Task* (105, Section 4).

Dr. Albert C. Outler was the first theologian to systematize the quadrilateral, as it is currently known, in his book *John Wesley*, published in 1964. Grounded in the Anglican tradition of the "three-legged stool" that already emphasized Scripture, tradition, and reason, Outler asserted that Wesley added the fourth—experience—as a source that enlivens and confirms faith.

See also: www.UMC.org ; Albert C. Outler, *John Wesley* (New York: Oxford University Press, 1964).

Quorum for Meetings

> The defeat of the plan for a delegated General Conference boded no good for the Methodist Episcopal Church. Many of the preachers from remote Conferences began preparations to return home, and Bishop Hedding states that, had they left at this crisis, it would probably have been the last General Conference ever held. All the members from the New England Conference were making arrangements to depart. In this emergency he entreated them to remain, and declared his own determination to remain until the close of the Conference, whatever might happen. —James M. Buckley, *Constitutional and Parliamentary History of the Methodist Episcopal Church* (New York: The Methodist Book Concern, 1912), 109–10.

The quorums set for various meetings are as follows: (a) charge conference—the members present and voting (246.6); (b) Church Council—members present and voting (252.6); (c) local boards of trustees—a majority of its members (2532); (d) annual conferences and their committees—as set by their bylaws; (e) General Conference—a majority of the number of the whole number of delegates, with some exceptions (506); for the following general agencies, a majority—CT (906.2), GCAH (1705), GCFA (805.2), and UMPH (1603); for other general agencies—see their bylaws; for GBOPHB (Wespath) (1502.3); for Judicial Council meetings—seven members constitute a quorum, except for questions regarding constitutionality, which requires nine (combination of members and alternates) (2608.2).

Prior to the General Conference of 1808, eligible delegates included all elders in full connection, and with each General Conference preceding it, the number of years of required service increased (from zero to two to four) as an additional criterion. The quorum was basically the number of preachers who showed up, resulting in tremendous inequity in representation from different parts of the country. The General Conference of 1808 focused its work primarily on the establishment of a delegated General Conference and Constitution necessary to perpetuate the organization. It nearly disintegrated after a long and contentious discussion, over whether or not annual conferences should be able to elect their presiding elders, resulting in a near walkout of the members of the New England Conference and a few from the western conferences. If this had happened, the prospect for developing the Constitution of The MEC would have been so severely disrupted that it might not have ever taken place. Once a delegated General Conference was in place, grounded in the principle of equal representation, quorums, as then established by the *Discipline*, were maintained.

See also: Annual conference bylaws or standing rules; Robert's Rules of Order.

Reaffiliation—*See also* Appendix

> The inadequacy of the plan (The Segregated Plan of Union) lies in its failure to provide for cooperation between white and colored Methodists in annual and jurisdictional Conferences and in local communities. We think we may safely say that the Commission on Unification did not make provision in the plan for more direct relationship between white and Negro Annual Conferences and white and Negro local churches. . . . —Women's Missionary Council of the Methodist Episcopal Church, South, 27th Annual Report (1936–37), 141. RRS, Vol. 2, 553.

The prospect of reaffiliation for previously disaffiliated churches was passed by the 2020/2024 General Conference as a replacement for the original Paragraph 2553 that created the means by which churches could disaffiliate. That original paragraph no longer exists in any form. The new paragraph requires that each annual conference create a process for churches that seek to reaffiliate with the denomination, with the required inclusion of a step in which the church reaffirms its commitment to the Trust Clause (2553).

Historically, the language surrounding disaffiliation and reaffiliation was that of division and merger, unification, and reunification. After going through major divisions in the nineteenth century, the predecessor denominations (The MEC, The MECS, and The MPC) sought to reunify. At the time the churches in the different denominations had been divided geographically, by withdrawal, or by expulsion. Beginning in 1870, conversations began seeking the establishment of relationships between The MEC and The MECS, and eventually The MPC and the Brethren-related churches. Not until 1939 did the unification of the "big three" take place, with the caveat that a segregated jurisdiction would exist for African Americans. Then in 1968 The Evangelical United Brethren and The Methodist Church merged to become The United

Methodist Church. "United" as the part of the name that represented the smaller EUB denomination.

See also: Paragraph 2553 in the Appendix; umc.org/en/content/ask-the -umc-the-umc-really-is-part-6-opening-the-door-to-re-affiliations.

Records Maintenance by the Local Church

Quest. 2. What is the duty of a Deacon? 9. To take an exact account of the numbers in the society, and bring it to the conference. 10. To send an account of his circuit every quarter to his elder [and] take a regular catalogue of the societies in the towns and cities, as they live in streets. —*Discipline*, 1789, §VI. "On the Constituting of Deacons, and their Duty."

The permanent membership records of a *local church* are defined by the *Discipline* (230-234). The *GCAH* provides a document called *Guidelines for the Management of Records for the Annual Conference* and *Local Church* that provides guidelines on all additional records, especially those required for *property* and *finances*.

Early histories of Methodism document "Numbers in the Church" reported with each *annual conference* and *General Conference*. *Deacons* were responsible for data collection on every circuit. Nathan Bangs, in each of his volumes, indicates the cumulative numbers as they were recorded in the Minutes and Journals of the *annual conferences*, monitoring the increase or decrease from the previous year.

See also: gcah.org/resources/guidelines/.

Related Organizations—*See* Ecumenical Relationships

Residency Program (Residency in Ministry)

Monday [November] 29 [1784, Worcester City, Pocomoke County, Maryland] I have now had the pleasure of hearing Harry preach several times.

I sometimes give notice immediately after preaching, that in a little time Harry will preach to the blacks; but the whites always stay to hear him. Sometimes I publish him to preach at candle-light, as the negroes can better attend at that time. I really believe that he is one of the best preachers in the world and he is one of the humblest creatures I ever saw. —Vickers, 37.

The residency program (called Residency in Ministry by the *GBHEM* and various other names by *annual conferences*) is the minimum two- or three-year interval (depending on the conference) between being commissioned with *provisional membership* and being ordained with *full connection* in the conference. During residency, *provisional members* are required to participate in a regular program of groups and events that are designed to assist with maturing persons in their identity and skills in ministry and preparing them to apply for *ordination* (325-326).

In the early MEC, the exhorters, local preachers, and deacons prior to becoming *elders*, worked alongside *elders* under their supervision.

Deacons were primarily responsible for the administrative responsibilities of the deacon-elder team. For any of these positions, this work could serve as a sort of internship because there was always a way to exit the work of ministry without shame. The deacon participated in the administration of the *sacraments*, supported the local preachers, oversaw the stewards, ensured the collections were taken, led watch-night services and Love Feasts, sold books to Methodist families, and handled the reports. Their "residency" took place as they worked and were supervised by a traveling or presiding *elder* in anticipation of being elected into *full connection* and ordained as *elders* themselves.

See also: gbhem.org.

Restrictive Rules

The general conference shall have full powers to make rules and regulations for our church, under the following limitations and restrictions, viz —*Discipline*, MEC, 1808, 15.

The Restrictive Rules are six articles defined in Division Two, Section III of the Constitution of The United Methodist Church (18-23). They define the structures and rules of United Methodism that cannot be changed by the General Conference. They can be changed only through the process of amendment following the directions in Division Five of the Constitution. Rules I and II require a supermajority of three-fourths of the General Conference and a three-fourths majority of the aggregate vote of the lay and clergy members of all the annual conferences. Changes to rules III–VI require a two-thirds majority, the same as the rest of the Constitution.

The Restrictive Rules protect the Articles of Religion, the Confession of Faith, the itinerant general nature of UM episcopacy, the privilege of clergy and members to a right to trial, the General Rules, and the use of certain funds for the support of retired or disabled preachers.

These rules have been, in very similar form, a part of the Constitutions of The UMC's predecessor denominations since the earliest Constitution was composed at The MEC General Conference of 1808. This General Conference shifted direct decision-making authority from Bishop Asbury and newly elected Bishop McKendree to the legislative processes of the General Conference. The Restrictive Rules and the establishment of the General Conference as a delegated conference have been a part of the Methodist identity ever since.

See also: www.umc.org/what-we-believe/glossary-restrictive-rules-the.

Ritual

And I have prepared a Liturgy little differing from that of the Church of England . . . which I advise all the Travelling-Preachers to use, on the Lord's Day, in all their Congregations, reading the Litany only on Wednesdays and Fridays, and praying extemporare on all other days. I also advise the Elders to administer the Supper of the Lord on every Lord's Day. —John Wesley, Letter to Dr. COKE, Mr. ASBURY, and our Brethren in NORTH AMERICA, in John Telford, ed., *The Letters of the Rev. John Wesley* (London: Epworth Press, 1931), 7:237–38, as in MEA II, 72.

The General Conference has the constitutional responsibility "to provide and revise the hymnal and ritual of the Church and to regulate all matters relating to the form and mode of worship" (17.6). The ritual of the Church includes the liturgies for special services, such as weddings and funerals, as well as orders and texts for use within the context of divine worship, including the sacraments of baptism and Holy Communion (Lord's Supper). The rituals of The UMC are found in *The United Methodist Hymnal* and *The Book of Worship*, as well as on the website for the GBOD (1113).

Original MEC liturgies and services were based on the Anglican tradition of John Wesley. Article XXII of the Articles of Religion, as revised by Wesley for the new MEC denomination, states that a diversity of "rites and ceremonies" is understandable due to differences in "countries, times, and men's [and women's] manners." The article also states, however, that those who decide "through private judgment" to change the ritual as it has been formed and approved by the denomination make it an offense "against the common order" and deserving of rebuke. (See 104.)

See also: www.umcdiscipleship.org/worship/worship-planning.

Sacraments

> I have accordingly appointed Dr. Coke and Mr. Francis Asbury, to be joint Superintendents over our Brethren in North America: As also Richard Whatcoat and Thomas Vasey, to act as Elders among them, by baptizing and administering the Lord's Supper. And I have prepared a Liturgy . . . which I advise all the Travelling-Preachers to use, . . . I also advise the Elders to administer the Supper of the Lord on every Lord's Day. —John Wesley, Letter to Dr. COKE, Mr. ASBURY, and our Brethren in NORTH AMERICA, in John Telford, ed., *The Letters of the Rev. John Wesley* (London: Epworth Press, 1931), 7:237–38, as in MEA II, 71.

The two sacraments observed in United Methodism—*baptism* and the *Lord's Supper* (Holy Communion, the Eucharist)—are visible means and signs of God's invisible grace, practiced or decreed by Jesus Christ, and thus, to be practiced by the Christian community. The sacraments help Christians acknowledge, experience, and grow in God's grace. They also serve as reminders of God's redemptive purpose for the world, expressed in and through Jesus's life, ministry, suffering, death, and resurrection (104, Articles XVI [Of the Sacraments], Confession VI [The Sacraments]).

Elders are ordained, in part, to the administration of the sacraments (303.2). By virtue of being licensed for ministry, provisional *elders* and *deacons* may also administer sacraments in the location where they serve (326.2, 328). *Deacons* are ordained and assist with this administration or preside in the celebration of the sacraments in offering grace to the world (328), *Local pastors* are approved for administering the sacraments in the *local church* to which they are appointed (340.2 *b)* (1)).

While reticent to allow a new Methodist *Church* to be established in the US following the Revolutionary War, John Wesley and leaders of the Methodist movement in the original colonies were deeply concerned about the lack of access to the sacraments in the Methodist societies. Priests of the Church of England had fled the colonies, and the newly formed Protestant Episcopal Church was not very welcoming to the more enthusiastic elements of Methodism. A key reason Wesley approved the new *Church* was because Methodist preachers needed to be ordained so that they could administer sacraments. A group of preachers in Virginia almost caused a schism because they began ordaining one another in order to offer sacraments to their people in 1780, prior to the formation of the *Church* in 1784. Francis Asbury was able to quell their rebellion long enough to establish the new *Church* and get the preachers ordained!

See also: John Wigger, *American Saint: Francis Asbury and the Methodists* (New York: Oxford Press, 2009).

Sacristy

Everything used in our worship services has a place to rest. When worship enhancing items are not in the sanctuary, they are respectfully stored in the sacristy. —From Memorial United Methodist Church, Avon, CT; www .avonunitedmethodist.com/content.cfm?id=439, accessed June 2, 2017.

A sacristy is a closet or room in a *local church* where the altarware and materials for the *sacraments* are kept safe and clean. Due to the spiritual and financial value of the equipment, the sacristy is often kept locked. Sometimes it is the same as the robing room for *clergy* and choir members, and sometimes it is located in or near the kitchen. A closet with a small refrigerator and large sink (not in a bathroom!) can be very helpful for maintaining the Communion elements and the cleanliness and beauty of the altarware.

In the early days of Methodism, the *Discipline* instructed that the stewards, the *lay leaders*, of the *charge* were responsible for providing the elements for the Holy Communion services. No mention is ever made about a sacristy. When Methodists gathered in small chapels, the traveling preachers often carried their own altarware for the *sacraments*. One can suppose that, as *churches* grew in number and Methodists grew in wealth, *churches* began to own their own altarware and thus needed a place for storage when it was not in use.

See also: www.youtube.com/watch?v=VcaMJotrOhA.

Safe Sanctuaries®

¶246. Great care shall be exercised in the selection of teachers, officers, and other workers in the church school. They shall be elected annually. —*Discipline*, MC, 1964.

Safe Sanctuaries® is a trademarked publication and process for the training and development of policies and procedures by any ministry involved with vulnerable populations. As a denominational strategy it is used to reduce the occurrence of sexual abuse of children, youth, and vulnerable adults while they participate in programs of the local church and other ministries. Every local church is expected to enforce Safe Sanctuaries® policies and strategies. The annual conference is responsible for monitoring compliance of local churches with Safe Sanctuaries® policies. The GBOD website has all of the approved Safe Sanctuaries® policies and steps that local churches should take to fulfill this obligation.

Safe Sanctuaries® came about through the establishment in 1990 of a fund by Frank O'Neal, a teacher from Tennessee. He sought to challenge clergy and congregations to create systems within the life of their churches that would prevent, intervene in, and eliminate child abuse in churches. Beginning as a brochure for youth ministries and building on resolutions of the 1996 General Conference regarding the rights of children and sexual misconduct of clergy, the work has now expanded so that every annual conference has a policy, and each local church is expected to participate in Safe Sanctuaries® training, policy development, and implementation.

See: https://store.umcdiscipleship.org.

Schools of Theology

> The demand for superior theological training in our Church shows itself in a two-fold form, arising from the upward tendency of Methodism, like any other successful and progressive principle, from the lower to the higher stratum of society. The people are hungry for a higher style of sermonizing, and they will have it, or leave our communion. We thus yearly lose large numbers of those whose intelligent influence we need the most. We train up children in the bosom of the Church, who leave us at the very time they are prepared for usefulness. —James Strong, "A Central Theological Seminary for Our Church," *Christian Advocate* (New York: 22 December 1853), 201.

Oversight of the schools of theology acceptable for the preparation of UM *clergy* is the responsibility of the University Senate within the *GBHEM* (1416.3 *d*)). All *clergy* in The UMC are required to complete a program of theological education. One can complete either a Master of Divinity (MDiv) degree (*elders* and most *deacon* candidates) or the Basic Graduate Theological Studies core curriculum (some *deacon* candidates) at an approved seminary or through the *Course of Study* (local *pastors* and some *elders*).

Official UM schools in the US include: Boston University School of Theology, Candler School of Theology (Emory University, Atlanta, GA), Claremont School of Theology (Claremont, CA), Drew University Theological School (Madison, NJ), Duke Divinity School (Durham, NC), Gammon Theological Seminary (ITC, Atlanta, GA), Garrett-Evangelical Theological Seminary

(Evanston, IL), Iliff School of Theology (Denver, CO), Methodist Theological School in Ohio (Delaware, OH), Perkins School of Theology (SMU, Dallas, TX), Saint Paul School of Theology (Leawood, KS), United Theological Seminary (Dayton, OH), and Wesley Theological Seminary (Washington, DC). These schools receive financial support from apportionments through the Ministerial Education Fund (1416.3 *a)-b)*).

The University Senate also maintains a list of non-UM theology schools, approved for UM students. *Central conferences* have the flexibility to establish schools as well.

While several other schools, now known as official UM schools of theology, were established earlier, Drew was the first actually established by a Methodist denomination. What is now the Boston School of Theology was established in 1839; other schools established in the nineteenth century include Garrett-Evangelical (a merger among three institutes), Iliff, Claremont, and Gammon, all by The MEC; United, by The UBC; and Wesley, by The MPC. The MECS opened Perkins, Candler, and Duke in the early part of the twentieth century.

See also: www.gbhem.org.

Scouts

> Truly, ours is a circle of friendships, united by our ideals. —Juliette Gordon Low (founder of Girl Scouts of the USA).

> Try and leave the world a little better than you found it. —Robert Baden-Powell (founder of Boy Scouts of America).

Scouting is an example of a civic youth-serving agency, which is encouraged and supported by the *GCUMM* and the *annual conference* scouting coordinator (648, Article 5, *d*); 671, Article 5 *b*); 2302.5). When a *local church* is involved with scouting it should have a scouting coordinator, who reports to the *Church Council*, and a partnership agreement (253, 256.4). It is extremely helpful, but not required, for the troop leader to be a *professing member* of the *local church*.

Scouting began in England in 1908, and in the US in 1910. According to the Boy Scouts of America, Protestant *churches* had established more than four hundred troops by 1915. Girl Scouts began in 1912. Both have official faith-based emphases that support a child's exploration of faith. The MC officially endorsed scouting in 1919.

See also: www.scouting.org; www.resourceumc.org/en/content/scouting -another-church-door.

Social Creed

> The rich have grown so very much richer as to widen the gulf between the man of very large means and the man who makes each day's livelihood by that day's work; and those who with sincerity, and efficiency, and deep conviction, back together for mutual help, as you are banded—not only for one to reach down and help another, but for each to extend his hand in help to, and to take the hand extended to him in help by his brother. Those of you who do that are those who can do most to keep the gulf from becoming too wide. —President Theodore Roosevelt, Address to The MEC, May 19, 1908.

The Social Creed, along with its Companion Litany, is a tool for use in Sunday *worship* that reminds worshippers of ways in which our *discipleship* leads to participation in the *mission* of God and the transformation of the world. (164). There is also A Companion Litany to Our Social Creed adopted in 2008 for use in worship and devotional settings (164).

First adopted by The MEC in 1908, the Social Creed grew in use in various Methodist denominations throughout the early part of the twentieth century. It was written as a theological statement against the social ills that resulted from the industrialization of the economy and the accompanying horrible conditions for workers. It was added as a resolution to the *Discipline* of the Uniting Conference in 1939, reinstated in the *Discipline* with the merger in 1968, and updated at the 2008 *General Conference*.

See also: www.umc.org/what-we-believe/social-principles-social-creed.

Social Media—*See* Media

Social Principles

> But what of the women—mothers of children—some of them leading kiddies by the hand or even trundling baby carriages in the picket line; middle-aged women; elderly women? They are of the European peasant type; many of them must within the decade have changed their old country life for the textile mills of New Jersey. They walked out of the mills with their men and their young folk. For three months now they have been living on meagre strike funds. And their spirits are still undaunted. —Winifred Chappell, "Women of Passaic," *Christian Century* 43, no. 18 (May 6, 1926): 582–83. (Winifred Chappell was a researcher/activist with the Methodist Federation for Social Service.)

The UMC inherited the concept of the Social Principles from The EUBC tradition. These principles function as a call to faithfulness, to instruction, and to prayerful dialogue. The Social Principles are not *church* law, but are a means by which the *General Conference* can "speak to issues in the contemporary world from a sound biblical and theological foundation" (Part V, Preface).

The *GBCS* is responsible for teaching and interpreting of the Social Principles. The *Book of Resolutions* is organized on the basis of the Social Principles and contains resolutions passed by the *General Conference*, most of which speak to contemporary, real-world dilemmas that relate directly to the Social Principles. The Social Principles are grouped together in four main sections:

(160) I. COMMUNITY OF ALL CREATION; PREFACE; CREATION IN PERIL; A. Destruction of Ecosystems; B. Global Warming and Climate Change; C. Dependence on Fossil Fuels; STEWARDSHIP OF CREATION; A. Environmental Racism; B. Sustainable Policies and Practices;

(161) II. THE ECONOMIC COMMUNITY; PREFACE; ECONOMIC CHALLENGES; A. Globalization; B. Poverty and Income Inequality; C. Human Trafficking and Slavery; D. Graft, Bribery, and Corruption;

ECONOMIC JUSTICE; A. Farming and Agricultural Production; B. The Dignity of Work; C. Corporate Responsibility;

(162) III. THE SOCIAL COMMUNITY; PREFACE; THE NURTURING COMMUNITY; A. The Family; B. Human Sexuality; C. Marriage; OTHER SOCIAL ISSUES; A. Substance Abuse, Alcohol, and Tobacco; B. Bullying and Other Forms of Violence; C. Colonialism, Neocolonialism, and Their Consequences; D. Death with Dignity; 1. Faithful Care of Dying People; 2. Euthanasia and Suicide; E. Gambling; F. Gender Equality and Diversity; G. Media and Communication Technologies; H. Pornography; I. Medical Experimentation and Research; J. Organ Donation and Transplantation; K. Reproductive Health and Abortion; L. Racism, Ethnocentrism, and Tribalism; M. Sexual Harassment, Abuse, and Assault;

(163) IV. THE POLITICAL COMMUNITY; PREFACE; GOVERNMENT RESPONSIBILITIES; A. Church and Governments; B. Civil Disobedience; C. Restorative Justice; D. Criminal Justice; E. War and Military Service; BASIC RIGHTS AND FREEDOMS; A. Health Care; B. Children and Young People; C. Elders and the Aging; D. Women and Girls; E. Indigenous, Native, and Aboriginal Communities; F. Migrants, Immigrants, and Refugees; G. People with Disabilities; H. Religious Minorities.

While both The MC and UB had embraced the Social Creed in the first decade of the 1900s, the Social Principles most clearly echo the principles established by the newly formed EUBC given voice in 1946. The "Basic Beliefs Regarding Social Issues" detailed six areas of social concern that clearly precede the "Communities" as defined in the current Social Principles: the *Church* and Economic Life, Community Life, Family Life, Moral and Social Conduct, Racial and Cultural Relations, and World Order. The former structure and content of the Social Principles were presented by a Social Principles Study Commission at the 1970 *General Conference* and approved in 1972. They were amended at each *General Conference* thereafter. The current form of the Social Principles was adopted at the 2024 General Conference.

See also: www.umc-gbcs.org; https://www.umcjustice.org/who-we-are/social-principles-as-adopted-by-general-conference-charlotte-2024.

Special Sundays

The College will be under the presidentship of the Bishops of our church for the time being: and is to be supported by yearly collections throughout our circuits, and any endowments which our friends may think proper to give and bequeath. —*Discipline*, 1789, §XXX. "On the Plan of Education established in Cokesbury College."

The *General Conference* identifies Special Sundays that emphasize a Church-wide calling to learn about and support (262). *UMCom* provides on their website promotional materials for *local churches* for all of these Special Sundays (1806.12).

Six of them have associated *offerings* that *local churches* are expected to remit along with *apportionments* that go to *general agencies* for distribution to special programs. The six with a general-church *offering* are: Human Relations Day (263.1, 825.1), UMCOR Sunday (263.2, 825.2, 1315.1 *c*) (5)), World Communion Sunday (263.3, 825.4), United Methodist Student Day (263.4, 825.3), Peace with Justice Sunday (263.5, 825.5), and Native American Ministries Sunday (263.6, 825.6).

The five Special Sundays without an *offering* are: Heritage Sunday (264.1), Laity Sunday (264.2), Organ and Tissue Donor Sunday (263.3), Men's Ministry Sunday (264.4), and Women's Ministry Sunday (264.5).

There are, in addition, five Special Sundays with a direct appeal for an *offering* for funds that remain for distribution and use within the *annual conference*: Christian Education Sunday (265.1, 1109.7), Golden Cross Sunday (265.2), Rural Life Sunday (265.3), Disability Awareness Sunday (265.4), and Volunteers in Mission Awareness Sunday (265.5). Annual conferences may also identify their own Special Sundays and *offerings*.

Prior to the establishment of regular weekly *offerings* during *worship* services (in the early 1900s) and annual *stewardship* campaigns that committed members to planned, regular, anticipated giving, every collection taken up at an event such as a Love Feast, meetings such as quarterly conferences, or a *worship* service was a direct appeal for a specific purpose. By 1912, The MEC was advocating for a systematic process for determining special *offerings* in conjunction with general-church *apportionments*. What emerged was a "consolidated *apportionment*" for most of the work of the *Church*. Today, only the *General Conference* determines the Churchwide Special Sundays.

See also: www.umcgiving.org/how-we-give#sundays.

Staff Employed by the Local Church

¶247.1. On nomination of the pastor, with the concurrence of the Commission on Education and the Committee on Pastoral Relations or the committee on lay Personnel, the Quarterly Conference may employ, or may annually request the bishop to appoint, a director or minister of Christian education or an educational assistant, . . . a director of or minister of music, or a music assistant. —*Discipline*, MC, 1964.

Employed staff of a *local church* are those hired under the auspices of the *Pastor/Staff Parish Relations Committee* and *Church Council*, who are not under *appointment* by the *bishop*. This includes both *laypersons* and *clergy* who are not under *appointment* or who are from another denomination. Staff are hired to do work best done by someone other than *volunteers* or the appointed *pastor(s)* and to maximize their "stewardship of time" (258.2). Each staff member shall have a written job description and job title as well as consultations with and support from the *Pastor/Staff Parish Relations Committee* for professional and spiritual growth and the pursuit of certifications in their specialty areas.

Practices for the management of staff should be outlined in *local church policies* and procedures that have been approved by the *Church Council*. In the absence of such policies and procedures, the *pastor* and *Pastor/Staff Parish Relations Committee* have the authority to handle all staff-related matters. In addition, the *Pastor/Staff Parish Relations Committee* and *Church Council* shall provide for adequate health insurance and life insurance, severance pay, and pension for lay employees (258.2 *g*) (12)).

Local churches are responsible for following all civil *laws* pertaining to employment practices, including but not limited to hiring and firing, personnel taxes, workers' compensation, background checks, and policies related to sexual harassment and violence in the workplace. The best resource for this information is Section III of the *Legal Manual* provided by the *GCFA* (258.2 *g)* (15)).

It is difficult to pinpoint when local *churches, annual conferences*, and agencies began to employ lay staff persons. In 1888, the order of *deaconess* was created, which called and employed laywomen to work, primarily with the poor, but that included a wide range of other possible activities as well. Since the reunification of The MEC, MECS, and MPC in 1939, lay professional staff have been hired on an increasing basis by *local churches*. While no evidence of direction regarding lay staff was evident in the 1940 MC *Discipline,* by the 1964 *Discipline*, specific directions were given for a Committee on Lay Personnel (145.3) as well as a separate Committee on Lay Personnel, responsible for establishing and maintaining policies and determining compensation and benefits. The 1972 *Discipline* of The UMC mentioned the responsibility for lay staff positions under the *Pastor/Staff Parish Relations Committee* and spoke to the importance of addressing benefits as well as compensation. The importance of job descriptions was added in 1984. Policies addressing lay employment by *general agencies* showed up in the 1988 *Discipline*. As the *Church* entered the twenty-first century, it became clear that local *churches* must establish and implement policies for employed staff in order to comply with both legal and ethical mandates of The UMC.

See also: www.umcdiscipleship.org.

Standing Committee on Central Conference Matters—*See* Central Conferences

Stewardship

Do You Know That: Christian stewardship succeeds even when consecration seems to fail? . . . is true consecration in work clothes? . . . is "cashing

up" on what has been consecrated? . . . is the only true test of actual consecration? . . . is in full accord with all Scripture readings? . . . begins with giving a tithe of our increase to God? . . . goes beyond the tithe by additional
free-will offerings? . . . does not increase the burden of giving in any case?
. . . brings back the joy experienced at conversion? . . . is recommended by
every one who has tested it? —*Western Christian Advocate* 80, 1082 (10)
(September 16, 1914).

Faithful stewardship is most holistically described as the generous and responsible management of the resources and gifts that God has given to people and
communities, including time, talents, personal resources, and the gifts of God's
creation. United Methodist stewardship is rooted in the Gospels, in Jesus's par-
ables of the faithful and unfaithful stewards. The *GBOD* describes stewardship
as the task of "nurturing generous living." It produces stewardship materials for
use by *local churches*. Faithful stewardship is encompassed by the vows taken
when a person joins a *church*, the promise to support the *local church* and The
UMC with our prayers, presence, gifts, service, and witness (217).

Local churches are strongly encouraged to establish stewardship ministry
groups, led by a coordinator who sits on the *Committee on Finance* (258.4).
Financial stewardship, however, is only one area of responsibility when stewardship is understood in a more biblical way. The stewardship ministry group
is responsible for planning approaches that enhance generosity, understood
both broadly and financially, in the *local church* (254).

Beginning with the 1785 *Discipline*, Section XXXIV was titled "On the
Qualification and Duty of Stewards," indicating the growing need for local lay leadership and management of the societies while preachers traveled
throughout their circuits. *Lay leaders* were, by definition, called to responsible
stewardship of all resources in their care. In the early 1920s, language in the
Discipline shifted from calling *lay leaders* "stewards" to defining stewardship
as a responsibility of all Christians. *Local church* committees and positions,
such as the director of stewardship for the Church School, and the Church
Committee on Stewardship were defined for the first time in the *Disciplines*
of the late 1920s.

See also: www.umc.org.

Tax-Exempt Status

Congress has enacted special tax laws that apply to churches, religious organizations and ministers in recognition of their unique status in American society and of their rights guaranteed by the First Amendment of the Constitution of the United States. Churches and religious organizations are generally exempt from income tax and receive other favorable treatment under the tax law; however, certain income of a church or religious organization may be subject to tax, such as income from an unrelated business. —*IRS Tax Guide for Churches and Religious Organizations*, Publication 1828; www.irs .gov/pub/irs-pdf/p1828.pdf.

Churches are considered tax-exempt with regard to most taxes throughout the US Tax laws in other countries may be applied differently. Tax-exemption is best protected through *incorporation of the local church* as a 501(c)(3) organization. The UMC applied for and received a group tax-exemption ruling from the IRS in 1974, so *local churches* are covered under this ruling. Some donors and grant-making organizations may require a *church's* tax-xempt certificate, and so it is important to be aware of and have easy access to the information needed to explain the group ruling (see below). It is in the best interest of some organizations to go ahead and establish their own 501(c)(3) status. Some states require that *churches* be registered as tax-exempt organizations.

This status prohibits a *local church* from supporting and advocating for votes for or against political candidates and issues. *Pastors* and *churches* may state personal opinions and be involved in political activities as individuals, but not as representatives of the *church* or in the course of an official *church* function. The IRS provides a tax guide for *churches* (see below). In addition, the *GCFA* provides an online application for tax-exemption (see below).

According to Elizabeth Livingston's article "A Bright Line Points Toward Legal Compromise" (see below), the tax-exempt status awarded to *churches* is rooted in millennia of similar practices traced to early Egypt and other ancient civilizations, which exempted priests and temples from taxes. Likewise, Constantine exempted *churches* from taxes, as did medieval societies. England also exempted charitable organizations, and included *churches* as one of four different types of charitable organizations. American colonies originally followed a European-like system of establishing a church-state relationship in which the established *church* received financial support through some form of taxation and likewise did not have to pay into taxes. The US Constitution abolished the remnants of this system, but most people believed that *churches* should be accorded some privileges with regard to tax-exemption. By 1802, the Congress had established a nationwide exemption from *property taxes* for *churches* and other nonprofit organizations. As stated in the UM *Legal Manual* (Section 4, page 17), tax exemption is not a guarantee protected by the First Amendment.

See also: www.gcfa.org; Elizabeth A. Livingston, "A Bright Line Points Toward Legal Compromise: IRS Condoned Lobbying Activities for Religious Entities and Non-Profits," *Rutgers Journal of Law and Religion* 9, no. 2 (Spring 2008): 2–4.

Taxes Churches Pay—*See* Property Taxes; Staff Employed by the Local Church

Tithe/Tithing

> The first of these is (he that heareth let him understand!) Gain all you can!
> . . . But this it is certain we ought not to do: we ought not to gain money at
> the expense of life, nor at the expense of our health. . . . II.1 . . . Save all you
> can! Do not throw the precious talent into the sea. III.6. Gain all you can,
> . . . Save all you can. Then give all you can. —Sermon 50, Luke 16.9, "The
> Use of Money," Wesley, *Works*, 266–69.

The roots of tithing are found in the biblical practice of returning one-tenth of one's harvest back to God as an act of thanksgiving. In Leviticus, a faithful Jew gave three tithes—one tenth each for the support of the priests (the Levites), for the temple and festivals, and for the poor. In United Methodism, the offering of a tithe of one's income is a spiritual practice of stewardship that acknowledges that all we have and have earned belongs to God, indeed, comes from God in the first place. A Christian understands that we hold property in "solemn trust" and it is to be "used responsibly for human good under the sovereignty of God" (104, Article XV, page 77). Tithing is a spiritual discipline that undergirds the importance of simple living and the General Rule "to do good" through frugality (104).

Tithing was introduced as a spiritual discipline in US Protestant churches in the mid-1870s. The concept first emerged in The MECS *Discipline* in 1922, in the name of a committee of the [local] Church Board of Lay Activities, the "Stewardship and Tithing" committee.

See also: www.umcdiscipleship.org.

Treasurer of a Local Church

¶196. Ans. 2. It shall be the duty of the stewards to organize by electing a chairman, secretary, and treasurer; to make estimates of expenses and provision for the support of the gospel; to take an exact account of all the money, or other provision, collected for the support of the ministry; to make an accurate return of every expenditure of money. —*Discipline*, MECS, 1914.

The treasurer of a *local church* disburses funds as represented in the *church* budget and as determined by the *Church Council*. The treasurer sends monthly installments on *apportionments* to the conference treasurer and makes regular, detailed reports of the income and expenditures of the *church* to the *Committee on Finance* and *Church Council* (258.4 *b*)). The records of the treasurer are subject to an annual audit (258.4 *d*)).

The treasurer is a member of the *Church Council* and the *Committee on Finance* (252.5 *f*), 258.4). The treasurer may be either a paid *staff* person or a *volunteer* elected by the *charge conference* (249.4). If *staff*, the treasurer shall serve on these committees with voice, but not vote (258.4). The treasurer shall not also hold the office of *financial secretary*, or be an immediate family member of the *financial secretary* or of an appointed *clergy* member's family (258.4).

Originally, in The MECS and MEC, the *church* treasurer was the equivalent of one of the three elected leaders of the board of stewards in each *charge*.

They were appointed by the *pastor*, but confirmed by and amenable to the quarterly conference. The actual position of treasurer emerged in The MECS *Discipline* of 1938.

See also: www.gcfa.org; Bruce J. Nuffer, *The Church Treasurer's Manual: A Practical Guide for Managing Church Finances* (Kansas City: Beacon Hill Press, 2008).

Trials

> Quest. 1. How shall a suspected member (of a society) be brought to trial?
>
> . . . First let private reproof be given by a Leader or Preacher; if there be an acknowledgement of the fault and proper humiliation, the person may remain. . . .
>
> Quest. 2. What shall be done in cases of improper tempers, word or actions, or a breach of the articles and disciplines (by clergy)? —*Discipline*, 1785, §XXXII. "On bringing to Trial, finding guilty, reproving, suspending and excluding disorderly Persons from Society and Church-Privileges."

Both laity and *clergy*, including *bishops*, are subject to the possibility of a *complaint* and chargeable offense that may result in an investigation and *church* trial. A trial takes place only when all other attempts to resolve a case have been unsuccessful. Steps are described in detail in the *Discipline* for filing a *complaint* that may be determined to be a chargeable offense by the *bishop*, proceeding through an investigation, determining whether or not to go to trial, and carrying out a trial (2701-2719). The right to a trial is protected by *Restrictive Rule* 21, found in Section III, Article VI of the *Constitution* (21). The *GCFA* has a handbook on the administrative and judicial procedures for this kind of process.

The right to trial of either a *layperson* or *clergyperson* was first established in the 1785 *Discipline*, Sections XXXII and XXXIII. It was codified in the original *Constitution* of 1808, as one of the *Restrictive Rules*. Even at the time, trials were viewed as a last resort after attempts to correct a person's misbelief or misbehavior had failed.

See also: www.umc.org/what-we-believe; www.gcfa.org, particularly Administrative & Judicial Procedures Handbook.

Trust Clause

> Question 4. What shall be done for the security of our preaching-houses, and the premices belonging thereto?
>
> Answer. Let the following plan of a deed of settlement, be brought into effect in all possible places, and as far as the laws of the states respectively will admit of it. —*Discipline*, MEC, 1798, ch. III, section 1.

The trust clause is a key characteristic of historic Methodism's connectional relationships and assists with holding our churches, agencies, and institutions accountable to the denomination (2501). A trust clause is required in all deeds for real property of local churches, general agencies, and institutions of The UMC. There are five versions of the actual language required in the deeds, the wording for which is dependent on the use of the property—as a place of worship, a parsonage, or for the more general benefit of the denomination (2501, 2503.1-5).

Even if a trust clause is absent from a deed, the property is still held in trust for the benefit of the denomination. The local church or agency or Board of Trustees is not absolved of this responsibility if one of the following three conditions is met: the property was conveyed to a UM church or predecessor denomination; it has used the name, customs, and polity of The UMC or a predecessor and is known to the community as a part of the denomination; and/or it has accepted pastors appointed by a bishop or employed by the district superintendent of the district or annual conference of The UMC or predecessor denomination (2503.6). A trust clause is unnecessary in only one instance: when a qualification is written into the deed that upon the termination of the property's use as a place of divine worship, the property is to revert back to the grantor of the deed (2503.1). The district superintendent and conference treasurer have been trained to assist organizations with the inclusion of the trust clause in deeds.

John Wesley instituted a "model deed" to protect English Methodist preaching chapels from being misused for teaching and preaching doctrines unacceptable to Methodism. A US version, called the "Deed of Settlement," was first written into the *Discipline* in 1796.

See also: www.gcfa.org.

Trustees—*See* Board of Trustees

United Methodist Church Website

> In the month of September this year (1826) was commenced the publication of the Christian Advocate, a weekly periodical devoted especially to the interests of the Methodist Episcopal Church and to general intelligence. The appearance of this weekly sheet, filled as it was, with useful and interesting matter, gave great satisfaction to the members and friends of our Church, and the number of subscribers in a very short time amounted to about thirty thousand. —Bangs, vol. 3, 322.

The official UM website is www.umc.org. It serves as a highly comprehensive source of information, resources, and news about The UMC and Methodism; as a tool for discovering the network of organizations that make up The UMC; and as a directory for leaders throughout its international connection.

The *Methodist Magazine* (1789–90) and the *Christian Advocate*, founded in 1826 by The MEC as a weekly newssheet, were the first official communications sources for early Methodists. The *Christian Advocate* continued until 1972. Eventually annual conferences published their own versions of the *Advocate*, and other newspapers. Now, however, many conferences have their own websites.

See also: www.umc.org.

United Methodist Committee on Relief (UMCOR)

> Compelled by Christ to be a voice of conscience on behalf of the people called Methodist, UMCOR works globally to alleviate human suffering and advance hope and healing. —UMCOR Mission Statement; www.umcor .org, accessed May 14, 2017.

The United Methodist Committee on Relief (UMCOR) is an incorporated 501(c)(3), nonprofit corporation responsible for helping UMs—persons, *churches, annual conferences,* and other units—engage directly in ministries of "relief, rehabilitation, and service" as these areas relate to the issues of "displaced persons, hunger and poverty, disaster response, and disaster risk reduction" (1315.1). The UMCOR is a highly rated charity because 100 percent of all designated giving goes directly to the ministry for which it has been given. It is supported by UMCOR Sunday offerings (see *Special Sundays*) and designated giving.

The UMCOR is directly related to the *GBGM* through the election of its board of directors and adherence to the policies and bylaws of the *GBGM* (1315.1 *b*)). The UMCOR's reach is global, working with conference units as well as ecumenical, interdenominational, and interfaith organizations, to identify, advocate for, and assist with their mandated areas of responsibility. The UMCOR carries out these responsibilities through direct service, training, and working with local leaders, and administering programs and the distribution of funds. The UMCOR ministries seek to preserve and improve human dignity and quality of life without restricting the populations they serve, while carrying out their responsibilities in the spirit of Jesus Christ (1315.1 *c*), *d*)).

The UMCOR was founded originally as the Methodist Committee for Overseas Relief in 1940, in response to the dire human suffering caused by World War II. It was renamed, and its mission was broadened to include response to other needs, especially those of natural disasters, in 1972.

See also: www.umcor.org/.

United Methodist Doctrinal Standards

Doctrinal standards seek to assist the worshipping community in developing this accountability to Scripture in six complementary ways in the Wesleyan tradition: (1) . . . serves as an authoritative guide to one seeking the essential and central truth of Scripture. (2) They serve as a dependable standard to which appeal can be made in matters of controversy. (3) They serve as a trustworthy source by which the truth is attested and received. . . . (4) . . . serve to regulate the teaching office of the churches. . . . (5) . . . unite a diverse church body in a common doctrinal purpose. And (6) they defend against abuses (such as the misuse of church property, a major motive for the Restrictive Rule to be written) by those who would demean or degrade these teachings. —Thomas Oden, *Doctrinal Standards in the Wesleyan Tradition*, Revised Edition (Nashville: Abingdon Press, 2008), 15–16.

The *Discipline* defines the Doctrinal Standards of The UMC as the Methodist *Articles of Religion*, The EUBC *Confession of Faith*, Wesley's Sermons, and *Explanatory Notes on the New Testament*. The *General Rules* are also included as an accompaniment to the Doctrinal Standards. Together they are framed as the UM "Foundational Documents" and are found in the 2020/2024 *Discipline* (103-104).

While the *Articles of Religion* have remained nearly unchanged, the *Confession of Faith* went through several revisions before merger. They were deemed congruent and united side by side in the 1968 *Discipline* of the newly merged UMC.

See also: https://www.umc.org/en/who-we-are/what-we-believe; Thomas C. Oden, *Doctrinal Standards in the Wesleyan Tradition* (Nashville: Abingdon Press, 2008).

United Methodist Foundational Documents—*See* United Methodist Doctrinal Standards

United Methodist Hymnal

> To remedy these inconveniences, measures have been adopted to prepare a revised edition of our Hymn Book, such a one as should exclude the defects and retain the excellences of the one heretofore published. The principal improvements which have been made consist in restoring those which had been altered to their original state, as they came from the poetical pen of the Wesleys; names that will ever be held dear and in high estimation by every lover of sacred poetry. —Preface of the new Hymn Book published in 1820, as reported in Bangs, vol. 3, 134.

From the beginning, Methodists have been a "singing people," and throughout its history the *Church* has produced the hymnals of a singing faith. The Wesley brothers used hymn singing as a means of teaching their Methodist theology, and Wesleyan hymnody continues to be a source and expression of UM doctrine. The *General Conference* provides for the hymnal (17. Article IV.6); the Worship area of the *GBOD* fosters resources for worship and recommends to *General Conference* the need for future editions; The *UMPH* publishes the official hymnal.

Charles Wesley wrote over 6,500 hymns during his lifetime, and many of these have been utilized in the *worship* of the *church* since his day. In 1784, John Wesley sent a new hymnbook to North America, which was adopted by the "Christmas Conference," and subsequent *General Conferences* have continued to publish in this spirit. The most recent *United Methodist Hymnal* was published in 1989. Since that time, additional hymnals and supplemental songbooks have been published in Spanish and English (1113.3).

See also: www.hymnary.org/hymnal/UMH; www.umc.org/news-and-media/gc2016-turning-the-page-on-the-united-methodist-hymnal; www.unitedmethodistreporter.com/2016/12/15/survey-seeks-input-for-new-united-methodist-hymnal.

United Methodist Men—*See* General Commission on United Methodist Men

United Methodist Publishing House (UMPH)

> By a reference to the books of the agency, in the handwriting of John Dickens, who was the first book-steward, it appears that the first book printed was A Kempis. This entry is dated August 17, 1789. The first volume of the *Arminian Magazine* was published the same year, also the *Hymnbook, Saints' Rest*, and *Primitive Physic*. —Bangs, vol. 1, 306.

The United Methodist Publishing House (UMPH) is the official publisher and distributor of resources for The UMC (1601). It is the descendant of The Evangelical Press and the Otterbein Press of the former EUBC, and the Book Concerns of the predecessor Methodist denominations. The UMPH is responsible for the publication of academic, professional, inspirational, and Sunday school/children and youth materials to be used by the denomination. Cokesbury is the main distributor for The UMPH. Abingdon Press is its most well-known imprint.

John Wesley emphasized the education of both preachers and laity. New preachers and Methodist laity needed resources to help strengthen their Methodist beliefs. He provided lists of books his preachers were expected to read. He also shipped books to the colonies for distribution among the preachers. Asbury educated himself by a diligent practice of reading Wesley's assigned texts and expected the preachers to do the same.

The MEC Book Concern was the first general agency of Methodism, established in Philadelphia in 1789. The Book Concern was established because most local printers were not interested in texts with a comparatively small circulation and highly selective, narrow appeal. After the Revolutionary War, they were not interested in publishing texts for people who had been led, originally, by a well-known Tory. The books were distributed and sold by the traveling preachers. The list of required texts evolved into the original Course of Study, which was then included in the *Discipline*. In 1796, the General Conference decided that the proceeds of the Book Concern would go to support retired and disabled clergy. Proceeds of The UMPH continue to help underwrite the cost of clergy pensions today.

In the early 1800s, clergy were not allowed to write books without the approval of their annual conferences. Following the schisms of 1828 and 1844, The MEC, MECS, and MPC each established their own Book Concern. They were brought together in the 1939 reunification.

See also: https://www.umph.org; www.cokesbury.com.

United Methodist Volunteers in Mission

Mission: To inspire change in the world, To inform, connect and equip volunteers, To interact as servants of Christ. — umvim.org.

A grassroots voluntary organization with *jurisdictional, annual conference*, and *local church* coordinators, United Methodist Volunteers in Mission (UMVIM) supports the development and work of short-term work teams and individual *volunteers* who travel to many different parts of the world. UMVIM is affirmed and provided guidance by the *GBGM* (1302.14). Teams work on a wide variety of projects, including construction, medical clinics, disaster response, and children's programs. The handbook "A Mission Journey: A Handbook for Volunteers" helps teams explore the best ways to be of service and to grow in their own spiritual lives while involved in *mission. Local church* coordinators are required to report to the *charge conference* on an annual basis (247.12).

UMVIM emerged as a lay-driven movement in the Southeastern Jurisdiction in 1972. It now has organizational leadership in each US jurisdiction.

See also: www.umcmission.org, particularly "Volunteers."

United Methodist Women—United Women in Faith

An earnest desire to develop among the ladies of our Church greater interest and activity in our Missions, together with the firm conviction that the pressing needs of our Foreign Missions demand our immediate attention, led, in the month of March, to the organization of the Women's Foreign Missionary Society . . . to meet as far as is possible, the great want experienced by our Eastern Missionaries, of Christian women to labor among the women of those heathen lands. —"Appeal to the Ladies of the Methodist Episcopal Church," *The Heathen Woman's Friend* 1, no. 1 (June 1869): 1–3, as in MEA II, 359.

United Methodist Women (UMW) is an official women's membership organization, the largest women's faith-based organization in the world, engaged in ministry that fosters spiritual formation, leadership development, and ministry with and advocacy for the poor and oppressed. It focuses on the needs of women, youth, and children; community-building among women; and growth in faith, leadership, mission education, and Christian social involvement at the local church, district, annual conference, jurisdictional, and national levels (1901–1902). It is the successor to fourteen historic women's organizations that were active in six Methodist and EUBC predecessor denominations (1905). The UMW also oversees the work of deaconesses, home missioners, and home missionaries (1913–1918).

Every local church is required to have a unit of the UMW, based on the authorized UMW Constitution (256.5). All pastors, including men, are ex officio members of the local UMW (256.5, Article 4). Constitutions for the district, annual conference, jurisdiction, and national units are also found in the *Discipline* (537, 647, 670, 1912). The UMC General Conference voted to make the national policy-making body of the UMW autonomous in 2012. The public-facing name of UMW is now United Women in Faith.

Created originally as a means through which women became missionaries and were empowered to be in missional support and ministry, the early organizations became very active, highly effective outlets for women's leadership in an era when women were neither ordained nor rarely licensed as local preachers, nor allowed to serve in lay leadership roles in the local churches and annual conferences. The MECS first proposed a women's missionary organization in 1872. The UBC organized the Women's Missionary Association in 1875, and The MEC, the Methodist Woman's Foreign Mission Society in 1869, and Women's Home Mission Society in 1880. The MEC also established the Wesleyan Service Guild for women who worked and could not attend weekday meetings. The MPC established the Women's Foreign Missionary

Society in 1879. The Evangelical Association started its Women's Missionary Society in 1884.

See also: www.unitedmethodistwomen.org.

Ushers

St. James understood the pew system when he instructed the ushers in his church as to their duties, "If there come into your assembly (or church) a man with a gold ring and goodly apparel, and there come in also a poor man in vile raiment: and ye have respect to him that weareth the gay clothing and say unto him, 'Sit thou here in a good place' (in the middle section with the four hundred) and say to the poor, 'Stand thou here or sit here (under the gallery) are ye not partial in yourselves and are become judges of evil thoughts?" —Elizabeth Grinnell, "The Pew System as it Worked in One Church," *Northwestern Christian Advocate* 45 (November 3, 1897): 11.

Often the first people that a visitor meets when coming to a *local church*, ushers, along with greeters, extend hospitality to attendees, guests and members alike. Ushers should be available to answer questions and to direct people to not only seats for *worship* but also resources in other parts of the *church*. They will also assist with ensuring that the sanctuary is prepared for *worship* and straightened up following the service. During the service, the ushers will usually take up the *offering*. In some traditions, the ushers direct the participants to the altar table for depositing the *offering*. In addition, they will often bring the elements to the altar table for the *Lord's Supper*, if the elements are not already stationed at the altar. Ushers should also be trained in the basics of medical emergency preparedness and security.

Throughout the history of the Christian faith, persons have been called to, assigned, or elected to a position that fulfilled the roles of the usher. The ministry of ushers is grounded in the tradition of the doorkeepers of the temple during the time of Jesus. In the third-century church, a clerical order of "ostiary" or "porters" was committed specifically to guarding the doors of a *church* against those who would disturb the services. Ushering has been such an assumed role in *worship* life that no attention has been paid to it in the *Discipline*.

See also: John Gilbert, *The Usher's Book: Creating a Welcoming and Safe Environment for Worship* (Nashville: Abingdon Press, 2005).

Vacation Bible School (VBS)

> In the panic connected with the paralysis epidemic all schools under the control of the Daily Vacation Bible School Association were ordered closed. But one school declined to obey the order. The pastor enlarged his staff . . . , arranged for daily inspection of every child . . . , and insisted that the children would be more safe in the cool, clean church under careful supervision than playing indiscriminately in the filth of the hot, burning streets. While the children all about the parish have been stricken, not one of the school children has contracted the dread malady. —"A Summer Bible School Not Stopped by the Infantile Paralysis Epidemic" [South Third Street MEC, Brooklyn], *The Christian Advocate* 91, 1194 (22) (September 17, 1916).

Vacation Bible school (VBS) is a summer spiritual-formation opportunity, primarily for elementary-aged children, but increasingly for all ages, offered by *local churches* in a week-long format. The format involves Bible study, music, crafts, recreational activities, *worship*, and other types of activities, depending on the length of time the program runs during the day and/or evening.

The earliest vacation-based school experiences have been traced back to the summer institutes started by The MEC at Lake Chautauqua, NY, in the early 1870s. By the 1890s, Baptists had picked up the idea and began summer programs for children in Hopedale, IL, and immigrant children in New York City. The program quickly became a part of the Church School movement. In 1921, Methodists, along with Baptists, Presbyterians, Congregationalists, and Christian Churches circulated a joint statement in support of vacation Bible schools. The Methodist Book Concern created its own "Vacation Day School" curriculum in that year.

See also: www.cokesbury.com/forms/DynamicContent
.aspx?id=296&pageid=2510.

Volunteers

> But wherever this is really fixed in the soul it will be shown by its fruits.
> . . . First: By doing no harm, by avoiding evil of every kind, especially that
> which is most generally practiced. Secondly: By doing good; by being in ev-
> ery kind merciful after their power; as they have opportunity, doing good of
> every possible sort. —John Wesley, The first two of the three General Rules
> included in "Rules &c. of the United Societies," 1742–1743.

Volunteers who serve The UMC, their *local church*, and the world, out of
a sense of calling as *laypersons*, are the driving force for "mak[ing] disciples
of Jesus Christ for the transformation of the world" (120). Whether serving on administrative committees or in soup kitchens, whether traveling
to another country on a *mission* team or building a Habitat for Humanity
house, whether trained as a certified *lay servant* or leading the *youth ministry*
in a *local church*, the *mission* and work of the *Church* is totally dependent
on volunteers.

Because of the nature of the world in which we live, volunteers must be willing to submit to background checks, cooperate with Safe Sanctuaries® policies, participate in training, and commit to practice spiritual disciplines as a
foundation upon which their activities are built. Volunteers should be disciples who are *professing members* of The UMC. Volunteers shall not be elected
as members of the *Church Council* unless they are *professing members* of the
local church.

Methodism was essentially a movement carried out by lay volunteers who led
class meetings and bands, and administered the societies as stewards. Local
preachers also served without compensation. Methodism in the American
colonies originated through the leadership of volunteers. Phillip Embury
(d. 1775), a local preacher who emigrated from Ireland to New York City,
was compelled by other Irish Methodists, especially Barbara Heck, to begin
preaching. As the society grew, and once the Wesley Chapel on St. John's

Street was established, it became clear that they needed more help, as Embury also had to work to support himself and his family. They appealed to Wesley for additional leadership. This was a strategic way in which societies expanded throughout the frontier of the new US.

See also: www.umc.org/how-we-serve/volunteer-opportunities.

Weddings

Quest. 1. Do we observe any Evil which has lately prevailed among our Societies? Answ. Many of our Members have married with unawakened Persons. This has had fatal Effects. They have been either hindered for Life, or turned back to Perdition. Let every Preacher publically inforce the Apostle's Caution, "Be ye not unequally yoked together with Unbelievers." —*Discipline*, 1785, §XXI. "On unlawful Marriages."

United Methodist clergy in the US are, by virtue of their *license for pastoral ministry*, agents of the state government for the purpose of performing wedding ceremonies and signing marriage licenses (340.2 *a*)(3)(*a*)). Likewise, in the US, *laypersons* may perform weddings and sign licenses if they are a notary. A *lay supply* or *certified lay minister* shall not perform weddings unless one is also a notary—and signs the license as such. Laws for what constitutes a legal wedding vary from country to country. Some US states require *clergy* to be bonded or registered. *Clergy* should check when performing weddings outside their own state.

The *Discipline* affirms marriage as "a sacred, lifelong covenant that brings two people of faith, an adult man and woman of consenting age or two adult persons of consenting age, into union with one another and deeper relationship with God and the religious community" (Part V Social Principles, ¶162. The Social Community, *The Nurturing Community*, D. Marriage, page 123). Clergy are not required, compelled, or prohibited from performing any marriage, union, or blessing, but "have the right to exercise and preserve their conscience when requested" (340.2 *a*)(3)(*a*)).

Issues regarding marriage have existed throughout the history of Methodism. Both Wesley and Francis Asbury believed that it was far better for Methodist preachers not to marry. Wesley wished he had not. Asbury never did. Such a rule was certainly unenforceable if The MEC was going to survive and grow. *Clergy* were, however, instructed to have a serious conversation with fellow preachers before deciding to marry.

As early as the 1785 *Discipline, clergy* were given boundaries for whom they should not and were not allowed to perform weddings. They were strongly dissuaded from marrying couples when one partner was not a Christian. They were not allowed to marry anyone who had been divorced. Rules regarding who one should marry and the injunction against marrying divorced persons loosened for both *clergy* and laity beginning in the early twentieth century.

See also: www.umcdiscipleship.org.

Wesley, Charles

"Oh, for a Thousand tongues to sing, my great redeemer's praise, The glories of my God and King, the triumphs of his grace." —*The United Methodist Hymnal: Book of United Methodist Worship* (Nashville: The United Methodist Publishing House, 1989), 57. Originally published in 1740, this hymn was written on May 21, 1739 and titled "For the Anniversary Day of One's Conversion" commemorating Charles Wesley's conversion on Whitsunday, May 21, 1738. *Collection of Sacred Poems for 1740*; https://divinity.duke.edu/sites/default/files/documents/05_Hymns_and _Sacred_Poems_%281740%29.pdf.

Charles Wesley, alongside his brother John, was a significant leader in the Methodist movement. He was an anglican priest, the facillitator of the initial Oxford Holy Club, a missionary to Georgia, and an itinerant preacher for a season. He later located in Bristol and London where he continued to serve. In addition, Charles was a prolific hymn writer producing an estimated sixty-five hundred texts during his lifetime, which was a major part of his contribution to the movement. Many of these not only inspired Methodist worship in the societies, but served as a means of teaching the theology of the movement.

Throughout his lifetime, Charles and his brother John published numerous hymnals that became the foundation for Methodist worship and devotion.

As a result, his hymnody has been published not only in Methodist churches for over two hundred years, but many of his hymns have become popular in other denominations as well.

See also: John R. Tyson, *Assist Me to Proclaim: The Life and Hymns of Charles Wesley* (Grand Rapids: Eerdmans Publishing Co., 2007).

Wesley, John

> After some time spent in prayer, the design of our meeting was proposed, namely, to consider, 1. What to teach; 2. How to teach; 3. What to do; that is, how to regulate our doctrine, discipline, and practice. —*Minutes* (June 25, 1744), §1, *Works*, 10:124.

John Wesley is often given credit for being the main organizer of the Methodist movement in England. He was an Anglican Priest, Oxford Fellow, a missionary to the Georgia Colony, and itinerant preacher. Following his Aldersgate experience, he joined the evangelical revival in England through field preaching, offering his message of God's grace in Jesus Christ.

As he sought to renew the faith of the Church of England, Wesley organized the awakened converts into bands, societies, and classes for spiritual growth and nurture, pastoral care, and mission, and built preaching chapels. He provided the General Rules for the United Societies to guide the Christian behavior and morality of those living out the gospel and encouraged the constant observance of the Means of Grace among his followers. Wesley inspired and trained up those among the laity, both men and women, who were called to preach, developed circuits, and held annual conferences with his preachers. His published sermons and *Explanatory Notes Upon the New Testament* secured by the Model Deed gave shape to the uniquely Methodist character of his theology. And he provided leadership and resources for the nascent Methodist Episcopal Church in North America through ordinations, the Sunday Service, the General Rules, and the *Large Minutes* from the preaching conferences.

Though Methodism and the emerging churches in the movement have often emphasized differing aspects of our heritage resulting in the world

Methodist family, most Methodists over two hundred years later still find in their polity elements of the doctrine, connection, and discipline of John Wesley's organization.

See also: Richard P. Heitzenrater, *Wesley and the People Called Methodists*, 2nd ed. (Nashville: Abingdon Press, 1995).

Wesleyan Way of Salvation *(Via Salutis)*

> Let us inquire, What is salvation? The salvation which is here spoken of is not what is frequently understood by that word, the going to heaven, eternal happiness. It is not the soul's going to paradise, termed by our Lord, "Abraham's bosom." It is not a blessing which lies on the other side death; or, as we usually speak, in the other world. The very words of the text itself put this beyond all question: "Ye are saved." It is not something at a distance: it is a present thing; a blessing which, through the free mercy of God, ye are now in possession of. Nay, the words may be rendered, and that with equal propriety, "Ye have been saved": so that the salvation which is here spoken of might be extended to the entire work of God, from the first dawning of grace in the soul, till it is consummated in glory. —Sermon 43, "The Scripture Way of Salvation," Wesley, *Works*, vol. 2, 156.

The UM understanding of the Christian life is grounded in the sermons and writings of John Wesley, as he preached, published, and conferred with people fearful about their spiritual salvation and resigned to their often-wretched states of human existence. Wesley's message was one that sought to save the lost and create a process of growth in *discipleship* that would ultimately result in what came to be known as "perfection in love (perfect love of God and neighbor)."

Essential to Wesley's understanding of grace was his belief that all persons suffered in a fallen state of original sin, but through prevenient grace are given free will to respond to God. In addition to the personal workings of the Holy Spirit, grace is available to all persons in the means of grace. The first is through practices instituted by God as the *ordinances* (also known as the instituted means of grace) or the works of piety. The second is by intentionally engaging in thoughtful and wise practices of holy living (also known as

231

prudential means of grace), such as: classes and bands, and works of mercy including visiting the sick and imprisoned. The third includes the more general means of grace such as self-denial, obedience, and taking up one's cross. Without a relationship with God, however, such means of grace would be experienced as either a form of works righteousness or simply meaningless practices. This also means, however, that a person, even having experienced the saving grace of Jesus Christ, can turn away (backslide) from God and salvation.

Beginning with his sermon "Free Grace," first preached at Bristol, England, in 1740, John Wesley was engaged in debate against the doctrines of election and predestination and, in contrast, held to the understanding of God's prevenient grace. Within Methodism, debate regarding Wesleyan theology has been rare. Differences of opinion have tended to focus on the marks of holiness as one moves through sanctification. From about 1857 to the 1880s, The UBC and EA debate focused on the theological issues of total depravity and sanctification, eventually contributing to splits in both denominations.

See also: www.umc.org; particularly Laceye C. Warner, *Who We Are and What We Believe* (Nashville: Abingdon, 2024); Randy L. Maddox, *Responsible Grace: John Wesley's Practical Theology* (Nashville: Kingswood Books, 1994).

Wespath

"Every worn-out preacher," say the rules, "shall receive, if he wants it, $64 a year; every widow, if she wants it, $53.33; every child shall receive once for all, if he wants it, $53.33. But none shall be entitled to anything from the fund till he has paid $6.67; nor any who neglects paying his subscription for three years together, unless he be sent by the Conference out of the United States." —wesley.nnu.edu/holiness-classics-library/history-of-the-methodist-episcopal-church/volume-2-book-iii-chapter-4/.

Previously known as The General Board of Pension and Health Benefits (GBOPHB), the board is now known as Wespath and has general administrative and supervisory responsibility over the pension for clergy and lay employees in The UMC, investing and disbursing retirement benefits (1501). Membership is composed of representatives from the Council of Bishops, the jurisdictional conferences, and the central conferences (1502.1). Wespath reports to the General Conference (1501.3).

From the early days of the movement, Methodism has shown concern for the well-being of active and retired pastors. Paragraph 23, Article VI of the Restrictive Rules prevented the use of income from publishing houses, the book concerns, or the Chartered Fund for anything other than the benefit of retired or disabled preachers and their families. Beginning as the Board of Conference Claimants in 1908, the pension and health benefit programs of the church have evolved under numerous names including: Board of Pensions and Relief (1924); Board of Pensions of The Methodist Church (1944); General Board of Pensions (1956); General Board of Pension and Health Benefits of The United Methodist Church (1992). In 2016, the agency was renamed Wespath as a way of honoring John Wesley and to indicate a pathway of financial success for clergy. Wespath is recognized in the US as one of the top one hundred pension-fund managers and the largest in the nonprofit arena.

See also: wespath.org.

World Methodist Council

As to the divisions in the Methodist family, there is little to mar the family likeness. For, first, there has been among the Wesleyan ranks no division as to doctrines Nor, secondly, is there any radical difference in usages. Even in the Connexional bonds there is general likeness; [such as in] the itinerant ministry, quarterly and annual conferences. . . . Differ as we may, there is something in all of us which the world recognizes. —Bishop Matthew Simpson, "Sermon at Opening Service," The Ecumenical Methodist Conference, City Road Chapel, London, September 1881.

The UMC is a member of the World Methodist Council (WMC) (433.1). The Council, which has grown to eighty member bodies, holds gatherings every five years, rotating its meeting to a different continent each time. These gatherings offer Methodists from all over the world the opportunity for fellowship, worship, shared learning, and relationship-building with a major focus on evangelism. The WMC has no legislative or executive power with any of its member churches.

The Council traces its roots back to an 1881 gathering in London of thirty Methodist churches from around the world. It had evolved into its present form by 1951.

See also, https://worldmethodistcouncil.org.

Worship

In divine worship, (as in all other actions,) the first thing to be considered is the end, and the next thing is the means conducing to that end. The end is the honour of God, and the edification of the Church; and then God is honoured, when the Church is edified. The means conducing to that end, are to have the service so administered as may inform the mind, engage the affections, and increase devotion. —John Wesley, *A Roman Catechism Faithfully Drawn out of the Allowed Writings of the Church of Rome: With a Reply Thereto* (London: Published and Sold by J. Kershaw, 1825; originally published July 18, 1749).

Worship is a "duty and privilege" of persons, who, in the presence of God, offer God adoration, thanksgiving, and praise. Communal worship is critical to the life of the *Church* and the *discipleship* of Christians. Both the *Articles of Religion* and the *Confession of Faith* speak to this essential nature of worship, and govern historic practices, especially as they relate to the *sacraments*, the language in which worship is heard, and Sunday/Lord's Day (104, Section 3. *Articles of Religion*—XIII, XV, XVI, XVII, XVIII, XIX; *Confession*—V, XIII, XIV).

Worship is a "nurturing ministry" of the congregation that must focus on the "needs of individuals and families of all ages" (252.2 *a)*). Actions that give shape to worship include invocation; confession and absolution; prayers of thanksgiving, lament; the hearing of the Word through the Scriptures, preaching, and hymnody; the celebration of the sacraments; offering ourselves, and being sent forth to join in God's *mission* in the world.

Leading worship is a primary responsibility of *elders* and *local pastors* (340.2 *a*) (1)). No *pastor* is permitted to stop offering worship services without the consent of the *charge conference* and *district superintendent* (341.2). Nor is a *pastor* allowed to offer services within the boundaries of the *charge* of another UM *pastor* without the consent of that *pastor* or the *district superintendent* (341.5).

Laypersons are encouraged to attend training that will prepare them to assist in leading worship, with, for example, the reading of the Scriptures, serving elements of Communion, leading congregational singing, the preparation of the chancel for the changing seasons of the *Christian year*, and the preparation of acolytes. *Laypersons* may also serve on a *Worship Planning Team* that assists the *pastor(s)* with worship design and coordination. The *GBOD* offers many resources for worship preparation and training on its website.

In the *General Rules*, Wesley included "the public worship of God" as one of the six "ordinances of God" to which all faithful Methodists must attend (104, Section 3, page 80). Until the founding of The MEC in the US, early Methodists participated in their own preaching services, but attended public worship and received the *sacraments* in the Church of England. With the withdrawal of the Church of England from the colonies during the Revolutionary War, it was imperative that Methodist preachers be able to offer public worship, including the *sacraments*, to Methodist disciples, hence the founding of the new denomination.

See also: www.umcdiscipleship.org.

Worship Planning Team (or Committee)

It is as the conductor of public worship that the minister takes the special place that is his. This is true whether he stands forth to preach or to pray, to announce a hymn or baptize an infant. He stands before his fellow mortals as the representative of the Deathless Immortal God; he directs and guides these fellow mortals to worship rightly and worthily praise this God He furthermore sets the example by his own public action and bearing in rightly representing and worthily speaking for Him whom he serves. —Harmon, EE, 128.

The *pastor* is the one person in the *local church* who is ultimately responsible for the oversight and quality of *worship* services. However, a Worship Planning Team or a Worship Committee may be formed as a ministry group or *program ministry* of a *local church*, made up of *laypersons, clergy,* and/or *staff,* with the responsibility of planning and implementing *worship* services in the *local church.* Chaired by the *pastor,* an assigned *staff* person, or elected *layperson,* this group is responsible for ensuring that everything related to the implementation of *worship* in the *church* is carried out. If the *church* has such a team, then other groups such as altar guilds, choirs, and worship bands are accountable to the team to ensure a unified and coordinated approach to *worship.*

Historically, the *rituals* and hymns of the *Church* were strictly monitored by John Wesley. He submitted for its use to the new *Church* in the US, the "Sunday Service of the Methodists of North America" in 1784. The *General Conference* took an increasing interest in the character of *worship;* eventually, the *rituals* for both the preaching service and the *sacraments* were included in the *Discipline.* Until the mid-twentieth century, when *churches* began to diversify the number and styles of worship services, the *pastor* had full responsibility for the content and liturgical form of the service. As *worship* services have become more diverse, informed and well-trained *volunteers* and *staff* are needed to assist with planning high-quality services.

See also: *The United Methodist Book of Worship* (Nashville: The United Methodist Publishing House, 1992); www.umcdiscipleship.org/worship /worship-planning.

Worship Ware

> "When I see an open Bible on the Lord's table I immediately know two things: first, that this Bible is not going to be read and, second, that today on this table the Lord's Supper is not going to be celebrated." —James F. White as quoted in Hickman, 60.

The care and placement of the various materials and items used for worship are carried out by altar guilds, Communion stewards, or other designated positions.

The cross, candles, and flowers are traditional altarware, located in the "chancel"—the area of the sanctuary where the pulpit, altar table, baptismal font, and often the choir are located. Additional pieces include offering plates and candle lighters. For Holy Communion, the bread is placed on a special plate called a paten; the juice is in a flagon or cruet—a special kind of pitcher—that is then poured into a chalice. Some churches use trays with individual Communion cups.

"Paraments" are the variously colored cloths that hang over the pulpit and altar table during other worship services, changed in accordance with the seasons of the Christian year. White linens are used for the Lord's Supper. During the season of Lent, the cross and other representations of joy may be veiled with purple. During the seasons of Advent and Christmas, Lent and Easter, items unique to these seasons may be used, such as an Advent wreath, Christ candle, and Paschal candle. Banners may also hang from the walls. In some churches, the altar is also the focal point for occasional, liturgically appropriate visual art based on the theme of a particular sermon series or high holy day.

Throughout the history of Christianity, the altar, also called the Communion Table, has always been the setting for the elements of the Lord's Supper. Methodists were originally inclined toward simple and useful design. In the late 1800s, Methodists had grown in wealth and social status in their communities, and by the turn of the twentieth century, larger, more ornate churches were built. The chancel and altarware became more decorative as well.

See also: Hoyt L. Hickman, *United Methodist Altars: A Guide for the Congregation* (Nashville: Abingdon Press, 1996); www.umcdiscipleship.org.

Worship Wear

Clerical Garb. "I shall not quarrel with a preacher who employs a symbolic dress for some occasions," said Henry Ward Beecher; "but no man should dress himself simply for the purpose of saying, 'I am a preacher.'" But Henry Wilder Foote says that if a man's Church expects a distinctive dress, let him wear it. There has been some argument about it; but after all, it is an inconsequential thing in principle. "The unforgivable crime," we once heard a minister say, "is for a man to stand in the pulpit with soiled linen upon his person." —Harmon, EE, 49, 168.

Decisions about who wears what while leading *worship* are unique to the location, type, and timing of *worship* services. Local culture and personal choices of *clergy*, leaders, and members most often dictate the decision. While accommodations to the event and setting, and personal tastes are important, it is critical that leaders' dress and vestments are respectful of their role in *worship* and do not draw undue attention to themselves.

When *clergy* wear vestments, they will most often wear an academic robe or an alb. Recently, new styles of robes have been designed that are also acceptable and better suited to different body types. There are two types of albs—the cassock and chasuble; either may also be worn by laity providing leadership in *worship*, such as acolytes and choir members. Choir members will often wear robes with an accessory that matches the color of the season of the *Christian year*.

Stoles are worn only by ordained *clergy*. The *deacon's* stole hangs over the left shoulder and joins just below the right hip. The *elder's* stole drapes across both shoulders and hangs down the front of the robe.

Clergy shirts with a collar may be worn by *clergy* either instead of or under a robe. They may also be worn when needing to indicate that one is involved in an official capacity, such as hospital visitation. Different colors of shirts are acceptable, with the exception of purple. Purple shirts are worn only by *bishops*.

The tradition of wearing robes in *worship* dates back to the early third–fourth-century *church* when priests and monks wore robes as signs of reverence and humility. Early Methodist preachers were strongly encouraged to dress plainly and to "not effect the gentleman." Few had the financial resources for an extra suit of clothes, much less vestments. Nathan Bangs, in his *History of the Methodist Episcopal Church*, describes that, quickly following the 1784 Christmas Conference, not only did the US Methodists dispense with the use of the *Book of Common Prayer*, they also stopped wearing "gowns" because of opposition to them. They were worn only for *sacraments* and *ordinations*. In the famous 1882 print depicting the ordination of Francis Asbury in 1784, he wears a suit, while each of those laying hands on him, Thomas Coke, Thomas Vasey, Richard Whatcoat, and Phillip Otterbein, wears a different style of robe, with or without a stole. Bishop Coke stands in a white robe wearing a traditional stole. Francis Asbury was well known for his frugality as a mark of piety. He is depicted in a simple suit with riding boots. The appeal of wearing vestments rose again with the growing wealth and social status of Methodists.

See also: www.umcdiscipleship.org.

Worship—Where

Thursday, 29. I left London and in the evening expounded to a small company at Basingstoke. Saturday, 31. In the evening I reached Bristol and met Mr. Whitefield there. I could scarcely reconcile myself at first to this strange way of preaching in the fields, of which he set me an example on Sunday; I had been all my life (till very lately) so tenacious of every point relating to decency and order that I should have thought the saving of souls almost a sin if it had not been done in a church. Monday, 2. At four in the afternoon, I submitted to be more vile and proclaimed in the highways the glad tidings of salvation, speaking from a little eminence in a ground adjoining to the city, to about three thousand people. —Wesley, *Works*, vol. 19, 46.

United Methodist *worship* can be held anywhere. In a *church* building, *worship* usually takes place in a sanctuary or a chapel. Some *churches* are now also holding services in gymnasiums, theaters, or arenas. New *church* plants will often begin in a local school, theater, storefront, funeral home, or hotel space. Special services may take place in institutional settings such as prisons, hospitals, and airports.

Worship services often take place outdoors, especially at community Easter sunrise services, at outdoor *baptism* and *wedding* services, and in camping and camp meeting settings. When planning an outdoor service, any necessary permits must be acquired, and *laws* pertaining to that particular site must be followed.

Many *local churches*, especially since the 2020 corona virus pandemic, livestream and post *worship* services and sermons on their websites and You-

Tube, providing access to persons who cannot or do not attend in person. While this technology provides important *connections* to people for a wide range of reasons, there is little consensus about the efficacy of the *sacraments* conveyed through *media*. A consultation was held on the topic of online *Holy Communion* in 2013; the *Council of Bishops* set a moratorium on the practice of online *Holy Communion* in 2014. During the pandemic, online Holy Communion was practiced in various churches. Now that churches have returned to in-person worship with continued online worship services, conversations about what is appropriate regarding online Holy Communion are continuing.

In the earliest days of the Methodist movement, upon the encouragement of George Whitefield, Wesley moved out into the fields to reach people with his message of the saving grace of Jesus Christ. While he originally described this move as "a vile act," it happened in part because Whitefield, Wesley, and other preachers were increasingly prevented from preaching in the churches of the Church of England. The New Room in Bristol, and the Foundery in London, were the first of more than four hundred buildings acquired and designated for preaching and organizing Methodist meetings and ministries. Sacraments, however, were not initially celebrated in the chapels, because very few of the Methodist preachers were ordained. In the US, chapels were built along circuits, in rural locations and cities. Camp meetings became an early practice of the societies, meeting under brush-arbors and tents for evangelistic services and sometimes quarterly conferences. In the late 1800s, Methodists began building larger churches following two main styles—the "Akron" and the "Gothic" styles of sanctuaries—both reflecting upward mobility among Methodists.

See also: www.umcdiscipleship.org/worship.

Year End Statistical Report

Quest. 2. What numbers are there in the society?

Ans. New-York,   180

Philadelphia,   180

New-Jersey,	200
Maryland,	500
Virginia,	100
(Preachers 10.)	1160

—Minutes of the first conference in the colonies, held in Philadelphia, July 4, 1773, Bangs, vol. 1, 80.

At the end of each calendar year, pastors are required to file Year End Statistical Reports on the membership, income, expenses, assets, and mission investments of the local church. The reports are divided into three tables: Membership and Participation, Church Assets and Expenses, and Church Income. The total operational costs (not including mission or capital expense) are used in calculating the apportionments each local church pays. The GCFA has developed a new electronic system for filing these reports known as EZRA (www.gcfa.org/umc.org-gcfa-data-services-datasync).

District superintendents and conference treasurers will know whether the conference is using EZRA. The accuracy of all records is certified by the pastor of the church (340.2 *c*) (2) *(f)*).

Beginning with the first annual conference, held in the American colonies on July 4, 1773, membership statistics have been maintained. In 1773, there were ten preachers and 1,160 members. By the annual conference of 1774, there were seventeen preachers and 2,073 members. The practice of the regular, mandated practice of reporting statistics was embedded in the first *Discipline* of 1785, in which the deacon was assigned the task of keeping the membership statistics, looking over the accounts of the local stewards, and keeping watch on the state of the circuit. Each of our predecessor denominations established a regular, unified system for keeping annual records, maintained since the beginning of Methodism in the US.

See also: www.gcfa.org.

Youth/Young Adult Ministry

Article 2. Object. The object of the League is to promote intelligent and vital piety in the young members and friends of the Church, to aid them in the attainment of purity of heart and constant growth in grace, and to train them in works of mercy and help. —*Discipline*, MEC, 1892, ¶325 article 2.

The spiritual care of both children and youth is a major responsibility of the *pastor* and other leaders who are involved with these age groups, such as teachers, *Scout* coordinators, and youth group leaders (226). "Young people" is now an inclusive term defining persons between "approximately twelve through thirty years of age in the United States and thirty-five in the *central conferences*" (256.3). The term "youth ministry" encompasses all the concerns of the Church and all activities by, with, and for youth. Youth are "all persons from approximately twelve through eighteen years of age in the United States and up to twenty-four in the central conferences." The term "young adult ministry" encompasses all the concerns of the Church and all activities by, with, and for young adults. Young adults are "all persons from approximately eighteen through thirty years of age in the United States and twenty-four through thirty-five years of age in the central conferences." Each *Charge Conference* is strongly encouraged to develop a youth leadership team when there are at least five youth in the congregation(s) (256.3.c).

Youth, in particular, are to be instructed in *confirmation* classes using UM materials, encouraged to make a profession of faith, and to continue in instruction through the *church* school and/or youth group. *Confirmation* classes are the responsibility of the *pastor* and shall occur annually (216, 226).

Youth who have become *professing members* have the same rights as adult *professing members* and may serve on *church* committees (226.5). There shall be at least one youth member on the *Church Council* (244.3). Youth also serve on the Charge Conference (246). Youth and young adults may serve as lay members of the *annual conference* and on conference committees, as *lay delegates to General Conference*, and as members of *general agency* boards (502.1 a); 705.3 c)).

242

The *GBOD* Division on Ministries With Young People, through the Young People's Connectional Network, provides resources and opportunities for youth, young adults, and their leaders, from local programming to international opportunities (1201-1211). The *GBOD* also provides materials for the development of *Safe Sanctuaries*® policies to prevent sexual abuse of both children and youth in local *churches*. The *GBHEM* provides a certification for youth ministry. The identification of "youth" as a group with unique *discipleship* needs did not emerge in the *Church* until the late 1800s. Prior to this era, children moved into adulthood at an earlier age. What have come to be called UMYF groups or youth groups were originally known as "Epworth Leagues," first established in The MEC in 1889, and constituted for the first time in The MEC *Discipline* of 1892. The MECS followed within the decade, as evidenced by its inclusion in their 1898 *Discipline*.

See also: https://www.umcdiscipleship.org/equipping-leaders/safe -sanctuaries.

Appendix

Commission on a Way Forward

> In the coming months we will move more deeply into the implications of being a global church that seeks to balance an approach to different and contextual understandings of LGBTQ identity with a desire for as much unity and connection as possible. We will be exploring this in the context of our mission and structure, and we will be developing models of listening and teaching in collaboration with the Council of Bishops and across annual conferences. —www.umc.org/who-we-are/the-way-forward-from -easter-to-pentecost, accessed July 15, 2017.

The establishment of the "Commission on a Way Forward" was recommended by the Council of Bishops and approved by the 2016 General Conference with the mandate to "do a complete examination and possible revision of every paragraph of the *Book of Discipline* concerning human sexuality and explore options that help to maintain and strengthen the unity of the church" (umc.org). This took place in response to delegates who took the very rare step of requesting the Council to figure out a way to break the impasse within the conference over the disciplinary paragraphs that address homosexuality. The commission is composed of persons selected by the Council and is moderated by three bishops: Sandra Steiner Ball (West Virginia), Kenneth H. Carter (Florida), and David Yemba (Central Congo). The moderators offer regular updates on umc.org.

The vision of the commission is to "design a way for being church that maximizes the presence of a UM witness in as many places in the world as possible, that allows for as much contextual differentiation as possible, and that balances an approach to different theological understandings of human sexuality with a desire for as much unity as possible. This unity will not be grounded in our conceptions of human sexuality, but in our affirmation of the Triune God who calls us to be a grace-filled and holy people in the Wesleyan tradition" (umc.org). The commission is meeting nine times and is preparing a proposal to be submitted to a called General Conference in 2019.

In the past, the bishops, by definition of their office, often had a much stronger voice and role to play in the decision-making processes of our predecessor denominations. For example, in 1844, the bishops intervened to try and prevent schism. In The MECS, the bishops sometimes functioned as a sort of judicial council and ruled on decisions of the General Conference. The request for intervention by the bishops at the 2016 General Conference was unprecedented in The UMC.

See also: www.umc.org/who-we-are/commission-on-a-way-forward.

Text of 2019 Paragraph 2553

Disaffiliation of a Local Church Over Issues Related to Human Sexuality—
1. Basis—Because of the current deep conflict within The United Methodist Church around issues of human sexuality, a local church shall have a limited right, under the provisions of this paragraph, to disaffiliate from the denomination for reasons of conscience regarding a change in the requirements and provisions of the *Book of Discipline* related to the practice of homosexuality or the ordination or marriage of self-avowed practicing homosexuals as resolved and adopted by the 2019 General Conference, or the actions or inactions of its annual conference related to these issues which follow.

2. Time Limits—The choice by a local church to disaffiliate with The United Methodist Church under this paragraph shall be made in sufficient time for the process for exiting the denomination to be complete prior to December 31, 2023. The provisions of ¶ 2553 expire on December 31, 2023, and shall not be used after that date.

3. Decision Making Process—The church conference shall be conducted in accordance with ¶ 248 and shall be held within one hundred twenty (120) days after the district superintendent calls for the church conference. In addition to the provisions of ¶ 246.8, special attention shall be made to give broad notice to the full professing membership of the local church regarding the time and place of a church conference called for this purpose and to use all means necessary, including electronic communication where possible, to communicate. The decision to disaffiliate from The United Methodist Church must be approved by a two-thirds (2/3) majority vote of the professing members of the local church present at the church conference.

4. Process Following Decision to Disaffiliate from The United Methodist Church—If the church conference votes to disaffiliate from The United Methodist Church, the terms and conditions for that disaffiliation shall be established by the board of trustees of the applicable annual conference, with the advice of the cabinet, the annual conference treasurer, the annual conference benefits officer, the director of connectional ministries, and the annual conference chancellor.

The terms and conditions, including the effective date of disaffiliation, shall be memorialized in a binding Disaffiliation Agreement between the annual conference and the trustees of the local church, acting on behalf of the members. That agreement must be consistent with the following provisions:

a) Standard Terms of the Disaffiliation Agreement. The General Council on Finance and Administration shall develop a standard form for Disaffiliation Agreements under this paragraph to protect The United Methodist Church as set forth in ¶ 807.9. The agreement shall include a recognition of the validity and applicability of ¶ 2501, notwithstanding the release of property therefrom. Annual conferences may develop additional standard terms that are not inconsistent with the standard form of this paragraph.

b) Apportionments. The local church shall pay any unpaid apportionments for the 12 months prior to disaffiliation, as well as an additional 12 months of apportionments.

c) Property. A disaffiliating local church shall have the right to retain its real and personal, tangible and intangible property. All transfers of property shall be made prior to disaffiliation. All costs for transfer of title or other legal work shall be borne by the disaffiliating local church.

d) Pension Liabilities. The local church shall contribute withdrawal liability in an amount equal to its pro rata share of any aggregate unfunded pension obligations to the annual conference. The General Board of Pension and Health Benefits shall determine the aggregate funding obligations of the annual conference using market factors similar to a commercial annuity provider, from which the annual conference will determine the local church's share.

e) Other Liabilities. The local church shall satisfy all other debts, loans, and liabilities, or assign and transfer them to its new entity, prior to disaffiliation.

f) Payment Terms. Payment shall occur prior to the effective date of departure.

g) Disaffiliating Churches Continuing as Plan Sponsors of the General Board of Pension and Health Benefits Plans. The United Methodist Church believes that a local church disaffiliating under ¶ 2553 shall continue to share common religious bonds and convictions with The United Methodist Church based on shared Wesleyan theology and tradition and Methodist roots, unless the local church expressly resolves to the contrary. As such, a local church disaffiliating under ¶ 2553 shall continue to be eligible to sponsor voluntary employee benefit plans through the General Board of Pension and Health Benefits under ¶ 1504.2, subject to the applicable terms and conditions of the plans.

h) Once the disaffiliating local church has reimbursed the applicable annual conference for all funds due under the agreement, and provided that there are no other outstanding liabilities or claims against The United Methodist Church as a result of the disaffiliation, in consideration of the provisions of this paragraph, the applicable annual conference shall release any claims that it may have under ¶ 2501 and other paragraphs of *The Book of Discipline of The United Methodist Church* commonly referred to as the trust clause, or under the agreement.

Text of 2020/2024 Paragraph 2553

Readmission of Disaffiliated Churches to The United Methodist Church. With a spirit of grace, we welcome those churches which have disaffiliated or withdrawn to rejoin The United Methodist Church. Where applicable, every annual conference shall have a policy of reaffiliation for the churches seeking to return to the connection. Each such policy shall require that reaffiliating churches affirm their commitment to the Trust Clause in ¶ 2503.

www.ingramcontent.com/pod-product-compliance
Lightning Source LLC
LaVergne TN
LVHW030356240725
816720LV00008BA/24